Better IEPs

How to develop legally correct and educationally useful programs

FIFTH EDITION

Barbara D. Bateman
Mary Anne Linden

Attainment Company

Authors:
Barbara D. Bateman, PhD, JD
Mary Anne Linden, PhD, JD

Editors: Joan Donovan and Tom Kinney
Graphic Design: Elizabeth Ragsdale

An Attainment Company Publication

Attainment Company
P.O. Box 930160
Verona, Wisconsin 53593-0160
Phone 1-800-327-4269   Fax 1-800-942-3865
www.AttainmentCompany.com

Contents

▶ ▶ ▶

FIGURES

About the authors

barbara Bateman, PhD, JD, began her special education career in the 1950s in public schools and institutions where she taught children who had mental retardation, visual impairments, autism, speech and language disorders, dyslexia and other disabilities. She conducted research on learning disabilities with Dr. Samuel Kirk at the University of Illinois. In 1966 she returned to Oregon and taught special education and special education law at the University of Oregon until 2000. In 1976 she graduated from the University of Oregon School of Law. Presently, Dr. Bateman is a consultant in special education law. She consults with and provides training to parents, attorneys, school districts and others involved in special education legal disputes. Her publications number over 100 and include *Writing Measurable IEP Goals and Objectives* (2006), *Why Johnny Doesn't Behave: Twenty Tips for Measurable BIPS* (2003) and *Better IEP Meetings* (2006), a companion volume to *Better IEPs* (2006).

Dr. Bateman's current professional priorities include evaluating IEPs, assessing program appropriateness for individual students, presenting IDEA to parents and school personnel and serving as an expert witness in special education cases. Less professional interests are travel and birding, in the largest possible doses.

mary Anne Linden, PhD, JD, is an attorney and has been an educator (K–12 teacher, administrator, and university faculty) for 23 years. She holds degrees in law, special education, and educational policy and leadership, and has been involved in teacher and administrator preparation since 1991. Dr. Linden's teaching and research activities focus on school law and policy, with particular emphasis on parent involvement in schooling, discrimination, alternative dispute resolution, and constitution law issues arising in public education. Dr. Linden provides training and consultation services on special education law and practice. She also has investigated special education complaints for the Oregon Department of Education.

Dedication and acknowledgments

o my sister, Jan, and the memory of our brother, Denny—the most loving, supportive and fun siblings on the planet. Sam Kirk, Zig Engelmann, my family and all my "special kiddos" have taught me what is educationally true and useful. I am grateful to them for this and more. In the preparation of this book, which is especially close to my heart because IEPs do matter, sincere thanks go to Tom Kinney, Claudia Vincent, Cindy Herr, and Pamela Bahnsen for their much-needed support.

—Barb Bateman

o my late father, who taught me to question conventional wisdom; my mother, who daily models quiet strength; my son, Jeremy, who makes me laugh when I need it most; and my sisters and brothers, who have been through it all with me. To Barb, whose example propelled me through my third year of law school, and who continues to encourage and inspire me. To my students, present and past, who remind me that special education is not a hypothetical endeavor but a real world filled with teachers and students and an apparently infinite number of novel situations that can change lives for better or worse. Last but not least, to Tom Kinney and Pamela Bahnsen, who kept us on task.

—Mary Anne Linden

Introduction

the purpose of this book is to give special educators, regular educators and parents the confidence and know-how to develop Individualized Education Programs, or IEPs, which are both legally correct and educationally useful. Currently, many IEPs are neither.

The IEP process is the centerpiece, the heart and soul, of the Individuals with Disabilities Education Act (IDEA). It is the procedure for fashioning the "free appropriate public education" (FAPE) to which every eligible child who has a disability and needs special education is entitled. In this book, we explain the role of the IEP in the larger context of the IDEA, and we present a child-centered, three-step IEP process.

Chapter One highlights the main components of the IDEA (Part B). We explain the sequential and interdependent relationships of evaluation, IEP development and placement. We also briefly review the IDEA's funding and due process provisions, which protect the rights of children and their families and govern dispute resolutions.

Chapter Two takes a close look at the IEP team and how it functions.

Chapter Three answers the most fundamental questions about how to prepare a squeaky-clean, legally correct IEP:

- ▶ **Who** develops it?
- ▶ **How** does the IEP team operate?
- ▶ **When** must the IEP team convene?
- ▶ **Where** does the IEP meeting happen?
- ▶ **What** must the IEP contain?

Chapter Four explains how not to develop IEPs. We dissect real-world examples of flawed IEPs and identify several common errors in IEP process and content.

Chapter Five describes a better way. We present the "Non-Form" and explain how to create an educationally useful IEP. We focus particular attention on the three-step IEP development process, illustrating each step with examples.

Chapter Six examines and evaluates standards-based IEPs.

Chapter Seven tackles some troublesome issues that have plagued schools since the IDEA was first enacted. We look at judicial decisions and agency rulings that elaborate and clarify these issues.

The US Department of Education Office of Special Education Programs (OSEP) is the federal agency responsible for promulgating regulations for and administering the IDEA. Some of the information in this book is found in two OSEP documents called Appendix C (1981) and Appendix A (1998) to the IDEA Regulations. They are a valuable resource for anyone who wishes to be knowledgeable about IEPs and the way OSEP interprets IDEA requirements. It is, of course, important to consider these interpretations in the light of later IDEA amendments, which may render some of them obsolete. However, our position is that the portions not in conflict with later changes represent good practice and offer helpful guidelines. In addition, we turn for guidance to topical Question and Answer documents that OSEP publishes from time to time[1] and OSEP letters[2] in response to inquiries regarding the interpretation of IDEA. Although the federal regulations promulgated by OSEP have the force of law, the OSEP guidance is advisory but not legally binding.

A well designed IEP can change a child's schooling experience from one of repeated failure, loss of self-esteem and limited options to one of achievement, direction, and productivity. Sadly, our experiences persuade us that legally correct and educationally useful IEPs are all too rare. We sincerely hope and believe this book can help change that situation.

Notes

1. Available at http://idea.ed.gov/explore/home

2. Available at http://www2.ed.gov/policy/speced /guid/idea/index.html and http://www2.ed.gov /policy/speced/guid/idea/letters/revpolicy /index.html

The IEP in perspective

Since 1977, every child in the United States who has a disability and needs special education has been entitled to a free appropriate public education (FAPE) under a federal law that is now called the Individuals with Disabilities Education Act (IDEA). The IDEA (Part B) has five major components:

1. Evaluation and Identification
2. Individualized Education Program and Related Services
3. Placement
4. Funding
5. Procedural Safeguards

In 1997, Congress amended the IDEA with the intention of: (a) strengthening the role of parents; (b) ensuring access to the general education curriculum and reforms; (c) focusing on teaching and learning while reducing unnecessary paperwork requirements; (d) assisting educational agencies in reducing the costs of improving special education and related services to children with disabilities; (e) increasing accommodation of racial, ethnic and linguistic diversity to prevent inappropriate identification and labeling; (f) ensuring schools are safe and conducive to learning; and (g) encouraging parents and educators to work out their differences by using nonadversarial dispute resolution.

The IDEA Amendments of 2004 reaffirmed the intentions of IDEA 97 but made a few changes, some good and some worrisome. On the positive side, they reflected increased emphasis on scientifically based interventions, improved academic and functional performance checks for students with disabilities, early intervening services, positive behavioral interventions, efforts to better serve minority students, and providing more effective transition services.

At the same time, however, parents' roles were significantly weakened, and short-term objectives or benchmarks were no longer required for a majority of special education students. Only time will tell how wise these changes have been. Except for the possible removal of short-term objectives, the essential components of IDEA have not changed since the law was first passed in 1975.

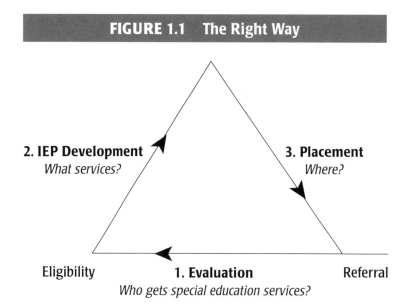

FIGURE 1.1   The Right Way

2. IEP Development
What services?

3. Placement
Where?

Eligibility

1. Evaluation
Who gets special education services?

Referral

Wisely, many districts have retained objectives, in spite of the change.

The heart of the IDEA is the **Individualized Education Program (IEP).** The centrality of the IEP is apparent in many ways. The **Evaluation and Identification** provisions determine who is eligible to have an IEP and contribute to understanding the unique needs of each child, which form the basis of the IEP. The **Placement** component calls for case-by-case placement decisions, based on a child's completed IEP. The **Funding** requirements guarantee a **free** appropriate public education, placing squarely upon school districts (or states) the financial burden of determining eligibility and implementing IEPs for children with disabilities. Finally, the **Procedural Safeguards** create a safety net for children and their parents. They were designed to ensure the development and provision of appropriate IEPs, to place parents and the school districts on a level playing field (although the US Supreme Court has changed this[1,2]), and to facilitate dispute avoidance and resolution.

In order to appreciate the role of the IEP, it is helpful to diagram the primary components in the sequence in which they affect a student (see Figure 1.1).

The first step of the process involves evaluating a child and making a decision on eligibility for FAPE. The second step is the development of an IEP based upon the child's unique needs. The third step is the determination of an appropriate placement based upon the IEP. Reordering this sequence violates the letter and intent of the IDEA.

The following sections of this chapter include brief descriptions of the five components of the IDEA. Each section ends with "Do's and Don'ts" in the form of advice to those wanting to employ practices that are both legally correct and educationally sound.

EVALUATION AND ELIGIBILITY

The purposes of the evaluation and identification provisions of the law are to gather academic, functional and developmental information necessary to determine whether a child has one of the disabilities defined in the IDEA, whether the child needs special education and related services, and the child's present levels of performance and individual educational needs.[3]

Both the 1997 and the 2004 Amendments to IDEA focused attention on the importance of the evaluation/assessment procedures exploring all the child's unique educational needs. Many evaluations prior to these Amendments looked only at eligibility. Now the eligibility determination, while still crucial, is on an equal footing with

FIGURE 1.2   IDEA 2004 Provisions: Evaluation and Eligibility

Evaluation

▶ The timeline from receipt of parental consent for evaluation through eligibility and needs determination is 60 days (or state timeline).

▶ Screening to determine appropriate instructional strategies to implement curriculum is **not** part of the evaluation process.

▶ Both eligibility **and** the child's educational, functional and developmental needs must be determined by the evaluation/ eligibility team comprised of qualified professionals and the parents.

Eligibility

▶ States **may prohibit** and **may not require** the use of **discrepancy** between ability and achievement as a criterion for SLD eligibility; states **must allow** Response to Intervention (RTI) as part of the SLD determination.

▶ A child may **not** be found IDEA-eligible if the determinant factor is lack of "appropriate instruction in the essential components of reading instruction (i.e., in phonemic awareness, phonics, fluency, vocabulary and comprehension strategies) or math."

▶ To be IDEA-eligible a child must (a) fit a category of disability as defined by IDEA **and** (b) must therefore need **special education** as defined by IDEA (i.e., "specially designed instruction").

the needs determination. Important changes to eligibility and evaluation made by the 2004 Amendments are shown in Figure 1.2. Every child who is eligible for an IEP is also entitled to an IEP team that has available to it a current, accurate description of his or her priority educational needs. These needs become the beginning point for the development of the all-important IEP. Every IEP team should insist on knowing these educational needs.

Evaluation must cover all areas related to a child's suspected disability, including, if appropriate, health, vision, hearing, social and emotional status, general intelligence, academic performance, communication needs, and motor abilities.

The IDEA specifies who participates in the evaluation process. First, the child's IEP team, including the parent, and "other qualified professionals" review existing evaluation data and decide what additional data are needed. The district then administers any needed tests and conducts other evaluation procedures. Finally, "a team of qualified professionals and the parent" makes an eligibility determination.

The team assembled to make the eligibility-needs determination **must** include members with the appropriate expertise to make the necessary decisions. The disability areas where the availability of this essential expertise is most problematic are learning disabilities, autism, traumatic brain injury, and intellectual disability (ID).

The difficulty with finding essential expertise in learning disabilities (LD) is that almost **one-half** of all identified special education students are labeled LD, and yet few (and fewer all the time) institutions offer advanced graduate work specifically in LD. With autism spectrum disorders

(ASD) the problem is the phenomenal and not fully understood explosion in numbers of children being diagnosed with ASD.[4] Traumatic brain injury is a relatively rare disability, but one whose diagnosis and educational planning require an extremely high level of training and expertise. The number of available experts is limited. Intellectual disability (ID) has become a disfavored diagnosis, to the extent that teams make an extraordinary effort, with or without deliberate intention, to avoid that diagnosis. Multiple disabilities, ASD, language disorders, emotional disturbance, or developmental disability are preferred. The upside of avoiding the ID diagnosis is that expectations can readily remain high. The downside is also that expectations can readily remain high, too often unrealistically so. Parents, perhaps more than some professionals, recognize the dangers inherent in misleading euphemisms.

The following "Do's and Don'ts" for school districts are derived from the law and from observation of practice in the real world.

Do's: Evaluation and Identification

▶ **Do** notify and fully inform the child's parents about the proposed evaluation, and obtain their written consent before conducting an initial evaluation, administering any new test as part of a reevaluation, or under other circumstances as required by state law or district policy. Remember that parents may withdraw their consent at any time.

▶ **Do** ask parents to participate in the evaluation and identification process and recognize their input as valuable to the evaluation process.

▶ **Do** inform parents that they have a legal right to an independent educational evaluation at public expense if they disagree with the district's evaluation and the district does not go to hearing and prove that its evaluation was appropriate.

▶ **Do** consider requesting a due process hearing or mediation if a child's need for special education is clear but the parents refuse consent for evaluation.

▶ **Do** use a variety of assessment materials and strategies that provide sufficient reliable and valid information to: (1) judge whether the child fits into one of the IDEA eligibility categories; (2) decide if the child, because of the disability, needs special education; and if so (3) determine the child's educational needs, laying the foundation for the content of the child's IEP.

▶ **Do** administer tests and other assessment materials in the child's native language or other appropriate mode of communication and rely extensively on observations, work samples, interviews, records, and other real-world data. Test scores can be important, but no more so than other data.

Don'ts: Evaluation and Identification

▶ **Don't** single out a child for testing, interviewing, or overt observation without notice to parents.

▶ **Don't** unreasonably extend prereferral intervention programs, such as "early intervening services" (**not** to be confused with early intervention services, which are totally different) and "response to intervention (RTI)," which have, or may have, the effect of delaying a child's special education evaluation or IEP. The child is entitled to a full, individualized special education in **all** areas related to the suspected disability and in all areas of educational need, even if not commonly related to the suspected disability. This entitlement to a thorough evaluation arises as soon as the district suspects or has reason to suspect the child has a disability.

▶ **Don't** equate evaluation with testing. Evaluation should also include observations, work samples, interviews, information provided by parents, cumulative files, etc. No one test comes close to being an adequate evaluation, legally or professionally. Some prefer the term "assessment." Either "evaluation or "assessment" must be broad-based and extend far beyond "testing."

- ► **Don't** rely on any particular battery of standardized assessments, and most definitely don't select tests solely from those "tabled" for use in a formula, or for any other purposes. Also beware of state or district policy which mandates or limits choice of "tests." Professional judgment must be the determining factor.

- ► **Don't** rely exclusively on any formula or quantitative guidelines to determine eligibility. The more elaborate the formula, the sillier it will appear to a judge. The law requires the exercise of expert professional judgment.

- ► **Don't** ask a professional, such as a physician or psychiatrist, whether a child has a particular disability. Instead, provide the IDEA disability definition, and ask whether the child fits that definition, especially if there are mental health issues. Without this precaution, the professional may rely on DSM-IV, DSM-IV-TR or, after 2012, DSM-V. IDEA definitions must prevail.

- ► **Don't** use evaluation methods that discriminate on the basis of race, culture, or native language. Evaluation that discriminates on the basis of sex is forbidden by other federal laws (ESEA, Title IX), but it is well known that almost twice as many boys as girls are in special education. It is noteworthy that no ethnic or racial disproportion approaches the size of the sex disproportion in special education.

INDIVIDUALIZED EDUCATION PROGRAM AND RELATED SERVICES (PROGRAM PLANNING)

Every child found eligible for IDEA services is entitled to an IEP. An IEP is a written document that describes a child's educational needs, and details the special education and related services the district will provide to address those needs. The IDEA lays out mandatory procedures for IEP development. Among other things, the law prescribes the membership of the team that designs an IEP, and it outlines the required components of an IEP. The remaining chapters of this book explore these requirements in detail, but brief highlights follow here.

Do's: Program Planning

- ► **Do** individualize the child's program. The IEP must reflect the child's unique needs, not the present availability of services in the district.

- ► **Do** figure out what supports the child might need to participate in the general curriculum. If there is no need for modifications or supplementary aids and services in the regular classroom, there is reason to question the child's eligibility. Every IDEA-eligible student must need and receive special education.

- ► **Do** consider the child's strengths and the parents' concerns for enhancing their child's education.

- ► **Do** specify and describe (not just name or list) all necessary special education, related services, supplementary aids and services, program modifications, and support for school personnel.

- ► **Do** include positive behavioral interventions and discipline strategies (a behavior intervention plan) when there is reason to believe that behavior is or may be an issue.

- ► **Do** meticulously observe all procedural requirements for IEP development and content.

- ► **Do** ensure full, equal, and meaningful parental participation.

- ► **Do** include objectives or other "progress markers" for each goal, even though IDEA no longer requires them on all IEPs.

Don'ts: Program Planning

- ► **Don't** worry about "opening floodgates." Providing certain services to one child does not set a precedent for other children. IEPs address the unique needs of individual children, so what one child needs has no implications for what the district must provide to others.

- ► **Don't** clutter IEPs with detailed goals and objectives for all the content standards in the general curriculum. Instead, focus on the accommodations and adjustments an individual child needs for appropriate **access** to and **participation** in the general curriculum. Goals should be prioritized and deal with large, important areas.

▶ **Don't** include more than three or four objectives or progress markers for each annual goal. Progress markers should describe "how far, by when" the child should progress toward achievement of each annual goal and ordinarily should coincide with grading periods.

▶ **Don't** use lack of funds or staff as an excuse for failure to provide a FAPE.

▶ **Don't** ever provide services categorically! For example, don't say that only emotionally disturbed students may have behavioral components in their IEPs, or that only students with learning disabilities may be allowed extra time on tests. All services must be based upon the individual child's needs without regard to disability category.

The US Supreme Court has held that a program is appropriate if it was developed according to the procedures required by the law, and if it is "reasonably calculated" to allow the child to benefit educationally. The Court offered the following guidance on the measure of appropriateness for certain students:

> The IEP, and therefore the personalized instruction, should be formulated in accordance with the requirements of the Act and, if the child is being educated in the regular classroom of the public education system, should be reasonably calculated to enable the child to achieve passing marks and advance from grade to grade. . . .[5]

The Supreme Court's analysis in *Rowley* dealt with the situation where a student with a disability is performing better than nondisabled children in the same regular classroom. Lower courts are still struggling with the issue of **how much** benefit is necessary for the program to be deemed appropriate when the student is not performing at the high level of Amy Rowley. There is, however, general agreement that the benefit must be "meaningful" and take into account the child's potential.

PLACEMENT

Placement lies at the center of an ideological storm in special education. Proponents of "full inclusion" insist that the proper learning environment for all children, with and without disabilities, is the regular classroom. The inclusionist movement has resulted in increased numbers of children with disabilities being placed full-time in regular classes. Many educators, adults with disabilities and advocacy organizations are resisting this trend, arguing that full inclusion deprives many children of the specialized services they need to meet their unique educational needs (see, e.g., Kauffman & Hallahan, 2005; Zigmond & Kloo, 2011).

While the storm rages, the law quietly remains unchanged. There is not now, and has never been, a requirement in the IDEA that all children with disabilities be "included" or "mainstreamed" in the regular classroom. In the 2004 Amendments, Congress again removed any doubts about a possible change in federal policy on this issue. The law continues to express a preference rather than a mandate for placement of children with disabilities in the regular classroom:

> To the maximum extent appropriate, children with disabilities, including children in public or private institutions or other care facilities, are educated with children who are not disabled, and special classes, separate schooling, or other removal of children with disabilities from the regular educational environment occurs only when the nature or severity of the disability of a child is such that education in regular classes with the use of supplementary aids and services cannot be achieved satisfactorily.[6]

"To the maximum extent appropriate" is the key phrase here. The IDEA recognizes that regular classroom placement might be inappropriate for some children. Least restrictive environment (LRE) is not a synonym for regular classroom. Technically, LRE refers to a set of procedures and requirements found in the IDEA regulations, and the least restrictive placement for a particular child is the placement decided on by the team, compliant with procedural requirements, and individually selected from a full continuum of alternative placements.

Once a placement has been selected, a district cannot change a student's placement unilaterally (except in some disciplinary situations) if the parents object to the change. If parents request a hearing to challenge a proposed change in placement, the child remains in the current placement until all administrative procedures and at least a first appeal (if any) are completed. This is called the "stay-put" provision.

The exception to stay-put is that the schools may unilaterally place the student in an alternative education setting for no more than 45 school days if the child carries or possesses a weapon at school, knowingly possesses or uses illegal drugs or has inflicted serious bodily injury upon another person.[7] The parent is entitled to an expedited hearing to appeal such action.

Predictably, disciplinary actions are a contentious issue in the placement of students with disabilities. Suspension for more than 10 days and expulsion constitute changes in placement. Schools that use exclusionary discipline for students with disabilities must follow a strict set of procedures (see Figure 1.3), and districts must continue to provide FAPE to students who have been excluded for more than 10 days. However, IDEA 2004 makes it significantly easier for schools to exclude students with disabilities, particularly by making it easier to show the disability did not cause the misconduct. Even so, districts should seek legal advice and proceed with caution before suspending or expelling students with IEPs.

Do's: Placement

▶ **Do** remember that program appropriateness is the primary IDEA mandate. As a federal district court judge has explained: "Nowhere in the Act is a handicapped child required to sink or swim in an ordinary classroom. . . . Congress certainly did not intend to place handicapped children in a least restrictive environment and thereby deny them an appropriate education."[8]

▶ **Do** make available the required continuum of various alternative placements, including resource rooms, special classes, special schools, etc., so children with disabilities can learn in the environment that is appropriate for them, based upon their individual needs.

▶ **Do** determine each child's placement at least annually. The placement decision must be individualized and based on the child's IEP.

▶ **Do** ensure that each placement decision is made by a group of persons, including parents, who are knowledgeable about the child, the meaning of the evaluation data, and the placement options.

▶ **Do** consider any potential harmful effects on the child or on the quality of services when selecting the LRE.

▶ **Do** make sure each child is educated with and otherwise participates with nondisabled children to the maximum extent appropriate.

▶ **Do** place each child in the school he or she would attend if nondisabled unless the IEP requires some other arrangement. IDEA does not entitle or require a child to attend the neighborhood school if the necessary services are better provided elsewhere.

Don'ts: Placement

▶ **Don't** remove a child with a disability from the regular education environment unless the disability is such that education in regular classes cannot be achieved satisfactorily, even with the use of supplementary aids and services.

▶ **Don't** substitute a policy of "full inclusion" for the continuum of various alternative placements required by the IDEA.

▶ **Don't** exclude parents from placement decisions.

▶ **Don't** forget to follow all the procedural requirements for all "changes of placement" including suspension of more than 10 days, expulsion and significant program changes.

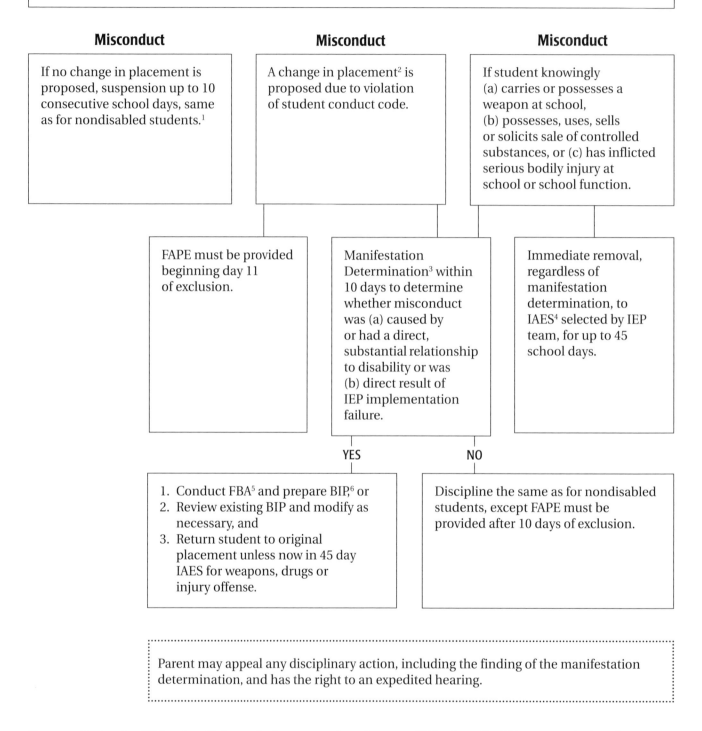

FIGURE 1.3 Discipline: IDEA 2004

Case-by-case consideration.
Notice to parents, including procedural safeguards, on day of decision to discipline student.

Misconduct

If no change in placement is proposed, suspension up to 10 consecutive school days, same as for nondisabled students.[1]

Misconduct

A change in placement[2] is proposed due to violation of student conduct code.

Misconduct

If student knowingly (a) carries or possesses a weapon at school, (b) possesses, uses, sells or solicits sale of controlled substances, or (c) has inflicted serious bodily injury at school or school function.

FAPE must be provided beginning day 11 of exclusion.

Manifestation Determination[3] within 10 days to determine whether misconduct was (a) caused by or had a direct, substantial relationship to disability or was (b) direct result of IEP implementation failure.

Immediate removal, regardless of manifestation determination, to IAES[4] selected by IEP team, for up to 45 school days.

YES   NO

1. Conduct FBA[5] and prepare BIP,[6] or
2. Review existing BIP and modify as necessary, and
3. Return student to original placement unless now in 45 day IAES for weapons, drugs or injury offense.

Discipline the same as for nondisabled students, except FAPE must be provided after 10 days of exclusion.

Parent may appeal any disciplinary action, including the finding of the manifestation determination, and has the right to an expedited hearing.

[1]Known as 10 "free days." [2]More than 10 days exclusion, consecutive or "patterned." [3]Conducted by LEA, parent and selected IEP team members. [4]Interim Alternative Educational Setting. [5]Functional behavior assessment. [6]Behavior intervention plan.

► **Don't** place a student on the basis of his or her disability category! Regardless of disability category, placement must be based upon the student's IEP.

THE RELATIONSHIP AMONG EVALUATION, IEP AND PLACEMENT

A firm understanding of the relationship among evaluation, IEP and placement can assist significantly in having IDEA operate smoothly and to the benefit of all.

Think for a moment, in a broad and loose way, about building a house. First, the foundation is laid. Evaluation is the foundation of the IDEA house. Great care is required to insure the foundation is solid. Next comes the framing of the house, built squarely on the foundation, with every nook and cranny corresponding to the foundation. That is how the IEP is supposed to fit on the evaluation. All the needs identified in the evaluation must be covered in the IEP. Finally comes the roof—the placement decision. The roof must fit the framing perfectly, just as the placement must fit (and is based upon) the IEP. If the fit between the evaluation and the IEP and the placement isn't perfect, the IDEA is creaky, leaky, and weak.

FUNDING

Special education and related services can be expensive, and the IDEA clearly places the financial burden of educating students with disabilities on school districts, with help from the state and federal government. The "F" in FAPE means free to parents. There are no exceptions to the requirement that a **free** appropriate public education must be made available to all children who have a disability and need special education.

Normally, cost may not be a consideration in selection of a child's program or placement. If evaluation reveals that a child with a disability needs a particular service, the district must provide that service even if it is costly. No court has ever allowed consideration of cost for common services, such as reading tutors or daily speech therapy.

In a few narrowly defined circumstances, cost may be a factor. For example, a district may select the less expensive of two suitable facilities for a child who requires residential placement. One circuit court of appeals has ruled that a district may consider costs for a placement so expensive as to impact the budget and significantly reduce the resources available to the other children in the district.[9]

Failure to provide FAPE can be more costly to a district than providing it would have been. Parents who believe their child's IEP is not appropriate may unilaterally place their child in a private school that does provide an appropriate program. Under most circumstances, parents must first notify the district of their dissatisfaction with the offered program, and of their intent to enroll the child in a private school at public expense. A district that receives such a notice should be very certain that its proposed program constitutes FAPE, or it may be ordered to reimburse parents for the cost of the private school. The US Supreme Court has advised that:

> . . . public educational authorities who want to avoid reimbursing parents for the private education of a disabled child can do one of two things: give the child a free appropriate public education in a public setting, or place the child in an appropriate private setting of the State's choice. This is IDEA's mandate, and school officials who conform to it need not worry about reimbursement claims.[10]

Do's: Funding

► **Do** base the content of the child's IEP on his or her educational needs without considering the cost of meeting those needs, at least sufficiently to constitute FAPE.

► **Do** make available a continuum of various alternative placements. Cost is no excuse for failure to do so. Small districts may not be able to maintain every conceivable placement a child might need, in which case they may choose to join in regional service plans, contract with other districts, or private facilities, etc.

- ▶ **Do** remember that attempts to cut corners can backfire. If the district fails to provide an appropriate program, parents can unilaterally place their child in an expensive private facility that does offer an appropriate program, and the district may have to pay for it.

Don'ts: Funding

- ▶ **Don't** compel parents to use private insurance to pay for any services a child needs in order to benefit from special education. If parents voluntarily use their insurance, the district must compensate them for any increases in premiums or reductions in benefits.

- ▶ **Don't** use a related service provider's schedule as a limiting factor on the amount of service available to a child. Districts must determine the frequency and duration of services case by case, based upon the individual needs of each child.

- ▶ **Don't** cite unavailability of personnel as a justification for failure to provide needed services. Districts should employ outside contractors if this is necessary to address a child's needs.

- ▶ **Don't** arbitrarily take a hard line with parents who disagree with their child's IEP. This is a high stakes gamble that the district can lose if it fails to offer FAPE and parents place their child in a private school that does offer an appropriate program.

PROCEDURAL SAFEGUARDS

Built into the IDEA is an elaborate system of procedural safeguards designed to ensure access to FAPE for children with disabilities.[11] Although a detailed discussion of procedural safeguards is beyond the scope of this book, a few points deserve mention here.

Parents have a right to participate in all meetings scheduled for the purpose of making decisions about their child's identification, evaluation, program, or placement. Districts should keep records that demonstrate a diligent effort to ensure parental participation. Parents need not be invited to informal or chance meetings, or to staff meetings held for the purpose of preparing for a meeting with parents.[12]

The IDEA requires informed parental consent before initial evaluation, initial provision of services and placement in special education, and administration of any new test during a reevaluation. State law may include additional consent requirements. If parents refuse consent for evaluation (but not for initial service or placement) a district may attempt mediation, or may seek a hearing officer's order to proceed without consent if that appears to be in the interest of the child. When considering actions that do not require consent, districts must still provide prior notice, and parents who disagree with the district's plans may file a complaint, initiate mediation, or request a hearing.

Procedural safeguards are effective only when parents know about and make use of them. School districts must provide parents with clear, detailed, and understandable explanations of their IDEA rights. This procedural safeguards notice must explain all safeguards related to: (1) independent educational evaluation; (2) parental notice and consent; (3) access to records; (4) students attending private schools; (5) opportunities to present complaints; (6) dispute resolution processes, including mediation, hearings and civil actions; (7) the child's placement during dispute resolution proceedings—the "stay put" provision; (8) procedures relating to suspension and expulsion; and (9) payment of attorneys' fees.[13]

Concern abounds, on the part of both parents and districts, as to what happens if IDEA procedural violations do occur. In order for procedural violations to constitute a denial of FAPE, a hearing officer must find that a district's procedural inadequacies (a) impeded the child's right to FAPE; (b) significantly impeded the parents' opportunity to participate in decision making; or (c) caused a deprivation of educational benefit.[14] Hearing officers and courts are becoming increasingly sensitive to what they call "pre-determination," where districts have foreclosed true parent participation by unilaterally deciding certain matters (typically placement or amount of certain services) beforehand, and not genuinely considering parental input.

IDEA 2004 made several technical changes which make it more important than ever for parents to know the procedural rules and/or to seek assistance from knowledgeable persons. Among other changes it is now more difficult for parents to (a) file an "acceptable" request for a due process hearing; (b) receive reimbursement for private placements even when the district failed to offer FAPE; and (c) collect attorneys' fees and costs when the parents prevail in a hearing.

Thus it is essential for parents, as well as school district personnel, to obtain totally accurate information on IDEA procedures and procedural safeguards.

Do's: Procedural Safeguards

▶ **Do** send parents prior written notice of proposed actions regarding their child. Parents are entitled to notice any time a district proposes or refuses to initiate or change anything about the child's identification, evaluation, program, or placement. Notice must describe the district's proposed action and the basis for it, inform parents of their rights, and be provided in a form that parents can understand.

▶ **Do** give parents a complete procedural safeguards notice when they request it and when: (1) their child is referred for evaluation and/or (2) a parent files a complaint or requests a due process hearing. Make sure this notice is provided in parents' native language, and avoid use of jargon.

▶ **Do** make mediation and resolution sessions available in order to resolve disputes between parents and schools in a nonadversarial fashion.

▶ **Do** provide parents with a genuine opportunity to participate in all decision making meetings relating to their child.

▶ **Do** notify parents and students in advance if state law provides for the transfer of parental rights to the student when he or she reaches the age of majority as defined by state law.

Don'ts: Procedural Safeguards

▶ **Don't** take any action regarding a child's identification, evaluation, program, or placement without sending detailed and understandable prior written notice to parents, as required.

▶ **Don't** restrict parents' access to their child's education records. Parents have a right to examine all their child's records, including student response forms for all tests, even though many districts are unaware of this and do not retain these forms.

Figure 1.4 illustrates the interrelationships among the IDEA components just introduced. The three sequential components—evaluation, program and placement—rest on a solid foundation of procedural safeguards, and public funding of all components ensures that all children with disabilities enjoy equal access to an appropriate education.

SUMMARY

The "IDEA Commandments" (see Figure 1.5) were first handed down in 1975 from "Mount Deecee" to public schools throughout the land, and are just as binding and important now. School districts break these commandments at their peril!

FIGURE 1.4 IDEA in a Nutshell

EVALUATION of educational needs

- Individualized evaluation
- Nondiscriminatory
- In all areas related to suspected disability
- Determines eligibility
- Specifies educational needs
- Delineates explicit instructional implications

WHO is entitled?

PROGRAM to address those needs at no cost to parents

IEP (partial)

1. Child's needs, characteristics, and present levels of performance (PLOPs)
2. Special education, related services, supplementary aids and services, accommodations, program modifications, and personnel support to address each need
3. Measurable, objective, behavioral goals to assess adequacy of services and to allow meaningful progress reporting at least every grading period

To WHAT services?

PLACEMENT based on IEP

- Individualized placement decision
- Decided after program (IEP) development
- Selected from full continuum of alternative placements
- In regular education environment when education there can be achieved satisfactorily
- Appropriate program is the primary mandate of the IDEA: Congressional preference for mainstreaming is secondary.

Delivered WHERE?

PROCEDURAL PROTECTIONS

FIGURE 1.5 IDEA Commandments

- Thou shalt base all eligibility decisions on professional judgment, not on quantitative formulae.

- Thou shalt open wide the door unto every needed service and placement for each eligible child.

- Remember thou that categorical delivery of services is an abomination.

- Each IEP shall be based solely upon the child's needs. He or she who looks instead to availability of services shall know the inferno.

- Maketh every IEP in the image of its child. An IEP like unto another is a graven image, despised by all who know IDEA.

- Place not all children in the same setting, but make available the entire continuum of alternative placements.

- Thou shalt not exclude parents from decisions that affect their children.

- Thou shalt not burden parents with the cost of their children's special education and services.

References

Kauffman, J.M., & Hallahan, D.P. (2005). *The illusion of full inclusion* (2d ed). Austin, TX: PRO-ED.

Zigmond, N., & Kloo, A. (2011). General and special education are (and should be) different. In Kauffman, J.M. & Hallahan, D.P. (Eds), *Handbook of Special Education*. NY: Routledge.

Notes

1. *Schaffer v. Weast*, 126 S.Ct. 528, 546 US 49 (2005).

2. *Arlington v. Murphy*, 126 S.Ct. 2455, 548 US 291 (2006).

3. 20 USC §1414.

4. One child in 10,000 births was diagnosed in the 1980s. As of 2011, it is approximately one in 100.

5. *Hendrick Hudson Bd. of Ed. v. Rowley*, 102 S.Ct. 3034, 458 US 176 (1982).

6. 20 USC §1412(a)(5)(A); 34 CFR 300.114(a)(2).

7. 20 USC §1415(k)(1)(G); 34 CFR 300.518.

8. *Visco v. Sch. Dist. of Pittsburgh*, 684 F.Supp. 1310 (WD PA 1988).

9. *Greer v. Rome City Sch. Dist.*, 950 F.2d 688 (11th Cir. 1991).

10. *Florence Co. Sch. Dist.Four v. Carter*, 114 S.Ct. 361, 510 US 7 (1993).

11. 34 CFR 300.500-537.

12. 34 CFR 300.501.

13. 34 CFR 300.504.

14. 34 CFR 300.513(a).

CHAPTER TWO

Working together: The IEP team

team collaboration is a key principle of all IDEA processes from initial referral of a student through termination of special education eligibility, with some exceptions regarding parent consent. Chief among these is the parent's right to unilaterally deny or revoke consent for provision of special education services.[1]

The term "IEP Team" has become a shortcut reference to any of several interlinked teams responsible for special education decision making. These teams are multidisciplinary in nature, which means that each member brings specific expertise that the other team members may not possess. Team members share professional knowledge and student-specific information that, in theory, combine to produce the three-dimensional picture of an individual student with a disability that is needed to develop an appropriate special education program for that student.

Multidisciplinary teaming is not a pointless procedural requirement but a system built into the law to ensure comprehensive understanding of the needs of each student with a disability, individualized program development based on the student's unique needs, and school-parent collaboration.

IDEA prescribes slightly different compositions for the teams responsible for eligibility, evaluation, IEP development or revision, placement, or discipline, but all teams represent some variant of the IEP team.

THE IEP TEAM

The core group in special education decision making is the IEP Team,[2] which is responsible for developing, reviewing, and revising the individualized educational program (IEP) for each student with a disability. Under normal circumstances, the IEP team also determines placement. The members of this team include, at minimum:

▶ The parent(s)

▶ At least one of the student's regular education teachers, if the student is, or may be, participating in the regular education environment

▶ At least one of the student's special education teachers or providers

- A representative of the school, district, or other public education agency who:
  - is qualified to provide or supervise specially designed instruction to meet the unique needs of children with disabilities,
  - understands the general education curriculum, and
  - knows about available resources

- A person who can interpret the instructional implications of evaluation information (this may be one of the persons listed above)

- Persons who have knowledge or special expertise about the student invited by the parent(s), or by the school or district or other public education agency

- When appropriate, the student with a disability

- A Part C program representative to participate in an initial IEP meeting for a child who had previously received services under IDEA Part C (early intervention for infants and toddlers), at the parent's request

The first five on this list are **mandatory** IEP team members. IDEA imposes no obligation on parents to participate but defines a critical role for parents on the team and requires districts to encourage parent involvement.

The next four members on the list—special education teacher or provider, regular education teacher, district representative, and the person who can interpret the instructional implications of evaluation results, must attend all IEP meetings unless the district and the parents have agreed in advance and in writing that their participation is not necessary.[3]

Persons in the final three categories on the IEP team list may or may not need to participate, depending on the circumstances, the parties' judgment, and the student's needs or age.

Parent

Under IDEA, the term "parent" encompasses a variety of people who function in a parental role.[4] A parent may be:

- The student's biological or adoptive parent

- A foster parent (unless state law forbids foster parents to act as parents)

- An authorized guardian (but not the state, if the student is a ward of the state)

- A person with whom the student lives, who acts in place of a parent, and who may be a grandparent, stepparent, or other relative (but not a legal guardian or foster parent)

- A person who is legally responsible for the student's welfare

- A surrogate parent[5] appointed by the district or a court to represent the interests of a student with a disability, when efforts to identify or locate a parent are unsuccessful

When more than one person attempts to serve as the student's parent for special education decision making and processes such as IEP development, the biological or adoptive parent is presumed to be the parent unless the biological or adoptive parent does not have legal authority to make educational decisions for the student. A biological or adoptive parent may lose parental rights through a court order for a variety of reasons, or a divorce settlement may grant educational decision making to only one parent. In such cases, another person who fits one of the descriptions listed above will serve as the parent for special education purposes.

Any errors that are made in deciding who is a parent, or which parent should participate in the IEP process, should favor inclusion rather than exclusion, since both the district and the parent may invite any knowledgeable person they wish to an IEP meeting, with the exception of a person whose presence is restricted by court order.

Special and Regular Education Teachers

Ideally, the special and regular education teachers are the student's current or recent teachers, who know the student and can share firsthand information about classroom performance and conduct. These members additionally offer expertise on curriculum, instruction and assessment, as well as effective methods of adjusting practices to meet the unique educational needs of the student. If it is not possible for teachers who know the student to serve on the team—for example, when a student has transferred to a new school or district—then the second-best option is teachers who will have the student in their classes. Filling these positions on an IEP team with teachers who neither know the student, nor will work with the student, misses the point.

A regular education teacher is not a mandatory IEP team member if the student does not currently participate and is not anticipated to participate, in the regular education environment. A special education provider such as a speech-language pathologist may fill the role of special education teacher on the IEP team, if the provided service includes specially designed instruction and is considered special education under state standards.[6]

Students with disabilities, especially at the secondary level, typically have more than one regular education teacher. Although IDEA requires only one to attend an IEP meeting,[7] it can be useful to get input from more than one. For example, a student's social studies teacher will be able to talk about the demands of the social studies curriculum, and about the student's struggles and achievements in US History, but lacks professional expertise in math education and firsthand knowledge about how the student's disability affects participation in Algebra.

Ideally, the special education teacher can gather information from all the student's regular education teachers, so the team has a clear and comprehensive view of how the disabilities affect participation and progress across the general education curriculum. Even when only one regular education teacher attends the meeting, all teachers and other service providers who have responsibilities to serve the student must: (a) have access to the IEP before beginning to work with the child, and (b) be informed of his or her specific responsibilities related to implementing the IEP, and of any accommodations, modifications, and supports that the IEP prescribes.[8]

District Representative

A school district has discretion to decide who serves on an IEP team as the district representative, as long as the person selected is: (a) qualified to provide or supervise the provision of specially designed instruction, and (b) knowledgeable about the general education curriculum and the availability of district resources. It is also important that the district representative have "authority to commit agency resources and be able to ensure that whatever services are described in the IEP will actually be provided."[9]

At an IEP review and revision meeting, when the issues and needed services are routine, the district may delegate authority to one of the other team members, such as the special education teacher.[10] When the student presents unique, complex, or unusually expensive needs, an administrator with greater authority should serve as district representative.

Failure of the district to include a properly authorized district representative on the team is a procedural error that violates IDEA. It would not, however, excuse a district's failure to implement an IEP. Authority to determine the needs of a student with a disability, establish goals, and identify needed special education and related services rests **solely** with the IEP team, and no one—neither parent nor district staff—may veto or refuse to deliver anything that the IEP prescribes.

The function of this team member is to develop a clear understanding of the student's needs, and to help the team determine how the team can draw upon district resources to provide appropriate special education and related services to the student. Neither the district representative (regardless of whether present at the meeting), nor any other individual or body, may override or ignore any consensus decision of the team.

Instructional Implications of Evaluation Expert

IDEA requires the IEP team to include a person who understands the instructional implications of evaluation results. The purposes of special education evaluation are to determine: (a) whether a student has a disability, and (b) the nature and extent of the special education and related services that the child needs.[11] Eligibility decisions, guided by state regulatory criteria, are relatively simple. Determination of a student's needed special education and related services is more challenging. IDEA prohibits cookie-cutter program decisions or placement based on disability category and expressly requires program decisions based on an individual student's unique educational needs.

Special education evaluation must be expansive enough to provide the team with a three-dimensional view of the student, assessing all areas related to the suspected disability. It must also consider test data as well as information from the parents, state and classroom assessment, observations from teachers and other service providers, and any other information that sheds light on the student's strengths and needs.

The role of the "instructional implications of evaluation" member is not merely to explain the meaning of arcane test scores but, more importantly, to help the team understand the crucial relationships between the information gathered during evaluation or reevaluation and the content of the IEP. The US Office for Special Education Programs (OSEP) has taken the position that this person need not be an expert in administration of diagnostic tests[12] and may be one of the other team members,[13] such as a special education teacher or speech-language pathologist.

Other Individuals

Just about anybody the parent or the district chooses can fill these wild card slots on the IEP team, as long as that person has important knowledge or expertise about the student, or about something relevant to the student's instructional and service needs. The party (district or parent) who invites an "other individual" determines whether that person has the required knowledge and expertise.[14] The team might include specialists such as a school psychologist, speech-language pathologist (SLP), occupational therapist (OT),

physical therapist (PT), audiologist, autism specialist, behavior specialist, counselor, nurse, or any other person with relevant knowledge of the student's needs, performance levels, learning modalities, etc. Parents might also invite an advocate, friend, family member, tutor, therapist, independent assessment specialist, or any other person they deem sufficiently knowledgeable about the student.

Increasingly, attorneys are attending IEP meetings, at the invitation of either district or parent(s). The status of attorneys at IEP meetings is unclear. In a 2001 letter[15] to then-Senator Hillary Clinton, OSEP implied that attorneys could be team members, citing the section of the IDEA regulations providing that the inviting party determines whether an invited member has "knowledge or special expertise" about the student. With a notable lack of enthusiasm, the OSEP letter stated that "The Federal rules pertaining to this situation do not disallow the school district from inviting the district's attorney to the IEP meeting." However, the OSEP letter also cited its own earlier guidance urging districts and parents not to invite attorneys to IEP meetings, explaining:

> Even if the attorney possessed knowledge or special expertise regarding the child . . . an attorney's presence would have the potential for creating an adversarial atmosphere that would not necessarily be in the best interests of the child.[16]

Anyone involved in special education knows all too well that conflict between families and schools does arise. Despite good intentions, either side may be unaware of what the law requires and may need to consult with an attorney. However, an IEP meeting is not a particularly appropriate venue for legal consultation. Attorneys at IEP meetings seldom possess any particular knowledge of the student unless they happen to also be family friends or relatives; their expertise is in the law, not in the student. Surely, IDEA does not contemplate the IEP meeting as a clash of competing teams, each led by a lawyer, but instead intends all members to be on one team that wins when a student with a disability receives special education and related services that address his or her needs.

The Student

The inclusion of the student on the IEP team "when appropriate" raises more questions than it answers. When is it appropriate? Is it permissive, or mandatory? Who decides? The answers are only partly clear.

It may be appropriate to include the student when the team believes the student is sufficiently mature to contribute ideas, or when the student's participation may increase his or her buy-in to the IEP. It may not be appropriate to include the student when discussion of disability-related concerns may be painful or confusing. Ultimately, the parent has sole authority to determine whether the student's participation is appropriate, as long as the student has not reached the age of majority under state law (typically age 18). While district personnel may discuss this issue with the parent, they may not override a parent's decision.

If the meeting includes consideration of postsecondary goals and transition services, the district must invite the student.[17] IDEA provides that transition must be part of the discussion and content of all IEPs, beginning with the IEP that will be in effect on the student's 16th birthday.[18] Although not currently required by IDEA, beginning transition planning earlier than the student's 16th year is better practice, as the postsecondary goals will have implications for high school coursework. With the parent's consent, the district must also invite representatives from any other agencies that will provide or pay for transition services.[19]

Transition planning must take into account a student's strengths, preferences, and interests,[20] so staff must seek this information from and about the student even if the parents refuse to permit the student to participate as an active team member. If for some reason the student does not attend an IEP meeting that includes discussion of transition, the team must still consider the student's preferences and interests.[21]

When a student reaches the age of majority, all parental rights under IDEA transfer to him or her unless the student has been found incompetent under state law.[22] This means that the student displaces the parent on the IEP team. Either the district or the student may invite the parent to participate as a person with special knowledge or expertise about the student. Under the terms of the Family Educational Rights and Privacy Act (FERPA), however, the district would have to obtain the student's consent to disclose confidential educational records to a parent if the adult student does not live at home and is not a dependent for tax purposes.[23] OSEP has advised that a district could invite the parents of a nondependent adult student even without the student's consent,[24] but it is difficult to understand how the parents could attend an IEP meeting without being privy to confidential educational records.

IEP TEAM MEETINGS

Let's be candid: Special education meetings are hard! The same feature that makes them so useful—the multidisciplinary composition—also carries the potential for turf-guarding, cliquing, and clashing claims of expertise. Liam's sad but true meeting demonstrates some of the ways a meeting can go wrong. This is a good time to read Liam's meeting (see Figure 2.1), and keep it in mind through the rest of this chapter.

A clear understanding of IDEA requirements and effective meeting facilitation limit the emergence of such pathologies and heighten the team's awareness that the meeting should be all about serving the interests of the student.

IDEA prescribes the participants, frequency, topics of discussion, and mode of decision making.

Meeting Attendance

Team members may participate on a long-term, intermittent, or short-term basis, depending on the nature of their contributions to the team and the student's needs. IDEA provides an excusal mechanism for mandatory team members, so they

FIGURE 2.1 **Liam's Meeting**

Attending

- a special education administrator
- a special education secretary
- the principal from Northside Middle School
- the principal from Liam's Southside Middle School
- a special education teacher
- an instructional assistant
- a social studies teacher
- a written language teacher
- a speech-language pathologist (SLP)
- an occupational therapist (OT)
- an autism consultant
- Liam's mother
- Liam's father

Setting

Northside Middle School Conference Room, a narrow, windowless space almost filled with two rectangular tables butted end to end.

Background

Liam was a sixth-grade student eligible for special education due to an autism spectrum disorder. His elementary school experience had been happy; his placement was the regular classroom with instructional assistance and pull-out instruction for reading and written language. However, the parents had been at odds with the district since the end of the previous school year, when the district had decided to place Liam in a program for students with autism and mild intellectual disability at a middle school on the other side of town. The parents had sought placement in the regular classroom at the middle school that was two blocks from their home. They accepted the district decision but after four months were convinced that Liam was not benefitting from his IEP or placement.

The school district members of the IEP team held a closed door pre-meeting for an hour before the scheduled IEP meeting. The attorney representing the school district, who was not listed on the meeting notice, attended the pre-meeting and remained available for consultation in a nearby office during the IEP meeting.

The Meeting

Liam's parents entered the conference room right on time and found 11 district staff members already sitting at the table. They knew only the two principals and Liam's special education teacher. The district had refused the parents' request to include teachers from the elementary school Liam had attended the previous year.

Darrel Lynch, a special education administrator who had no firsthand knowledge of Liam, facilitated the meeting. Liam's father complained that the existing IEP did not reflect the decisions of the team, and Darrel replied, "That's why we're recording the meeting." The parents said they planned to record it also.

Darrel distributed a draft IEP and explained that it was just a draft that the team could alter or develop. He announced that the first step was to talk abut Liam's strengths and present levels of performance. Liam's mother spoke of the supplemental tutoring she and her husband provided to Liam and said he had particular strength in math and social skills. Several staff members agreed with her description.

Darrel then moved on to discussion of Liam's needs. The language arts teacher said that Liam was three years below grade level in reading comprehension. Liam's father says that Liam does better reading at home and is improving comprehension; he can identify the main idea and some details without prompting. Darrel said staff had seen no indication of these skills in the school setting and added, "We will just have to agree to disagree about Liam's skills."

The parents expressed concern about a lack of homework and low expectations on the part of some of Liam's teachers. The social studies teacher pointed out that she posted homework assignments on her webpage but added that she did not expect Liam to do written assignments or homework, because she had "no reason to believe that he was capable of doing it" and "it would be frustrating to both of us." Liam's father said that homework was important. Darrel replied, "Your concerns are duly noted."

In a lengthy discussion, the parents and staff again and again reported different levels of skill and performance. Although the parents provided specific examples of Liam's work, Darrel said that the staff could not corroborate the parents' observations, the meeting minutes would reflect the parents' point of view, and the meeting would have to move forward.

Darrel redirected the team to IEP goals. He announced that they would keep the same reading fluency goal that was in the existing IEP. Liam's special education teacher recommended changing the reading comprehension goal, but Darrel said the current goal would carry over to the new IEP. When the team moved on to discussion of written language goals, Darrel announced that Liam was making progress. Liam's mother passed out copies of a writing sample that Liam had produced the previous year, at his elementary school. The district staff on the team said they had never seen this writing sample. Liam's mother pointed out that in the 4 months that Liam had been in the middle school, the staff had not become familiar with his skills and past achievements. Darrel said, "We are going to agree to disagree on where Liam is right now." Liam's mother asked to see examples of Liam's current work. The special education teacher passed a writing sample to the parents, but Darrel said now was the time to discuss goals. When the parents protested, Darrel threatened to end the meeting.

Parents agreed to move on to a discussion of math goals. They said they were concerned because Liam's math activities were no more than review of things he already knew how to do. Darrel replied that they were following the normal scope and sequence of sixth-grade math.

The cycle of parent concerns continued, followed by Darrel's explanations of why the district's goals were appropriate. At every point of disagreement, Darrel said that "The meeting minutes will reflect your concerns," or "We will have to agree to disagree." Three times during the meeting, Darrel left the conference room to consult with the attorney.

The discussion turned to the services. The parents asked to add access to a computer as an accommodation. They said that Liam could type 30 wpm and could write much better when using a computer, and they objected to the requirement of one current teacher that he handwrite his assignments. Darrel dismissed the parents request that Liam be allowed to use a computer, saying "I have no information indicating that keyboarding is a necessary accommodation." The parents protested, pointing out that Liam had received occupational therapy services since second grade and had always used a computer. Darrel said it wasn't possible to guarantee that a computer would always be available. When asked, the OT said she had not spent much time with Liam but she thought he could work on his handwriting. The parents again protested, and Darrel said the team needed to move on, or he would terminate the meeting.

The autism consultant spoke next. He apologized to the parents for "dropping the ball," explaining that he had not known about Liam. He said it would be important to significantly increase the minutes of services he would provide, and to put in place a system for communicating with the parents.

The discussion turned to placement. The parents again stated their belief that Liam should be in a regular classroom with an aide and resource room support. Darrel said that the placement had been decided when the current IEP was written the previous June, and that the staff did not believe Liam could do the work required in a regular classroom. He polled the district members of the team, most of whom agreed that they thought Liam's current placement was appropriate for him.

Finally, after 4 hours, the meeting ended.

may attend only part of a meeting or not attend at all.[25] It is unreasonable to expect busy professional people to attend a meeting in which they have little or no contribution to make. Perhaps an SLP may wish to attend a meeting only for that portion during which the team discusses the student's speech or language needs, services, and goals. A regular education teacher may ask to be excused from the meeting entirely if his or her area of curriculum is not on the agenda.

The district and the parent(s) must agree in writing and in advance to excuse any mandatory team member for any reason. It is improper to announce an absence at the meeting and ask a parent to sign an excusal agreement at that time! If the district and parents agree to excuse a team member whose area of professional expertise is on the agenda, that team member must submit written input before the meeting, so the team can consider the information as they are developing the IEP.[26]

Schools must inform parents about any proposed IEP team meeting. The notice must: (a) specify the purpose, time, and location of the meeting; (b) identify who will attend; and (c) let parents know they may invite others who have knowledge or special expertise about the student.

If the student will turn 16 during the time the IEP will be in effect, the notice must also inform parents that one purpose of the meeting will be to discuss postsecondary goals and transition services, and that the school will also invite the student.[27]

School personnel must take steps to encourage one or both of a student's parents to attend each IEP Team meeting. First, the school must notify parents of the meeting early enough to ensure that they can attend.[28] IDEA does not define what "early enough" means; we can assume that it means something like "a reasonable time." Second, the school must schedule the meeting at a mutually agreed on time and place.[29] In a recent case, *Drobnicki v. Poway Unified School District*, the Ninth Circuit Court of Appeals held that a district violated IDEA when it made no effort to reschedule a meeting after a parent said she was unable to attend on the scheduled date; instead the

district allowed the mother to participate only by telephone.[30] The court concluded that the district had significantly restricted parental participation in the IEP formulation process.

Schools routinely schedule IEP meetings within work hours defined in staff collective bargaining agreements; on this practice, OSEP has recently stated:

> Although [IDEA] does not prohibit public agencies from scheduling IEP Team meetings in the evening, it does not require that they do so. Therefore, it is not unreasonable for public agencies to schedule meetings of the IEP Team only during regular school hours or regular business hours because it is likely that these times are most suitable for public agency personnel to attend these meetings.[31]

If neither parent can attend an IEP meeting, the district must facilitate another mode of parent participation,[32] such as telephone conference call, videoconference, email, etc. Note that this is mandatory, not optional! Many parents face significant challenges in scheduling, transportation, child care, or work schedules that limit their ability to get to the school for meetings. In such circumstances, IDEA requires districts to find another way to ensure meaningful parent participation.

A district may hold an IEP meeting without parent participation only if it has been unsuccessful, after genuine and repeated efforts, in persuading the parents to participate.[33] In such circumstances, the district must maintain detailed documentation of its efforts to secure parent participation, including phone call logs and notes, copies of written correspondence, and records of home visits.[34] Where a parent's own conduct unreasonably delays an IEP meeting, however, courts are likely to find no IDEA violation if the district conducts an IEP meeting without the parent.

Failure to hold a meeting and develop or revise and IEP, even in the face of perceived parent recalcitrance, can be a costly mistake. In *Hogan v. Fairfax County School Board*,[35] a parent either ignored or did not receive two letters from a school district regarding an IEP review meeting. The district did nothing at all for more than five months, leaving the student without a current IEP. Finally, in late August, the parent inquired about the student's IEP for that school year. The district proposed to place the student, a girl who had a severe reading disability, in a program for males with emotional and behavioral disabilities. The parents rejected the placement, engaged in a dispute with the district about additional evaluation, and placed the student in a private program for students with reading disabilities.

Meanwhile, the district still did not convene an IEP meeting. Ultimately, a hearing officer concluded that, while the parent bore some responsibility, the district had failed to provide the free appropriate public education to which the student was entitled. The federal district court concurred and ordered the district to reimburse the parents for the cost of the private services the parents had obtained.

How Often Does the IEP Team Meet?

The simple but not-so-simple answer to the question, "How often does the IEP team meet?" is "As often as necessary." This may be surprising to those who think that an IEP is on a strict one-year review schedule. In fact, IDEA provides that the IEP team must review an IEP "periodically, but not less than annually,"[36] and must revise the IEP to address:

▶ lack of expected progress toward annual goals
▶ results of any reevaluation
▶ information about the student provided to, or by, the parents
▶ student's anticipated needs
▶ other matters

If a student is progressing as the team anticipated at the last IEP meeting, and no relevant new information about the student emerges either at school or at home, an annual IEP meeting satisfies IDEA. However, if the student is floundering despite conscientious implementation of the IEP, or if the student develops new problems that the team did not know about, or if the district or parents have new evaluation information

with implications for the appropriateness of the student's program, the team should revisit the IEP as soon as possible, even if the IEP has been in effect for only a few weeks or months.

Where Does the IEP Team Meet (or Does It)?

IEP teams customarily meet at the student's school. This is certainly a reasonable and sensible practice, as most team members are already at the school. If, however, parents are unable to get to the school, it is important for the school to consider other options for the parents to participate.

IDEA provides that parents and schools may agree to use alternative means of conducting an IEP or placement meeting, using such conventional modalities as telephone or video-conference.[37] In addition, many options are now available for interactive video communication from almost any location via personal computer or smart phones. If necessary, a parent who cannot take time off work to attend an IEP meeting could participate from the workplace.

Alternative meeting formats offer a number of potential advantages. Of course, they increase opportunities for active meeting participation by all team members, and may also encourage better meeting preparation by all parties. They can be very efficient and productive, especially when the team works well together and is in general agreement, and when the purpose of the meeting is to make relatively minor adjustments to an existing IEP. However, alternative meeting modes are not appropriate for initial IEP development, when the team is just beginning to understand the student's needs and the parent may not yet know very much about special education. A face-to-face meeting provides team members the opportunity to examine and easily share documents and work samples, and to begin the essential process of building strong working relationships.

From time to time, districts might encounter parents who have an unusually high need to meet and review their child's IEP. If staff are confident that the IEP in effect is producing the expected results, and the student is doing well, the district can refuse to convene additional IEP meetings. The district would have to provide prior written notice to the parent of its refusal to call a meeting, and the parents could use any IDEA dispute resolution mechanisms to challenge that decision.

We all know that school personnel are tremendously busy, and nobody wants to encourage unnecessary meetings. IDEA expressly encourages meeting consolidation,[38] and the district and the parents may agree to amend an IEP after an annual IEP review without holding a formal IEP meeting.[39] If this happens, the district must produce a written document that specifies the modifications to the IEP, and must inform the IEP team of the changes. In addition, the district must provide the parents a copy of the IEP with the revisions incorporated into it upon request.[40]

COLLABORATION AND DECISION MAKING

Parent Participation

Parents are full team members, not mere adjuncts to the team. When a dispute arises on any of the special education multidisciplinary teams, district personnel often state that "the team decided" rather than correctly stating that "the district staff on the team agreed." This is not a minor rhetorical distinction but rather reflects a common misconception that parent participation in special education decision making is a *pro forma* requirement rather than a substantive right. The constitutional right of parents to direct their children's education is well established,[41] and parents do not relinquish this right when their children become eligible for special education. IDEA states that:

> Almost 30 years of research and experience has demonstrated that the education of children with disabilities can be made more effective by . . . strengthening the role and responsibility of parents and ensuring that families of such children have meaningful opportunities to participate in the education of their children at school and at home.[42]

One of the stated purposes of IDEA is "to ensure that the rights of children with disabilities and parents of such children are protected."[43] Since enactment of IDEA in 1975, parents have been members of their children's IEP teams, and each time Congress has amended the law, express parent involvement rights have broadened. As of 2011, IDEA specifically includes explicit rights to: (a) be involved in every stage of referral, evaluation, and eligibility determination; (b) participate in IEP development, review, and revision; (c) be part of the placement team; and (d) take part in disciplinary proceedings, including manifestation determinations, location of interim alternative educational setting, and disciplinary change of placement. In addition, IDEA requires schools to ensure that parents can understand and participate in meetings by providing interpreter services for parents who are deaf or whose native language is not English.[44]

Although IDEA expressly includes parents in all special education decision making, the nature of parent involvement varies tremendously from place to place and from court decision to court decision. Even the terminology is inconsistent from source to source. Is it parent participation, or parent input, or parent attendance? OSEP has always taken the position that parents are "equal participants"[45] or "equal partners"[46] with district staff on the team. OSEP further explained how parents participate in IEP development:

> This is an active role in which the parents (1) provide critical information regarding the strengths of their child and express their concerns for enhancing the education of their child; (2) participate in discussions about the child's need for special education and related services and supplementary aids and services; and (3) join with the other participants in deciding how the child will be involved and progress in the general curriculum and participate in State and district-wide assessments, and what services the agency will provide to the child and in what setting.[47]

Clearly, this means more than formalistic meeting attendance or token opportunity to provide input.

IDEA contemplates a process in which parents contribute expertise on their own children and possibly also informed views about teaching and learning, while district members of the team primarily contribute professional expertise in curriculum, instruction, assessment, school policy and also, ideally, specific knowledge about the student. Equal partners means equal partners, each with valuable contributions to the team and to the student!

Preparing Parents for Meetings

School personnel can and should provide direction to parents to help them prepare for the IEP meeting and encourage active parent participation. District staff are generally required to send meeting notice to parents on standard forms, but such forms are impersonal and uninviting. For an initial IEP, we encourage special educators to send a letter of invitation in addition to whatever form the district requires.

Parents need to understand the purpose(s) of the meeting. The letter would inform the parents that the purpose of the meeting is to accurately identify the student's unique educational needs and present levels of performance; to establish annual goals; and to plan a program of specially designed instruction, related services, and accommodations designed to enable the student to move from present levels to goals. The letter should also explain to parents that they are equal partners with the district, and that their contributions are valuable. Above all, the letter should ask the parents to arrive at the meeting prepared to share ways in which they would like the district to individualize their child's educational program. The law requires the IEP team to consider the strengths of the child and the concerns of the parents for enhancing their child's education. Parents need to know this!

We know that special educators have plenty of work to do already, and we do not wish to burden them unduly with yet another bit of paperwork. However, the invitation letter we propose could be a form letter that needs only to be personalized with the parents' names, the student's name, and the correct pronouns. We suggest one possible format (see Figure 2.2), but experienced special education teachers may prefer to write their own. The important thing is to make the parents feel welcome, and help them to understand their role in IEP development.

Though parents are entitled to participate and are, indeed, essential partners in special education processes, they do not necessarily know how to contribute effectively to team discussions and decisions. We know few special educators who have time or resources to offer guidance to parents so they understand the value of their role as IEP team members and develop the skills to contribute effectively. Fortunately, parents can seek assistance from Parent Training and Information (PTI) or Community Parent Resource Centers (CPRC). Information about these organizations (and much more) is available from the National Dissemination Center for Children with Disabilities (NICHCY).[48]

IDEA provides funding for these organizations in order to ensure that parents of children with disabilities have access to information about IDEA, about special education, about resources available to them in their localities, and about effective involvement in decision making related to their children's special education. PTIs and CPRCs help parents develop skill in negotiating and advocating on behalf of their children. They offer workshops, book and video libraries, and referral services to other agencies and organizations. Some even provide trained volunteers who review IEPs or attend IEP meetings with parents.

Staff Preparation for Meetings

IDEA expressly permits the staff members of IEP teams to meet without the parents present to prepare for a full team meeting.[49] The purpose of a staff pre-meeting is to ensure that all district team members have the information they need to efficiently fulfill their responsibilities as team members. Articulating a district proposal or a district response to a parent proposal is also acceptable, assuming that the proposal or

FIGURE 2.2   IEP Meeting Invitation

Dear Parents,

As you know, we recently determined that your daughter Abigail was eligible for an Individualized Education Program (IEP) to meet her special academic, social, behavioral, physical, or other needs. She is now legally entitled to: (1) special education, which is specially designed instruction to meet those needs; (2) related services such as transportation or occupational therapy, which she may need to benefit from special education; and (3) any services, aids, modifications, or accommodations she may need if and when she is in regular education classes, including support for the staff working with her.

We need to have a meeting to plan Abigail's IEP. At this meeting, we will discuss her strengths, her unique characteristics and needs, services appropriate for her, and ways we can judge how well the services are helping Abigail make progress at school.

I will be at the meeting, and so will the people listed on the Meeting Notice form. You are welcome to bring anyone you wish to the meeting. Some organizations, such as the Parent Training and Information Center, may be able to help you prepare for the meeting or provide a volunteer to attend the meeting with you. I encourage you to call them and ask for information.

You may bring Abigail for all or part of the meeting, if you wish. It can be useful for a student to participate, and she may feel more involved with and committed to her IEP goals. If you decide not to bring Abigail to the meeting, please consider bringing a picture of her to remind us all that the only purpose of the meeting is to plan an educational program just for her.

You are a full and equal partner with school staff in deciding what will be in Abigail's IEP. I am enclosing a draft IEP with my ideas of what Abigail's IEP might include, but this is not a final IEP! You know Abigail better than anyone, and we invite you to help us to know her better. Please tell us about your concerns for her and what you think she needs. We urge you to give some thought to these matters ahead of time, so we can exchange ideas at the meeting. Feel free to bring any information and materials you think will help us to understand Abigail!

We have tentatively scheduled this meeting for February 2 at 3:00 PM here at McAuliffe Elementary. If this is not convenient, please call and we will arrange another time. In addition to the draft IEP, I have enclosed a brochure explaining your legal rights. Please look it over. If you have any questions, we can discuss them at the meeting.

Sincerely,

Anita Hill

Anita Hill

Abigail's Teacher

response is an agenda item for discussion at the team meeting and not intended as a final decision.

Staff members of the IEP team must also be aware of any accommodations needed to facilitate team communication and meaningful parent participation. If the parent is deaf or does not speak English fluently, the district must make sure that an interpreter attends the meeting.[50] In addition, staff must provide a copy of the Procedural Safeguards Notice in the parent's native language, if possible. Although the Procedural Safeguards Notice is widely available in Spanish, Chinese, Vietnamese, and other common languages, most states and districts lack the resources to publish documents in every language spoken by students and their families. In such cases, it is particularly important that the district offer careful explanations of the parent's and student's rights at the meeting through the interpreter.

Because IEP meetings typically take place at school, the responsibility for finding a suitable meeting space rests on staff. It should be as physically comfortable and free of distractions as possible. Try to arrange seating so that all meeting participants can easily make eye contact with one another; a round, oval, or horseshoe configuration is ideal. If meeting in a classroom is unavoidable, at least make sure that adult-scale chairs and table are available for the team. Make sure that any needed documents, records, work samples, or instructional materials are available to all team members. It may be necessary to set up a speaker phone or other technology to facilitate the participation of any team member who cannot be physically present. It may also be useful to set up a white board or chart paper for brainstorming or mapping the links between the student's needs, goals, and services.

Schedule ample time for the meeting so no one feels rushed. At the same time, it is important to prepare a draft agenda to keep the meeting focused and on-task. Initial IEP meetings may require an hour or even more. Annual reviews can often be shorter. Difficult and complicated IEPs can take several hours or sessions, especially if communication and trust have broken down, or if the student has complex needs.

Draft IEP

Although districts may not lawfully predetermine program or placement, staff may draft an IEP as a basis for discussion at the IEP meeting. In its commentary on the final federal regulations to the 2004 IDEA amendments, the US Department of Education discussed this issue in detail:

> We encourage public agency staff to come to an IEP Team meeting prepared to discuss evaluation findings and preliminary recommendations. Likewise, parents have the right to bring questions, concerns, and preliminary recommendations to the IEP Team meeting as part of a full discussion of the child's needs and the services to be provided to meet those needs. We do not encourage public agencies to prepare a draft IEP prior to the IEP Team meeting, particularly if doing so would inhibit a full discussion of the child's needs. However, if a public agency develops a draft IEP prior to the IEP Team meeting, the agency should make it clear to the parents at the outset of the meeting that the services proposed by the agency are preliminary recommendations for review and discussion with the parents. The public agency also should provide the parents with a copy of its draft proposals, if the agency has developed them, prior to the IEP Team meeting so as to give the parents an opportunity to review the recommendations of the public agency prior to the IEP Team meeting, and be better able to engage in a full discussion of the proposals for the IEP. It is not permissible for an agency to have the final IEP completed before an IEP Team meeting begins.

It is simple, really. In most cases, the student's special educator drafts an IEP and brings this draft to the IEP meeting. It adds only one step to distribute copies of the draft to the team—including parents, of course—before the meeting along with a request that all team members bring questions, concerns, and suggestions to the meeting.

Predetermination

Predetermination is a relatively new term used to describe an old problem—the selection of services or placement by the district before the IEP meeting. In an early IDEA case, *Spielberg v. Henrico County Public Schools*,[51] the district had placed a student in a residential setting. The district later developed its own program and informed the parents that the district would no longer pay for the residential placement, and the student must return to the public school. The court held that the district violated IDEA by first selecting a placement and developing an IEP to carry out their decision. This district action not only ignored the prescribed IEP Placement sequence, but also violated "the spirit and intent" of the law by infringing parent participation. "After the fact involvement is not enough," the court explained.

Predetermination of services sometimes occurs through institutionalized bad habits rather than intent to sidestep IDEA requirements. Typically, a special education teacher writes an IEP that closely resembles the current IEP except for updated (one hopes) present levels of performance and goals, reviews the new IEP at a brief ritualized IEP meeting, and asks the parent(s) to sign it. Joshua's meeting, which took place only last spring, illustrates this common scenario (see Figure 2.3).

Predetermination may also occur through a more calculated process in which the district holds a pre-meeting to make sure all staff present a united front on non-negotiable decisions regarding program or placement. One of the authors recently attended a meeting for Leilani that illustrates the way a district can appear cordial and invite parent participation without actually considering any options other than the one the district has already selected (see Figure 2.4).

Whether it occurs through careless practice or by design, predetermination undermines the fundamental principle of school-family collaboration via the IEP team process. Courts have held that predetermination deprives parents of their right to meaningful participation in IEP development, a procedural IDEA violation that constitutes a denial of FAPE.

One of the most blatant cases of predetermination is *Deal v. Hamilton County Board of Education*.[52] The Court found the school had an unofficial policy of refusing to provide one-on-one applied behavior analysis (ABA) programs, even when the parents shared ABA's impressive results with their son and district personnel openly admired the child's progress. The court believed the district was immovable, regardless of ABA's efficacy.

In another recent case, *Berry v. Las Virgenes Unified School District*,[53] the Ninth Circuit Court of Appeals affirmed a lower court decision that found predetermination when a school district decided to transfer a student from a private placement to a public school placement. The trial court did not find the testimony of district staff credible when they claimed that they had been open to considering options other than returning the student to public school.

Too frequently, courts do not delve deeply into the authenticity of the collaboration at an IEP meeting. If parents attended the meeting and spoke, a court may take it for granted that the district members of the IEP team gave serious consideration to the parents' preferences, reasoning, or supporting data.

Consensus, Disagreement and Dispute Resolution

An IEP team has the sole authority to determine the content of an IEP, based on student-specific information. Although IDEA does not mandate any particular decision making process for the IEP team, OSEP asserts that consensus is the appropriate model but does not elaborate on what consensus looks like. Consensus does not mean unanimous decision or decision by majority rule but rather general agreement. Disagreement within the IEP team often pits parents against school team members, which may by sheer weight of numbers suggest "general agreement," but which parents may understandably view as coercion.

Sometimes conflict arises because staff and parents disagree about what the team actually agreed to. The parents may receive a final copy

FIGURE 2.3   Joshua's Meeting

Background

Joshua is a 15-year-old freshman, eligible for special education as a student with a learning disability and "other health impairment" (ADHD). He mostly takes regular classes but has also been going to the resource room for services in math and reading.

The Meeting

Attending the early morning meeting were the resource (special education) teacher, a regular classroom teacher, Joshua, and his mother. The principal who was to serve as the district representative did not attend, but the resource teacher said, "She will sign later."

The resource teacher began by explaining that the meeting "is a 3-year reevaluation and an annual IEP planning meeting." The mother listened and nodded. Joshua wrote in his journal through most of the meeting.

The resource teacher talked about Joshua's assessment scores, comparing them to his scores from the previous year. She also talked about Joshua's progress compared to that of his sister, who was her former student. She talked about Joshua's strengths in glowing terms. She announced

that Joshua was now on grade level in math and was "no longer qualified in math . . . as long as the team agrees with me." Hearing no objection, she continued the meeting, telling the mother about how ADHD would affect Joshua's future. She also spoke about Joshua's frequent absences from school. The mother continued to nod her head, and Joshua doodled in his notebook.

The resource teacher reviewed the state assessment scores. The classroom teacher said that she needed to get to her room before her first-period students arrived. The resource teacher quickly turned to the goals page of the current IEP. She said they needed to drop the math goals because Joshua had reached grade level. She also said they needed to change the reading goals from fourth to fifth grade level. She then rushed through the rest of the IEP form and announced that Joshua's time in the resource room would be 60 minutes/day now that Joshua did not need math. She asked if everybody agreed that the resource room "best meets Joshua's needs."

At this point the classroom teacher asked if she could sign the IEP, and then she quickly left. The mother also signed the IEP, said good-bye, and left.

---

of the IEP and find components that differ from what they expected. District staff may remember it differently, and meeting notes may be too vague or inconclusive to resolve the disagreement. A simple way to avoid the stalemate that occurs when parents and district had different recollections of the meeting is to record the meeting. Access to recording equipment should not be a problem. Digital audio and video recorders are readily available, inexpensive, and unobtrusive. IDEA is silent about recording meetings. The most recent guidance from OSEP states that:

> [A state department of education or school district] has the option to require, prohibit,

limit, or otherwise regulate the use of recording devices at IEP meetings. If a public agency has a policy prohibiting the use of these devices at IEP meetings, that policy must provide for exceptions if they are necessary to ensure that the parent understands the IEP or the IEP process or to implement other parental rights guaranteed under Part B. Any recording of an IEP meeting that is maintained by the public agency is an "education record," within the meaning of the Family Educational Rights and Privacy Act ("FERPA"; 20 USC 1232g), and would, therefore, be subject to the confidentiality requirements of the regulation under both FERPA (34 CFR Part 99) and Part B (Sec. 300.560-300.575). Parents wishing to use audio or video recording devices

FIGURE 2.4   Leilani's Meeting

Background

Leilani is a 12-year-old sixth grade girl who has Down Syndrome, with mild intellectual and speech disabilities, whose home school district is tiny. She had an IEP current until the following November, and a placement in a larger district nearby. In June, after determining that serving Leilani in her home district would be less costly than the out-of-district placement, the district convened a meeting identified as an "IEP placement meeting," although no new IEP was proposed. The home district did not yet have a program suitable for Leilani but planned to have something in place when the new school year began.

The Meeting

The parents' view was clear; they did not want to transfer Leilani to the local school, citing several reasons. In her current placement, Leilani has peers (disabled and nondisabled) and a best friend. She would enter middle school with her sixth grade friends and would also be with older "life-skills" students in the eighth and ninth grades who would be models for her. The proposed new placement, a combination life-skills and general education class, would include only two other students with disabilities, both boys, and one much younger than Leilani. In her present placement, Leilani has access to the larger community and its activities and opportunities. In the proposed placement, Leilani would have access to limited community resources and activities, only a general store and a service station. Her parents felt it would be wrong to jeopardize the success Leilani has experienced in the city school by moving her to a hypothetical new program in an underresourced village school.

The discussion at the meeting was lengthy and civil. Staff were friendly, and they seemed interested in Leilani. The parents had plenty of opportunity to express their views. It was clear, however, that the district had no intention of seriously considering the option of allowing Leilani to stay in her present program. The facilitator of the meeting was knowledgeable about the law and skilled at giving every appearance of full parent participation. It seemed to this observer to be a well-designed but predetermined sham.

At the end of the meeting the parents said they would seek due process. Based purely on documentation of this meeting, it is possible that a hearing officer could conclude that the parents were able to fully exercise their right to participate in the decision. Fortunately, the parties settled without going to hearing. With the strong encouragement of their attorney, the district agreed that Leilani could stay in her present placement for the next school year.

---

at IEP meetings should consult State or local policies for further guidance.[54]

Regardless of whether the meeting is recorded, it is important to write detailed meeting notes. Specific details are better than bullet lists and cryptic sentence fragments. Using a computer would avoid the problem of indecipherable handwritten notes. Ideally, a person who is not a central player would be responsible for recording meeting notes, as some people find it difficult to take good notes while participating in discussion.

What happens when team members lack communication and collaboration skills, or when the "equal partners" of school and parents disagree? OSEP has consistently taken the position that:

> The [school district] has ultimate responsibility to ensure that the IEP includes the services that

the child needs in order to receive FAPE. It is not appropriate to make IEP decisions based upon a majority "vote." If the team cannot reach consensus, the public agency must provide the parents with prior written notice of the agency's proposals or refusals, or both, regarding the child's educational program, and the parents have the right to seek resolution of any disagreements by initiating an impartial due process hearing.[55]

Due process hearings are expensive, resource-intensive proceedings. They can permanently damage relationships between the parents and school. Of course, due process hearings may be unavoidable in some circumstances, but we recommend the use of informal negotiation or alternative dispute resolution mechanisms before resorting to the adversariality of formal due process. If district staff and parents are unable to resolve disagreements on their own, they might try any of the following options:

▶ **Facilitated IEP meeting,**[56] in which a neutral party not associated with either the district or other parents conducts the meeting and acts to promote clear communication among team participants, pinpoint disagreements, and focus the team on the task of developing an appropriate IEP. IDEA does not mention facilitated IEP meetings, but some state departments of education offer this service.

▶ **Mediation,** which is negotiation between the parties facilitated by an impartial third party, can be an effective tool for breaking through an impasse. IDEA requires state departments of education to make this option available at no cost to parents, but mediation is possible only when both parties agree to participate.

▶ **State complaint investigation** is another option, if parents believe that the disagreement reflects one or more IDEA violations. State departments of education bear the burden of ensuring that school districts comply with IDEA and must investigate allegations that a district is out of compliance.

Parents interested in pursuing any of these alternatives to a due process hearing should contact the special education department at their state department of education,[57] or a PTI or CPRC.

Meeting Well

A little good will and planning can go a long way toward avoiding conflict and eliminating, or at least reducing, the need for dispute resolution processes. This may seem overly idealistic or even unattainable, but in fact it happens every day in schools across the country. We have seen many good meetings and include an abbreviated description of Madeleine's pretty good meeting (see Figure 2.5).

Madeleine's meeting illustrates both procedures and behavior that encouraged the team to work effectively as a multidisciplinary team should.

▶ One person facilitated the meeting but did not dominate the discussion.

▶ The meeting space was adequate for the size of the group, and the seating arrangement enabled all participants to see one another.

▶ Everybody arrived on time, showing respect for the schedules of all participants.

▶ The facilitator set a friendly but businesslike tone. She kept the meeting on task while providing ample opportunity for all team members to contribute.

▶ Team members introduced themselves, ensuring that everyone understood the role of every other person at the meeting.

▶ A prepared agenda identified the key tasks of the meeting, and team members had an opportunity to add to it.

▶ The facilitator actively sought information from the parents about the student.

▶ Each team member contributed information related to their areas of expertise.

FIGURE 2.5   Madeleine's Meeting

Attending

- ► Special Education Teacher
- ► Regular Education (first-grade) Teacher
- ► Speech-Language Pathologist (SLP)
- ► S-K District Psychologist
- ► Principal
- ► Madeleine's mother
- ► Madeleine's father

Setting

Ponderosa Middle School Conference Room, a bright, square space with doors on two sides and a window showing an interior hallway. Meeting participants sat on moulded plastic chairs around a large round table.

Background

Madeleine is six years old and halfway through first grade. Last month, in January, she was found eligible for special education as a child with an intellectual disability. The parents were not sure they agreed, but they did not challenge the evaluation team's conclusion. The district scheduled a meeting to develop an IEP two weeks after the eligibility decision.

The Meeting

Cindy, the school psychologist, arrived first and set a pitcher of ice water and some paper cups on top of a bookcase. On a white board above the bookcase, she wrote the date and an agenda:

- ► Purpose: Maddie's IEP
- ► Procedural Safeguards
- ► Parental concerns
- ► Teacher concerns and observations
- ► Review assessments
- ► Draft IEP
- ► Placement

As team members arrived, Cindy greeted them with a friendly smile and said they could sit wherever they liked. The principal, who seemed a bit harried, arrived last and sat near the hallway door.

Cindy started the meeting at 2:45, right on schedule, and began, "Thank you all for being here this afternoon." She asked everyone at the table to introduce him- or herself, as the parents had not previously met the special education teacher or the SLP. "Now that we're all here, I will pass the IEP cover page. Please sign and date it, to document that this meeting took place and that you attended." She then asked if anyone wanted to add to the agenda, but nobody did.

Cindy picked up the Procedural Safeguards handbook and handed it to Madeleine's parents. "This is for you. It explains your rights as a special education parent." The parents said they already had one at home. Cindy told the parents they could call or email her any time they had any questions about it.

Cindy then asked the parents to "paint a picture of Madeleine" and share any concerns they had about her.

The father replied that Madeleine is cheerful and friendly and fun, but that her behavior was frequently out of control when she was disappointed, or when asked to do something she did not feel confident about. The mother said she worked with Madeleine at home and was worried because "Maddie gets something one day and then forgets what she learned, so I have to teach her all over again." The father said they were worried that if Madeleine did not make much progress in reading this year, she would fall further behind next year. Cindy said, "That's why we're here today. We are going write an IEP, so Maddie can get the help she needs."

Cindy thanked the parents for their observations and then asked the first-grade teacher to share her information about Madeleine. The teacher replied that she enjoyed having Madeleine, whom she described as happy, chatty, and helpful but a bit reticent with her peers. She observed that Maddie is often off-task and becomes stubborn and resistant when attempts are made to redirect her. "Maddie has a short attention span. She has not learned all her letters yet but can write her name using a visual model. She can recognize numbers up to 9, and she can count using manipulables, but she does not yet understand how to add single-digit numbers. The special education teacher agreed that these were the immediate areas of concern and recommended that Madeleine come to the resource room for 1:1 work on letter sounds and number skills with an instructional assistant. She also suggested that she and the first-grade teacher meet once a week to monitor Madeleine's progress.

Cindy asked the SLP to discuss Madeleine's speech and communication needs. The SLP said that Madeleine had some articulation problems, and she itemized them specifically. She added that an audiology screen indicated no problems, and Madeleine had surprisingly good receptive language. She recommended focusing on speech therapy this year.

Cindy said, "It sounds like we have a pretty good idea of what Maddie needs, so now we need to write her IEP." She added that she had been filling in the present levels of performance and recommended services on the IEP form as the team was talking. "Let's go through the form and make sure we are meeting all the requirements." She led the team through the IEP form, and when they got to the question about whether the student's behavior impeded her learning or that of other students, the team discussed the possibility of adding behavior support. The parents felt certain that behavior was a problem that needed to be addressed. The special education teacher suggested that Madeleine's misbehavior reflected frustration at facing academic expectations that she was unable to meet, and Cindy said she tended to agree. The parents disagreed, as did the first-grade teacher. After a few minutes of discussion, the team agreed to draft an IEP that included goals and services in reading, writing, and math to go into effect as soon as possible. However, they also agreed to conduct further assessment to help the team determine whether to add a behavior plan to Madeleine's IEP. The parents signed a prior written notice and consent for the behavioral assessment.

Cindy suggested that they reconvene to reconsider the behavior issue. She and the special education teacher estimated that the assessment could be accomplished within a couple of weeks. After checking their calendars, the team members agreed to meet again in 3 weeks.

Cindy thanked everybody for their contributions. The meeting adjourned less than an hour after it began.

► Team members appeared to feel safe expressing differences of opinion.

► The entire team listened with genuine interest to the parents' concerns and decided to take action in response to them.

► The team prepared an action plan and scheduled a new meeting to revisit the issue and consider new information.

► The team made efficient use of almost every minute of the meeting and reached a conclusion in less than an hour.

Madeleine's meeting presents a sharp contrast with Liam's meeting, in which:

► The meeting space was cramped, stuffy, and uncomfortable. The narrow table forced participants to twist around awkwardly when somebody sitting on the same side of the table was speaking.

► An unnecessarily large number of district staff attended the meeting, raising the suspicion that the district might be deliberately trying to intimidate the parents.

► The team appeared to have made decisions about the student's program and placement before the meeting and did not seriously consider information that the parents provided.

► The overall tone of the meeting was hostile. The facilitator openly discounted the parents' contributions and became threatening, when the parents insisted on trying to communicate their concerns and provide information from their own knowledge of the student.

► Although the attorney for the district was not in the room, and the meeting notice had not indicated that the attorney would be present, the facilitator consulted with him several times during the meeting.

► The meeting took an unreasonable amount of time but ended up where it started, with the district standing firm in the same decisions staff brought to the meeting four hours earlier.

Liam's meeting demonstrates an extreme case. Seldom have we encountered such flagrant disregard for the decision making processes that IDEA requires. Most IEP meetings inhabit a space somewhere between the conscientious attention to the letter and spirit of IDEA that Madeleine's meeting illustrates and the contemptuous travesty of IDEA requirements in Liam's meeting.

We would like to think it goes without saying that team members should treat one another with respect and courtesy. Still, team members sometimes let their emotions get the better of them and make intemperate comments. One of the authors attended an IEP meeting not long ago in which a mother recounted in elaborate detail the admitted multiple failings of her child's special education teacher, who had recently been dismissed. The mother continued her litany of complaints for so long—perhaps ten minutes

or more—that her husband looked slightly embarrassed. The staff members of the team listened without interruption except to admit that the problems with the former teacher had been serious, and had been allowed to continue far too long. Finally, the mother exhausted her need to vent, and the meeting proceeded briskly to a resolution that satisfied everyone. A situation that could have devolved into an exchange of recrimination and defensiveness instead resolved through team members' compassion, affirmation, and restraint.

Some of the advice in this section may seem counterintuitive. Planning for and facilitating meetings as we suggest may seem burdensome to teachers and other staff who have plenty of other responsibilities. Wouldn't it really be best to streamline meetings, keep them on a strict agenda, and discourage parents from talking too much and stretching the meeting out for hours? Well yes, sort of, and no. Efficiency is a good thing, especially for busy teachers, service providers, and administrators. By all means, have an agenda, but don't stick to is slavishly when it becomes clear that some agenda items need more time than originally scheduled. And squelching parent participation may seem efficient, but dissatisfied parents or those who feel disregarded may demand far more time down the road. Think of IEP meetings and collaboratively developed IEPs as an investment in the future. This is the best opportunity school personnel have to show parents that they take a genuine, personal interest in the student and truly want him or her to be successful. It's worth the effort!

The IEP meeting has only one purpose—to develop or review and revise an individualized educational program that meets the unique educational needs of a student with disabilities. Clarity about the IDEA requirement of collaboration, and good meeting facilitation and interpersonal skills, enables the team to achieve this purpose. We conclude with **Tips for Effective IEP Meetings and Positive Relationships** (Figure 2.6) that every team member—parents and staff alike—should review before each meeting.

FIGURE 2.6 Tips for Effective IEP Meetings and Positive Relationships

Prepare for the Meeting

- ▶ Identify a meeting time and place that enables parents to participate.
- ▶ Give parents information in advance, so they can prepare to participate meaningfully in the meeting.
- ▶ Convene a staff pre-meeting to share important information, but do not make decisions without parents.

Structure Meeting

- ▶ Identify the meeting facilitator.
- ▶ Spend no more than five minutes identifying and prioritizing topics for discussion.
- ▶ Define problems concisely and focus greater time, energy, and creativity on discussion.
- ▶ Accurately record all discussion and decisions.

Communicate, Communicate, Communicate!

- ▶ Effective communication may not be everything, but without it, nothing else is enough.
- ▶ Communication works two ways. TALK and LISTEN!
- ▶ Model active listening, and ask clarifying questions as needed to ensure mutual understanding.
- ▶ Take time to explain or define unfamiliar concepts or terminology.
- ▶ Communication involves discussion, not simply conclusions.
- ▶ Accept reality of emotional responses and avoid personalizing them.

Collaborate

- ▶ All team members offer important information, perspectives, and priorities.
- ▶ Avoid drawing lines in the sand. Compliance with law is the only non-negotiable.
- ▶ Remember this is about the student and his or her needs!

Maintain Climate of Mutual Respect

- ▶ Maintain pleasant facial expressions and relaxed body language.
- ▶ Ask participants how they prefer to be addressed.
- ▶ Assume good will and ignore provocations.
- ▶ Avoid "experts v. amateurs" or "us v. them" positioning.
  - Parents are experts on their children; however, they may **also** be knowledgeable about teaching and learning.
  - Staff are the experts in their professions; however, staff may **also** be knowledgeable about the child.

Tell the Truth

- ▶ Honesty builds trust. Nothing alienates so much as being lied to.
- ▶ Some truths are difficult, but speak the truth always.
- ▶ Support statements of fact with evidence.
- ▶ Avoidance and omission of important information is untruthful.
- ▶ Deliver painful information with compassion.

Admit Mistakes

- ▶ Everyone makes mistakes. Humility and candor earn respect.
- ▶ Don't make excuses. Just say "I was wrong!" and make amends.

Reach Decisions, Record Action Plan, and Follow Through

- ▶ Clearly articulate decisions and their rationales to be sure everyone understands.
- ▶ Note disagreements and their reasoning.
- ▶ Establish timelines and assign tasks. Commit action plan to writing!
- ▶ Define process for ensuring implementation of all decisions.
- ▶ Implement all decisions faithfully.

Adapted from: Kriha, D.L. (October 7, 2009). Can't we all just get along? Tips for effective IEP meetings. Presentation at the 26th Annual Pacific Northwest Institute on Special Education and the Law.

Notes

1. 34 CFR 300.300(b).

2. 34 CFR 300.321.

3. 34 CFR 300.321(e).

4. 34 CFR 300.30.

5. 34 CFR 300.519.

6. 34 CFR Part 300, Appendix A, Question 23 (1999).

7. OSEP. (January 2007). *Questions and Answers On Individualized Education Programs (IEPs), Evaluations, and Reevaluations*, Question C-2.

8. 34 CFR Part 300, Appendix A, Question 23 (1999).

9. US Department of Education Comment in IDEA regulations. Federal Register, v. 71, No. 156, p. 46670 (Monday, August 14, 2006).

10. 34 CFR 300.321(d); 34 CFR Part 300, Appendix A, Question 22 (1999).

11. 34 CFR 300.15.

12. US Department of Education Comment in IDEA regulations. Federal Register, v. 71, No. 156, p. 46670 (Monday, August 14, 2006).

13. 34 CFR 300.321(a)(5).

14. 34 CFR 300.321(b).

15. *Letter to Clinton*, 37 IDELR 70 (OSEP 2001).

16. 34 CFR Part 300, Appendix A (1999).

17. 34 CFR 300.321(b)(1).

18. 34 CFR 300.320(b).

19. 34 CFR 300.321(b)(3).

20. 34 CFR 300.43(a)(2).

21. 34 CFR 300.321(b)(2).

22. 34 CFR 300.520.

23. 34 CFR §99.30.

24. *Letter to Bieker*, 102 LRP 9204 (OSEP 2000).

25. 34 CFR 300.321(e).

26. 34 CFR 300.321(e)(2)(ii).

27. 34 CFR 300.322(b)(2).

28. 34 CFR 300.322(a)(1).

29. 34 CFR 300.322(a)(2).

30. 358 F App'x 788 (9th Cir. 2009).

31. *Letter to Thomas*, 51 IDELR 224 (OSEP 2008).

32. 34 CFR 300.322(c).

33. 34 CFR 300.322(d).

34. 34 CFR 300.322(d)(1), (2), (3).

35. 645 F. Supp. 2d 554 (ED VA 2009).

36. 34 CFR 300.324(b)(1)(i).

37. 34 CFR 300.328.

38. 34 CFR 300.324(a)(5).

39. 34 CFR 300.324(a)(4)(i).

40. 34 CFR 300.324(a)(6).

41. *Pierce v. Society of Sisters*, 268 U.S. 510 (1925).

42. 20 USC §1400(c)(5)(b).

43. 20 USC §1400(d)(1)(b).

44. 24 CFR 300.322(e).

45. 34 CFR Part 300, Appendix C (1981).

46. 34 CFR Part 300, Appendix A, Question 9 (1999).

47. 34 CFR Part 300, Appendix A, Question 5 (1999)

48. NICHCY home page http://nichcy.org and resources specifically for parents http://nichcy.org/families-community. A NICHCY document describing PTIs and CPRCs is available here: http://nichcy.org/wp-content/uploads/docs/bp3.pdf

49. 34 CFR §501(b)(3).

50. 34 CFR 300.322(e).

51. 853 F.2d 256 (4th Cir. 1988).

52. 392 F.3d 840 (6th Cir. 2004).

53. 370 F.App'x 843 (9th Cir. 2010).

54. 34 CFR Part 300, Appendix A, Question 21 (1999). See also *Letter to Anonymous*, 40 IDELR 70 (OSEP 2003).

55. 34 CFR Part 300, Appendix A, Question 9 (1999). See also OSEP. (July 20, 2010). *Letter to Richards.*

56. http://www.directionservice.org/cadre/pdf/Facilitated%20IEP%20for%20CADRE%20English.pdf

57. Contact information for the special education departments of all state departments of education is available online at http://nasdse.org/MeettheDirectors/tabid/60/Default.aspx

CHAPTER THREE

The legally correct IEP

the most important thing to be said for legal, technical and procedural correctness in IEP development is that it goes a long way toward ensuring a meaningful, useful IEP. It isn't a guarantee, but it surely is a good start. On the other side of the coin, the big risk in failing to employ squeaky-clean procedures is that the resulting program could be declared legally inappropriate. This finding of an inappropriate program, in turn, can obligate the school district to pay for parentally obtained private services, even a residential placement. So, developing IEPs is serious business. A great deal is at stake, most especially the education of children.

In one typical case, the administrative law judge ruled that the remedy for the district's procedural violations was to award reimbursement for all the costs of a private residential placement, plus physical therapy three times per week and daily language and occupational therapies. The procedural violations included: (1) the amount of related services offered was based not on the student's individual needs but on the district's predetermined service schedule; (2) an IEP meeting was held without a district representative

who had the power to allocate district resources; (3) the IEP goals were the same as the previous year; (4) the IEP failed to contain objective, measurable criteria, and evaluation procedures; and (5) the district failed to consider the need for an extended school year (ESY) *(Cobb Co. Sch. Dist.)*.[1]

Parental expenses for tutoring and more were awarded in a leading case in the Ninth Circuit Court because of these fatal and common procedural errors by the district: (1) an IEP was developed with no input from the private school the student was attending; (2) the IEP proposed placing the student in a program the district had predetermined to offer, apparently because it was available; and (3) the district failed to consider the recommendations of the people most knowledgeable about the student. Together, these violations showed the IEP was not reasonably calculated to allow educational benefit and so it denied FAPE *(W.G. v. Target Range Sch. Dist.)*.[2] One district's change in placement was invalidated by a court because of the district's failure to have a district representative present at the IEP meeting *(Smith v. Henson)*.[3] In general, the courts have taken the position that minor procedural flaws will be overlooked provided the essence of the process was intact, the parents had an opportunity for meaningful participation, and the result was an otherwise appropriate program (see, e.g., *Doe v. Defendant I*).[4] Major procedural flaws, however, will likely be a denial of FAPE and can result in awards such as those described.

In one such case where the court found serious procedural flaws, the court said: "Here, the [parents] are entitled to reimbursement. The School System deprived Zachary of a FAPE by predetermining the placement and by failing to ensure the attendance of regular education teachers at certain IEP meetings" *(Deal v. Hamilton Co. Bd. of Ed.).*[5]

Among the most vital principles of IEP development, about which there will be little if any judicial forgiving or overlooking, are these:

▶ Parents must have a genuine opportunity for full and meaningful participation in the IEP process.

▶ The services offered—special education, related services, supplementary aids and services, modifications, personnel support and accommodations—absolutely must be based on the child's needs, not on the availability of services or the category of disability. This principle is equally true of the placement decision, which must be based on the IEP.

▶ The district must not predetermine the program or placement and expect the parents to merely acquiesce.

▶ The parents must be given full notice of all their procedural rights related to their child's services, as well as to all other aspects of his or her education.

WHAT MUST THE IEP CONTAIN?

The federal requirements for the content of the IEP are straightforward. The individualized education program for each eligible child must include:

(I) a statement of the child's present levels of academic achievement and functional performance, including—

(aa) how the child's disability affects the child's involvement and progress in the general education curriculum;

(bb) for preschool children, as appropriate, how the disability affects the child's participation in appropriate activities; and

(cc) for children with disabilities who take alternate assessments aligned to alternate achievement standards, a description of benchmarks or short-term objectives;

(II) a statement of measurable annual goals, including academic and functional goals, designed to—

(aa) meet the child's needs that result from the child's disability to enable the child to be involved in and make progress in the general education curriculum; and

(bb) meet each of the child's other educational needs that result from the child's disability;

(III) a description of how the child's progress toward meeting the annual goals described in subclause (II) will be measured and when appropriate periodic reports on the progress the child is making toward meeting the annual goals (such as through the use of quarterly or other periodic reports, concurrent with the issuance of report cards) will be provided;

(IV) a statement of the special education and related services and supplementary aids and services, based on peer-reviewed research to the extent practicable, to be provided to the child, or on behalf of the child, and a statement of the program modifications or supports for school personnel that will be provided for the child—

(aa) to advance appropriately toward attaining the annual goals;

(bb) to be involved in and make progress in the general education curriculum in accordance with subclause (I) and to participate in extracurricular and other nonacademic activities; and

(cc) to be educated and participate with other children with disabilities and nondisabled children in the activities described in this subparagraph;

(V) an explanation of the extent, if any, to which the child will not participate with nondisabled children in the regular class and in the activities described in subclause (IV)(cc);

(VI)(aa) a statement of any individual appropriate accommodations that are necessary to measure the academic achievement and functional performance of the child on State and districtwide assessments consistent with section 612(a)(16)(A); and

> (bb) if the IEP team determines that the child shall take an alternate assessment on a particular State or districtwide assessment of student achievement, a statement of why—

>> (AA) the child cannot participate in the regular assessment; and

>> (BB) the particular alternate assessment selected is appropriate for the child;

(VII) the projected date for the beginning of the services and modifications described in subclause (IV), and the anticipated frequency, location, and duration of those services and modifications; and

(VIII) beginning not later than the first IEP to be in effect when the child is 16, and updated annually thereafter—

> (aa) appropriate measurable postsecondary goals based upon age appropriate transition assessments related to training, education, employment, and, where appropriate, independent living skills;

> (bb) the transition services (including courses of study) needed to assist the child in reaching those goals; and

> (cc) beginning not later than 1 year before the child reaches the age of majority under State law, a statement that the child has been informed of the child's rights under this title, if any, that will transfer to the child on reaching the age of majority. . . .[6]

In addition the IEP team must consider the strengths of the child and the parents' concerns for enhancing their child's education, in addition to the results of the initial or most recent evaluation and the academic, development and functional **needs** of the child.[7] Documentation of this consideration on the IEP is strongly urged and will probably be required by states and districts. It is the **fact** of consideration having been given, not the content, that needs to be documented.

Furthermore, under certain circumstances additional special factors must be considered and documented:[8]

▶ In the case of a child whose behavior impedes the child's learning or that of others, consider the use of positive behavioral interventions, strategies and supports to address that behavior;

▶ In the case of a child with limited English proficiency, consider the language needs of the child as these needs relate to the child's IEP;

▶ In the case of a child who is blind or visually impaired, provide for instruction in Braille and the use of Braille unless the IEP team determines, after an evaluation of the child's reading and writing skills, needs, and appropriate reading and writing media (including an evaluation of the child's future needs for instruction in Braille or the use of Braille), that instruction in Braille or the use of Braille is not appropriate for the child;

▶ Consider the communication needs of the child, and in the case of a child who is deaf or hard of hearing, consider the child's language and communication needs, opportunities for direct communications with peers and professional personnel in the child's language and communication mode. Consider also the child's academic level and full range of needs, including opportunities for direct instruction in the child's language and communication mode; and

▶ Consider whether the child requires assistive technology devices and services.

If during any of these deliberations the IEP team determines the child needs a particular device (excluding medical implants) or service (including an intervention, accommodation, or other program modification) in order to receive FAPE, a statement to that effect should be included in the IEP. Figure 3.1 summarizes the essential IEP components.

Present Levels of Performance (PLOPs)

Some special educators now use the longer phrase "present levels of academic and functional performance" and its acronym PLAAFP. We will continue to use the more pronounceable PLOP. The Department of Education's guidance is explicit about the child's present levels of performance (PLOPs) and what must be stated about them on the IEP:

> The statement of present levels of educational performance will be different for each handicapped child. Thus determinations about the content of the statement for an individual child are matters that are left to the discretion of participants in the IEP meetings. However, the following are some points which should be taken into account in writing this part of the IEP.
>
> The statement should accurately describe the effect of the child's handicap on the child's performance in any area of education that is affected, including: (1) academic areas (reading, math, communication, etc.), and (2) nonacademic areas (daily life activities, mobility, etc.).
>
> The statement should be written in objective measurable terms, to the extent possible. Data from the child's evaluation would be a good source of such information. Test scores that are pertinent to the child's diagnosis might be included, where appropriate. However, the scores should be: (1) self-explanatory (i.e., they can be interpreted by all participants without the use of test manuals or other aids), or (2) an explanation should be included. Whatever test results are used should reflect the impact of the handicap on the child's performance. Thus, raw scores would not usually be sufficient.
>
> There should be a direct relationship between the present levels of educational performance and the other components of the IEP. Thus, if the statement describes a problem with the child's reading skill, the problem should be addressed under both: (a) goals . . . and (2) specific special education and related services to be provided to the child.[9]

FIGURE 3.1 IEP Components

For all students

► Present levels of performance
► Measurable goals
► Assessment status
► Nonparticipation with nondisabled students
► All needed services fully described (amount, frequency, etc.)
► Progress measurement and reporting

For some students

► Transition goals and services, including transfer of parental rights to students
► Behavior plan
► ESL needs
► Braille
► Communication needs
► Assistive technology
► Short-term objectives or benchmarks

The 1999 Appendix A provides no further guidance beyond the basic directive that the statement of present levels of performance must include: (1) how the disability affects the student's involvement and progress in the general curriculum and (2) for preschool children, how the disability affects participation in age-relevant developmental abilities or milestones that typically developing children of the same chronological age would perform or achieve.[10]

A problem sometimes encountered with present levels of performance (PLOPs) is that some teachers think they must copy reams of test data from other sources onto the IEP form. This is probably not necessary. If required, it is because of state or district policy, not federal rules. Documents such as evaluation reports or test protocols may be incorporated into the IEP, and could simply be attached. The risk in this is that the data might not be intelligible standing alone, and that would be unacceptable.

So, what is a proper PLOP? It is an objectively measured and described performance of the child in an area of unique need for that child. Some unique needs involve the **conditions** needed for the child to learn, such as a quiet work area or 1:1 presentation of new concepts. These needs are addressed by specification of accommodations and modifications. Other unique needs are for improved **performance,** such as better handwriting, anger management, or social skills, etc. These are the needs which require the PLOP be determined.

The PLOPs need be written **only** in the areas of the child's unique needs which will be addressed by the special services. In effect, the PLOP is (1) an objective descriptor of the unique need and (2) the starting point for specifying services to address the need, and to develop goals and objectives to evaluate the results of the services. Suppose, for example, a child needs better anger management skills. That is the unique need to which a specific service must be addressed. The PLOP might be that the child has 10 to 15 inappropriate anger outbursts per week. Or suppose a child needs to learn accurate decoding

skills to replace his or her present excessive guessing at unknown words. His or her PLOP might be that the child reads second grade materials at 20–30 words correct per minute with five to eight errors, and he seldom, if ever, self-corrects. The PLOP is, in essence, a mandated, objective way of presenting a child's needs which the remainder of the IEP must then address. The PLOP also provides the beginning point against which progress must be assessed, so it must be measurably stated. A PLOP that is not both measurable and measured is useless. Here is what one administrative appeals office said about PLOPS:

> . . . Mother's participation in the IEP process was seriously impaired by the absence of a clear explanation of Student's current levels of performance in reading; of clear goals and objectives defining what progress could reasonably be expected within the next semester; and by the absence of regular reports which documented the rate of Student's progress toward his reading goals. . . .

> [T]he continued absence of a clear evaluation of Student's current levels of performance in reading and of Student's progress toward measurable goals in the area of Student's greatest deficiency made it nearly impossible for the IEP team to devise a program which adequately addressed Student's needs. Both Parents and other team members lacked information essential to devising an appropriate individualized plan because of the procedural defects identified above.[11]

Measurable Annual Goals and Progress Markers (Benchmarks or Short-Term Objectives)

According to Appendix A to the 1999 IDEA Regulations, the

> . . . measurable annual goals . . . are instrumental to the strategic planning process used to develop and implement the IEP for each child with a disability. Once the IEP team has developed measurable annual goals for each child, the team can: (1) develop strategies that will be most effective in realizing these goals, and (2) develop measurable, intermediate steps [progress markers] . . . that will enable families, students, and educators to monitor **progress** during

the year, and, if appropriate, to revise the IEP consistent with the child's instructional needs.[12]

Thus the purposes of annual goals and progress markers are to assess the appropriateness of the special services, and to monitor the child's progress. They should be written only for the special services necessary to meet the child's needs arising from the disability, not for the child's total program, unless all areas are so affected.[13]

IDEA 2004 deleted the requirement that all IEPs must contain short-term objectives or benchmarks. Now they are required only for the IEPs of those students who, for purposes of No Child Left Behind (2001), are "assessed against alternate standards" rather than against grade level standards.

Our view is that the requirement of mandated "progress markers" and reporting for all IEPs and short-term benchmarks or objectives for some IEPs can best be met, legally and educationally, by continuing the practice of including short-term objectives for each annual goal. One objective— measurable and measured each grading period— satisfies the progress marker need. Most districts are wisely continuing to use short-term objectives. Such objectives state **when** the student will do **what** and **how well,** for example:

> By the end of the first nine weeks the student will read the 200 most frequent sight words in 2 minutes with only self-corrected errors; **or**

> During the final nine weeks of the school year, the student will receive zero demerits, detentions, or office referrals; **or**

> By the end of the 2nd grading period, given 20 words from the spelling words presented up to that time, the student will spell at least 19 correctly on the first try.

Throughout the remainder of this discussion we assume that each annual goal will have objective, measurable progress markers or benchmarks. Parents should absolutely insist that, however it is done, the IEP must contain crystal-clear indictors of how progress will be measured and reported. Without this, the IEP is all but useless.

That having been said, we move on, including progress markers as part of the IEP. In practice the goals and progress markers are often the first items addressed in the IEP meeting, or perhaps second after a discussion of evaluation test results and present levels of performance. The next chapter will describe a different procedure. Since the purpose of a goal is to assess the effectiveness of services, it would seem it could be written with the specific service already in mind.

There are IEPs in which the entire contents are nothing but a reflection of the Woodcock-Johnson (W-J) or some other single test, no more, no less. On one such IEP one goal was written in each of the subtest areas in which the student was weak. The PLOP was the W-J score, the service was a check mark by "special education," and the goal was four months' progress as measured on the W-J. The PLOPs and the annual goals must indeed be directly related. However, the service to be provided is a better connector between the two than is a standardized test.

A common source of substantial difficulty and undue effort in writing IEPs is confusion about whether goals and objectives need to be written for the related services to be provided. Most people have assumed related services must have goals and objectives. However, this is incorrect. Notice that the related service provider need not attend the IEP meeting, and that typically his or her written input would address the nature, frequency, location and amount of services, not goals and objectives.

If one assumes that a related service is being provided, as it should be, because **it is necessary to enable the student to benefit from special education,** then it follows logically that a goal which evaluates the effectiveness of the special education thereby evaluates the supporting related service This is precisely the position taken by OSEP:

> . . . [W]hile there is no Part B requirement that an IEP include **separate** annual goals or short-term instructional objectives for related services, the goals and objectives in the IEP must address all of the student's identified needs that the IEP team

has determined warrant the provision of special education, related services, or supplementary aids and services, and must enable the team to determine the effectiveness of each of those services.

For example, if the IEP team has determined that a student needs speech and language therapy services as a component of free appropriate public education (FAPE), the IEP must include goals and objectives that address the student's need to develop and/or improve communication-related skills. It would not be necessary, however, to label the goals and objectives as "speech therapy" goals and objectives. Therefore, if the IEP includes goals and objectives which appropriately address the student's need to develop communication-related skills, no additional or separate "therapy" goals and objectives would be required. . . . If a related service such as air conditioning is necessary to enable the student to attend school, but that service is not intended to increase the student's skills, no goals or objectives are necessary. Similarly, if transportation is being provided solely to enable the student to reach the school, no goals or objectives are needed. If however, instruction will be provided to the student to enable the student to increase the student's independence or improve the student's behavior or socialization during travel to school, then goals and objectives must be included to address the needs to increase independence or improve behavior or socialization.[14]

A still-important note to the 1999 IDEA regulations explains that:

The new emphasis on participation in the general education curriculum is not intended by the Committee to result in major expansions in the size of the IEP or dozens of pages of detailed goals and benchmarks or objectives in every curricular content standard skill. The new focus is intended to produce attention to the accommodations and adjustments necessary for disabled children to access the general education curriculum and the special services which may be necessary for the appropriate participation in particular areas of the curriculum due to the nature of the disability.[15]

Standards-based IEPs, now gaining in popularity, do exactly what the federal regulations say should **not** be done, as will be discussed in Chapter Five.

Special Education and Other Special Services

The IEP must include

a statement of the special education and related services and supplementary aids and services, **based on peer-reviewed research to the extent practicable** [emphasis added], to be provided to the child, or on behalf of the child, and a statement of the program modifications or supports for school personnel that will be provided for the child to (1) progress toward the annual goals, (2) be involved in and make progress in the general curriculum and participate in extracurricular and other non-academic activities, and (3) be educated and participate with children with and without disabilities.[16]

One of the potentially most significant changes made to IDEA is the requirement that the special education and related services, and supplementary aids and services, included in the IEP must be **based on peer-reviewed research to the extent practicable.** The phrase "to the extent practicable" may be at the center of many disputes.

At least two points of view exist about the effect of this requirement that special education services included in the IEP be based on peer-reviewed research. Pete Wright, a respected and well-known special education attorney has said:

The services are to be based on peer-reviewed research, i.e. which method has stood the test of research. Anecdotal claims of success and beliefs about a program are insufficient. In litigation, a school district's reliance upon an 'eclectic approach' will become the kiss of death for that district. Assertions that the district takes 'the best parts of the best' methods and modifies them to a particular child will become less frequent. One Court, in commenting on such testimony and ruling for a child, said that the school district obviously had no expertise in any research based method.[17]

The other viewpoint is that "to the extent practicable" will provide a loophole through which any service can be driven. Time will tell. Perhaps the best guess is that some experts, ALJs, attorneys, hearing officers and courts will truly examine and evaluate the research behind the services being contested, and that others will not.

As of this writing, the majority of courts seem to reject evidence as to which service or method is more effective or appropriate. They inquire only as to whether the district's program or method addresses the problem and seems reasonably calculated to result in educational benefit. Courts continue to view *Rowley* as the standard in spite of several changes Congress made in IDEA indicating a higher standard. According to the Ninth Circuit Court of Appeals in *J.L. v. Mercer Island SD,*[18] Congress must explicitly, rather than implicitly, overrule *Rowley*.

Nevertheless, the clear language of the statute requires that the services in the IEP must be based on peer-reviewed research to the extent practicable. Perhaps as more experts and advocates address this requirement and the available research evidence, courts will become more receptive.

In the area of teaching beginning reading, the research-based evidence is clear and indisputable, and therefore IEPs from now on should provide for the same proven-effective teaching reading methods, programs and procedures approved in No Child Left Behind (2001). That law incorporates the findings of the National Reading Panel,[6] created at the direction of Congress. Shaywitz was one of the reading experts appointed to the National Reading Panel, which released its report in 2000, after examining more than 6,000 articles. She described the panel's work as "the most thorough report ever to be undertaken in American education" and notes it provides a "road map" to the "most effective, scientifically proven methods for teaching reading" (Shaywitz, 2003). Thus, one of the biggest areas of contention in special education should no longer be in dispute, as long as the readily available evidence is consulted.

Most authorities also agree that there is a large, persuasive research base for intensive, early intervention based on principles of applied behavioral research and discrete trial training for children who have autism. It will be incumbent upon district personnel, parents and advocates

alike to become increasingly familiar with research results, to stay abreast of new developments in research findings, and to become increasingly sophisticated in interpreting research and its implications.

The IEP must include all of the special education and other services needed by the child, whether or not they are available in the district. The IEP team's agreement that a service is needed gives rise to a commitment and a duty on the part of the district to provide the service, directly or indirectly:

> The public agency must ensure that all services set forth in the child's IEP are provided, consistent with the child's needs as identified in the IEP. It may provide each of those services directly, through its own staff resources; indirectly, by contracting with another public or private agency; or through other arrangements. In providing the services, the agency may use whatever State, local, Federal, and private sources of support are available for those purposes (see Sec. 300.301(a)), but the services must be at no cost to the parents, and the public agency remains responsible for ensuring that the IEP services are provided in a manner that appropriately meets the student's needs as specified in the IEP. The SEA and responsible public agency may not allow the failure of another agency to provide services described in the child's IEP to deny or delay the provision of FAPE to a child.[19]

A major element in service delivery is who will deliver the services. The short answer is "highly qualified personnel." An important aspect of the 2004 reauthorization of IDEA was the alignment of IDEA with NCLB, especially as to the qualifications of teachers and paraprofessionals. Special education teachers must now be "highly qualified," i.e., hold a bachelor's degree, and obtain full state special education certification or equivalent licensure. They cannot hold an emergency or temporary certificate. Special education teachers who teach English, reading or language arts, math, science, foreign languages, civics and government, economics, arts, history, or geography must meet additional requirements related to competence in the core academic subjects taught.[20]

Paraprofessionals who have instructional support duties (except translating for children with limited English proficiency) must have a high school diploma and, if hired after Jan. 8, 2002, must have completed two years of college. Alternatively, paraprofessionals may qualify through formal academic assessment where they must meet a "rigorous standard of quality."[21]

Under the IDEA, only students who need special education are eligible for services; therefore all IDEA students need special education provided by qualified special educators. One can only wonder what issues the future will bring as more and more children with disabilities are served exclusively by regular educators who do not work under special education supervision, and who are themselves responsible for providing whatever services the child needs.

NCLB has become so controversial that it is difficult to predict its future shape, if any. IDEA may or may not continue to be aligned with it.

The required statement of services to be provided is a very important but often neglected portion of the IEP. Services are typically described only by a number of minutes, for example, 90 minutes per quarter, or by check marks on the face sheet of the IEP. Special education may be indicated only with a check mark next to "resource room," or by the word "consultation," etc. Even a cursory perusal of the many IEP rulings which have been reported reveals that a much broader and detailed view of specification of services is required.

The service should be described sufficiently that a parent or other observer can determine whether it is being delivered. If, for example, a child has a reading disability, it is not appropriate to simply state "45 minutes of special education daily plus necessary accommodations." What is 45 minutes of special education? Is it sitting in the resource room doing worksheets? Is it reading with a study buddy from the highest reading group? Or is it intensive remedial instruction with a qualified teacher using a research-proven method in a group of no more than four similarly performing students? Substantial specificity is essential. Vague generalities in service description invite abuse. "Necessary accommodations" is also a

vague descriptor to be avoided. Who decides when and what accommodations are necessary? Does "necessary" mean only oral testing will be available, or does it also mean that the seventh grade student who reads at a second grade level will be provided content (science, history, etc.) information at or near his or her reading level? Parents and teachers alike should insist on a meaningful level of specificity. Including a service on the IEP in an unambiguous way goes far toward insuring it will be provided. In fact, most service descriptions are so vague they guarantee nothing whatsoever.

The range of services that must be included on the IEP is indirectly defined by the fact that, unless state law requires more, each student is entitled only to a program that is reasonably calculated to allow benefit, not a "best" or "most appropriate" program.[22] On the other hand, the scope of the services is also driven by the fact that all of the student's academic and functional needs must be addressed. The scope of this is very broad and can include self-esteem, coping skills to deal with rejection, feeding, gross motor activities, motor-sensory stimulation of a comatose student, self-help, vocational and prevocational skills, social skill development, organizational and attentional skills, academic tutoring, language and much more.

Rulings on related services have mandated assistive technology (e.g., auditory trainers, computers, spellers, wheelchairs), catheterization, parent and family counseling, extended school year, toileting assistance, special diets, interpreters, sign language training for parents, medical evaluations, occupational therapy, cognitive therapy, after-school aides, summer music programs, expressive therapy, early transportation to SAT review courses, music therapy, note-taking services and much, much more, including residential placements.

The amount of time to be committed to each of the various services must be appropriate to the child and included in the IEP in a way that is clear to all who develop and implement the IEP. OSEP has said that a range of times is not sufficient to indicate the necessary commitment of resources.[23] This position appears to require an exact specification of minutes, hours, or other units appropriate to the service. One sad but foreseeable result of this policy is that often only a bare minimum of services is written into the IEP. Suppose a child is believed to need speech therapy for 30 minutes daily and the district is willing and able to provide that amount. Many district personnel believe they must provide every minute that is written, and that if the student or therapist misses a day, or is late, or if the school is closed for a snow day, the district will "owe" the missed time and/or be "liable" for not providing the missed service. In fact, if there is an interruption in service one must look to the reason, the duration, and the effect on the student to determine whether it is a denial of an appropriate program.[24]

Since districts believe they cannot write an honest range, such as four to five sessions of 25–30 minutes weekly, they will sometimes specify the lowest that might be foreseeable, such as four 25-minute sessions weekly. That represents a significant loss (150 minutes versus 100 minutes) from what the district personnel believe is needed and are actually willing to provide. The use of reasonable ranges would seem to be a better practice, but it is apparently prohibited by OSEP.

A practice many would like to see prohibited is that of using service descriptors such as 1080 minutes per quarter or 1350 minutes per day. In at least one state this use of minutes is dictated by the IEP software program all schools are required to use. An IEP might describe one service in minutes per day, one in minutes per week, one in minutes per month, and yet another in minutes per quarter. It is hard to believe this lends clarity to the IEP or to the parents' understanding of what services the child will receive.

Related Services

The test for whether a service is a "related" service that must be included on the IEP and provided at no expense to the parents is whether the service is **necessary to enable the student to benefit from special education.** Some people mistakenly believe the test is whether the child can benefit from the service. Another erroneous position is that the child is entitled to a related service if it allows him to benefit from general education. However, the only real question is whether the child needs the service to benefit from special education.

One hearing officer ruled, obviously mistakenly, that accommodations in the **regular** class need not be provided under the IDEA because related services, by definition, are limited to those necessary to benefit from **special education**.[25] However, even if that were correct, all IDEA-eligible students are also entitled to the protections of Section 504 and the Americans with Disabilities Act, both of which require such accommodations. The history teacher who was personally assessed $15,000 damages for refusing to modify tests for a student with learning disabilities can also attest to the necessity of complying with needed modifications.[26]

What is a related service for one student might not be for another. And what is a related service for a student at one point in time may not be later. A common error is to think that a particular service is or is not a related service, and to overlook the fact that it depends upon student need.

Service Animals

Increasing attention and interest are being focused on the use of service animals by persons who have disabilities.[27] These animals include but are not necessarily limited to guide dogs, psychiatric service dogs (**not** including comfort or emotional support animals), hearing (signal) dogs, autism service dogs, mobility assistants, and seizure alert dogs. The Americans with Disabilities Act (ADA) defines service animal as a dog individually trained to perform certain work or perform tasks for an individual with a disability.[28] A separate provision in ADA also allows for miniature horses as service animals where reasonable.[29]

For students with disabilities, it appears that service animals can be an accommodation allowed under §504/ADA and/or a related service under IDEA. This raises some interesting questions! If a service animal is included in the IEP as a related service, must the district provide it? If so, would the animal belong to the student or to the district? Who would be responsible for feeding, cleaning, veterinary costs, etc.? ADA says staff are not required to provide care or food, but IDEA is silent.

A handful of service animal cases have arisen in IDEA hearings. In Florida, a hearing officer ruled the service dog did not need to be included in the IEP because the student's human aide could provide comfort and secure the student in the event of a seizure.[30] However, arguably, the dog would still be allowed to accompany the student in school under §504/ADA, if it were individually trained to deal with the seizure possibility.

In another case, a service dog was not a related service because it would be "more restrictive" than a one-on-one aide.[31]

In Ohio a state review officer held that a district violated IDEA when it denied consent for a service animal that enabled a student who had anxiety and social phobia to attend school.[32]

School personnel should note that ADA does **not** favor persons who have allergies or fear of dogs over persons who need service animals. Districts should accommodate both by designating appropriate spaces for each either within a classroom or in separate classrooms.

Medical and Health Services

A difficult and potentially very expensive related service determination involves the distinction between **medical treatment** that need not be paid for by the district (or other public agency) and **health services** that must be paid for by the district. The US Supreme Court has developed a two-part inquiry to determine whether a service is a related service which must be provided at no expense to the parents of a child with a disability:

▶ Is the service "required to assist the child to benefit from special education?" If not, it is not a related service. If so, ask:

▶ Is it excluded from IDEA coverage as a "medical service rendered for other than diagnostic or evaluative purposes"? If not, the LEA must pay.

To answer this inquiry one must know what "medical service" means. In *Irving Ind. Sch. Dist. v. Tatro,*[33] the Supreme Court articulated a "bright line" test which held that excluded medical services are ". . . services provided by a licensed physician" that serve other than diagnostic or evaluative purposes. The context of *Tatro* was the provision of clean intermittent catheterization, a relatively simple, inexpensive procedure which could be done by a trained aide.

The question that arose in subsequent decisions was whether this "bright line" medical services definition of *Tatro* should be applied when the services, unlike catheterization, are complex, expensive and risky. The lower courts were thoroughly split on the question. For example, *Detsel v. Auburn Sch. Dist.*[34] rejected the *Tatro* rule and held that the exclusion of extensive, therapeutic health services (e.g., tracheotomy and gastrostomy, requiring the constant and undivided attention of a nurse) was "in keeping with the spirit" of the regulatory definition of related services, and the district did not have to provide them.

Bevin H. v. Wright[35] adopted the *Detsel* reasoning and cited the "private duty" nursing requirement (i.e., life-threatening circumstances requiring constant attention) as distinguishing this case from *Tatro.* The court held that the ". . . nursing services required are so varied, intensive and costly, and more in the nature of 'medical services' that they are not properly includable as 'related services.'"

However, *Macomb Co. v. Joshua S.*[36] strenuously rejected *Detsel* and *Bevin* for departing from the *Tatro* analysis. *Macomb* found no basis to believe that states are free to decide on the basis of cost and effort which services are to be excluded. Therefore, the *Macomb* court relied simply and directly on *Tatro,* and held the complex and expensive health services had to be provided at no cost to the parents.

The issue was settled by the US Supreme Court in 1999 in a case where the student required continuous nursing care, bladder catheterization, suctioning of his tracheotomy, ventilator setting checks, ambu bag administrations, blood pressure monitoring and more. The court reiterated the bright line *Tatro* test, holding again that the clear language of IDEA and its regulations require schools to pay for medical services, except those that can only be provided by a physician, when they are necessary to allow school attendance. These services could be provided by a nurse, and so the district must pay for them as related services.[37]

Psychiatric Services

The Ninth Circuit Court had to decide whether a placement in a psychiatric hospital was a related service for which the district was financially responsible, or an excluded medical service. The court focused on the **purpose** for the placement and explicitly rejected the "licensed physician" criterion of *Tatro* as the sole criterion. The court also found that a program clearly aimed at curing a mental illness does not become a related service just because it can be implemented by staff other than physicians. This view raises difficult questions about most behavioral treatments for seriously emotionally disturbed children. The court specifically rejected the proposition that the IDEA requires schools to fund treatment for psychiatric illnesses.[38]

Not only do psychiatric placements pose these difficult medical treatment exclusion issues, but so do more simple therapeutic interventions that don't involve placement. Under *Clovis,* one must wonder whether, for example, behavioral therapy focused on reducing phobic or compulsive behavior would be excluded as "treatment for psychiatric illness." This is a difficult area. Nevertheless, three tentative rules have emerged:

▶ Residential placements made for educational reasons (purposes), or made for "inextricably intertwined" medical-behavioral-educational reasons (purposes), are related services.

▶ Residential placements made for non-educational reasons are not related services; however, a FAPE must be made available in or during that placement.

▶ In determining whether psychotherapy, apart from the setting, is a related service, the *Tatro* rule of whether it must be provided by a licensed physician would seem to be applicable.

Extended School Year

Extended school year (ESY) services may also be required as a related service. The common ESY pattern is summer school, but extended days or services on the weekend are also possible. The IEP team has the authority to determine on an individual basis whether an ESY program is necessary. The most widely used test for entitlement is whether the ESY services are necessary to prevent undue regression and/or undue difficulty in regaining lost skills.[39]

Six common district sins related to the failure to offer and provide ESY were all flagrant in *Reusch v. Fountain*[40] and still occur too often. The *Reusch* court held these ESY practices all violate the IDEA:

▶ Failing to provide adequate notice regarding ESY to parents of disabled students.

▶ Utilizing procedures that delay decisions regarding provision of ESY to disabled students.

▶ Making decisions on ESY too late in the school year.

▶ Failing to address ESY at annual review meetings, and failing to document the required discussions of ESY.

▶ Failing to apply a proper standard for the determination of whether students should receive ESY as part of their IEPs.

▶ Failing to comply with requirements for an individualized program, including LRE considerations, when ESY is offered.

Too many districts seldom, if ever, offer a truly individualized, tailor-made ESY. Instead, they still offer a special education "track" in their traditional summer school offering. This may be appropriate for some children, but not for all.

Methodology

Too many frustrating confrontations in IEP meetings have occurred around the issue of whether a specific methodology should be included in the IEP. Parents often believe passionately that a particular method should be used with their child, often because they believe that only that method has benefitted him or her in the past.

School personnel typically believe that methodology need not be written into an IEP. That view was arguably correct until the 1999 IDEA Regulations were finalized and issued. An important change was made to the definition of "specially designed instruction" (which is the crucial element in the definition of special education). The word "methodology" was added to the definition of specially designed instruction. The US Office of Education explained the significance of adding "methodology" to the IDEA Regulations:

> In light of the legislative history and case law, it is clear that in developing an individualized education there are circumstances in which the particular teaching methodology that will be used is an integral part of what is "individualized" about a student's education and, in those circumstances, will need to be discussed at the IEP meeting and incorporated into the student's IEP. For example, for a child with a learning disability who has not learned to read using traditional instructional methods, an appropriate education may require some other instructional strategy.

> Other students' IEPs may not need to address the instructional method to be used because specificity about methodology is not necessary to enable those students to receive an appropriate education. There is nothing in the definition of "specially designed instruction" that would require instructional methodology to be addressed in the IEPs of students who do not need a particular instructional methodology in order to receive educational benefit. In all cases, whether instructional methodology would be addressed in an IEP would be an IEP team decision.[41]

In spite of this directive, many school personnel still decline to specify methodology on IEPs. A compromise that is often suggested is that parents' preferred methodology be described, rather than named. However, the difficulty with this is that it is very easy to claim that whatever is being done fits the given description. For example, when parents request a "multisensory" reading methodology, they usually mean the very specialized Orton-Gillingham method or one of its derivative programs. However, to many school personnel, any and every reading program, method or eclectic practice is "multisensory."

We highly recommend that parents invest energy in obtaining objective assessment of a child's progress with whatever methodology is used rather than just concentrating on getting particular services. If progress is shown objectively to be inadequate, it is then far easier to obtain the desired methodology. The combination of No Child Left Behind and IDEA may or may not eventually compel the use of only proven-effective programs and methods for children with disabilities as well as for others.

As discussed earlier, courts have been slow and reluctant to take seriously the current IDEA requirement that services in the IEP be based on peer-reviewed research. Similarly they are not generally responsive to arguments about methodology. A district's chosen method or eclectic approach is likely to prevail, in spite of evidence to the contrary.

Classroom Modifications

Classroom modifications are commonly made by regular education personnel, with assistance, consultation, or monitoring by special educators. Modifications may be required in tests, texts, homework, assignments, grading, or more. By spelling these out in the IEP one can ensure that all necessary changes are made in a consistent way whenever and in whatever classes they are needed. (In the next chapters some practical tips for maximizing the appropriateness and helpfulness of these modifications are suggested.) Too often classroom modifications have not been addressed by IEP teams, sometimes because of the erroneous belief that the IEP team lacks the authority to require regular teachers to make changes.

The regular education teacher who is on the IEP team can provide valuable input to help determine the classroom and program modifications, the needed supplementary aids and services, and necessary supports for school personnel.[42]

Transition Services

One purpose of IDEA is to emphasize preparing students with disabilities for post-school life, including employment, independent living and further education.[43]

Transition services are defined as

a coordinated set of activities for a child with a disability that:

(A) is designed to be within a results-oriented process that is focused on improving the academic and functional achievement of the child with a disability to facilitate the child's movement from school to post-school activities, including post-secondary education, vocational education, integrated employment (including supported employment), continuing and adult education, adult services, independent living, or community participation;

(B) is based on the individual child's needs taking into account the child's strengths, preferences, and interests; and

(C) includes:

(i) Instruction;

(ii) Related Services;

(iii) Community experiences;

(iv) The development of employment and other post-school adult living objectives; and

(v) If appropriate, acquisition of daily living skills and functional vocational evaluation.[44]

Beginning when the child turns 16 years old, each IEP must contain (a) appropriate **measurable** **postsecondary goals** based upon age-appropriate transition assessment related to training, education, employment and where appropriate, independent living skills; (b) the transition services (including courses of study) needed to assist the child in reaching those goals, and (c) a statement the child has been informed of the rights that will transfer to the child reaching the age of majority.[45]

Some confusion has arisen over the exact role of the school with regard to other agencies that are to be involved in providing or paying for transition services. First, the school should invite a representative of such an agency. If the agency doesn't send someone, then the school should take other steps to get that agency to participate in planning. If another agency fails to provide agreed-upon transition services then the school, consistent with being the ultimately responsible agency (the place where "the buck stops"), must initiate a meeting to examine the transition goals, and perhaps to revise the IEP and/or identify alternate strategies to meet the objectives.[46] The 1999 IDEA Regulations elaborate:

This interagency planning and coordination may be supported through a variety of mechanisms, including memoranda of understanding, interagency agreements, assignment of a transition coordinator to work with other participating agencies, or the establishment of guidelines to work with other agencies identified as potential service providers. If an agreed-upon service by another agency is not provided, the public agency responsible for the student must exercise alternative strategies to meet the student's needs. This requires that the public agency provide the services, or convene an IEP meeting as soon as possible to identify alternative strategies to meet the needs of the transition service needs of the student, and to revise the IEP accordingly. Alternative strategies might include the identification of another funding source, referral to another agency, the public agency's identification of other district-wide or community resources that it can use to meet the student's identified need appropriately, or a combination of these strategies.[47]

Nothing in the IDEA excuses any other agency of its responsibilities to provide transition services, but the bottom line is that the school district still must ensure that the student has FAPE available, one way or another. And since the "F" in FAPE stands for "free to the parent" the district might end up paying a private organization to provide a transition service a federal or other state agency was supposed to, but failed to, provide.

Two 1994 due process hearings against an Iowa district resulted in rulings that the district's failure to provide appropriate transition planning and services precluded the district from graduating the students, and obligated it to provide further vocational programs.[48,49]

A federal court in South Dakota also evaluated all too common district transition practices. In this case the district falsely believed that it

> . . . fulfills its responsibility to develop and implement interagency participation in transition services if it communicates to the disabled student and her parents the kinds of agencies in the community that may be able to help the student in the future and provides the student and her family with a "linkage" to those agencies.[50]

Specifically, the transition plan adopted for this college-bound student who had orthopedic disabilities stated that:

> . . . vocational rehabilitation services, Supplemental Security Income, and "other programs available" were explained and that Tracy will need "Public and private transportation with assistive devices when appropriate." The District wrote that, "If Tracy is eligible for SSI he [sic] will also be eligible for Medicaid," and that "Prairie Freedom Center will be contacted by Angie Schramm." In the block for "Advocacy and Legal Services," the District wrote, "Not applicable." In the remaining areas of "Personal Management and Family Relationship," "Financial and Income," "Living Arrangements," "Leisure and Recreation," and "Medical Services and Resources," the district provided no other transition planning. Tracy and her parents were assigned follow-up responsibility in every area with [two] exceptions. . . .[51]

The court declared quite simply and directly that ". . . such a minimal approach to school district responsibility for transition services.

. . . fails to comport" with the IDEA, and that their transition plan does not satisfy any of the legal mandates. The district's failure to understand its own responsibilities caused it to fail to inform the family adequately of the nature and scope of transition services available to them.

Nonparticipation with Nondisabled

The IEP must contain an explanation of the extent, if any, to which the child will **not** participate with nondisabled children in the regular classroom, and in extracurricular and other nonacademic activities.[52] Some IEPs contain only a statement (rather than an **explanation**) of when the student will not so participate. However, if the parents are fully informed and appreciate the basis for any and all nonparticipation, that may be more important than the difference between a statement and an explanation.

State and Districtwide Assessment of IDEA Students

Concern has abounded that special education students were not being vigorously assessed and held accountable in state or districtwide testing and/or that when they were included in such assessments, their scores were neither included nor reported. This concern has now switched to a question of whether state and districtwide assessments using grade level standards may be too rigorous for some special education students, and thus not fairly reflect their actual achievement. As part of NCLB, students are now to be assessed (for state/district purposes) under one of four plans:

▶ Regular assessment against grade-level standards;

▶ Regular assessment with allowable accommodations (which do not affect the test validity) against grade level standards;

▶ Alternate assessment against grade level standards; or

▶ Alternate assessment against alternate standards.

No more than 1% of the entire grade level population (roughly 7.7% of the special education population) may be reported as "proficient" under alternate standards. This means that about 90% or more of all special education students will be deemed "not proficient" if they fail to meet **grade level** standards. This is obviously problematic, and educators will undoubtedly continue efforts to change or evade this NCLB regulation.

Federally mandated testing (NCLB) and public reporting of the results has resulted in scandals alleging that educators—teachers and administrators—have deliberately cheated by fraudulently increasing test scores. The scandals have erupted in Atlanta, Washington DC, Los Angeles, New York and Houston, among other cities. Many believe that much of the pressure on education comes from holding the huge majority of special education students to the same academic standards as nondisabled students. If any group of students (special education, English language learners, racial minorities) fails to meet projected yearly progress (AYP), the school is deemed to be "failing."

The focus of both NCLB and IDEA on assessing special education students using "regular" assessments and grade level standards based on the general education curriculum arguably represents a movement away from offering special education curricula. In any event, under NCLB, the IEP team no longer decides whether a student will participate in state or district assessment but determines only whether a student will need accommodations, modifications, or an alternative assessment.

Progress Reporting

IDEA requires that IEPs contain "a description of how the child's progress toward meeting the annual goals . . . will be measured and when periodic reports on the progress . . . toward the annual goals will be provided."

The IDEA requirement that the child's progress toward meeting the IEP's measurable annual goals be measured and reported to parents is absolutely critical to the success of IDEA and of each child. As Congress has explicitly recognized, emphasized and reemphasized, children who have disabilities are entitled to an appropriate educational program. An appropriate program is one which is effective, i.e., in which the child makes progress.

Parents must insist on measurable and measured progress markers in the IEPs at least every grading period. Objective, real measurement of progress is the only way to insure that the services being provided are effective, and are resulting in increased performance levels.

If a progress reporting system such as a traditional A, B, C report card is proposed, an IEP team member should immediately ask what would be meant, for example, by a C+ in anger management. Similarly, subjective evaluations such as "teacher observation" must be supplemented or preferably replaced by objective measures. Parents, as much or more than any other team members, need to be sure that the progress reporting proposed on the IEP is objective, sufficiently precise, understandable and meaningful to them, the parents.

Suppose the measurable annual goal for a youngster who has limited expressive language (the PLOP is that he currently speaks four words, intelligible only to his parents) is that he will have an intelligible expressive vocabulary of 100 words, all used when prompted, and at least 30 used spontaneously. If the proposed progress reporting system consisted of the teacher checking "emerging" (which seems to mean no progress yet, but we are hoping), "making progress," or "almost mastered," the parents and anyone else looking at the report would have almost no idea how much progress has been made. That is not acceptable.

Perhaps some would prefer a progress report by letter grade, with an asterisk. Suppose the measurable goal for a nonverbal 10-year old was that she would **always** signal her need to have a bowel movement and that her present performance is that she **never** so indicates. What information about her progress would be conveyed, for example, by a "C" at the end of the grading period?

Parents should be anything but apologetic in requesting measured, objective and completely understandable PLOPs, progress markers and goals. They are the key to knowing promptly and with certainty whether and how much a child is progressing, and whether the special education and related services are appropriate. Progress measurement is absolutely essential to IDEA working as it is designed, and without it the primary purpose of the law—providing effective education—is made farcical. The simpler and more direct the proposed measurement, the more likely it will happen.

Parents should insure that they are completely satisfied with each and every proposed PLOP, progress marker and goal. The team should avoid relying on subjective measures such as teacher judgment or observation. For example, suppose the team's first try at a goal for Jeremy is that he needs to "show respect for adults." How could one measure that objectively? The only way is to reformulate the goal, PLOP and progress marker so they deal with countable behaviors such as "using inappropriate verbal or body language in addressing school personnel." Now the team can agree that Jeremy currently does this five to 10 times daily (his PLOP). The goal then becomes zero inappropriate verbal or body language toward school personnel.

An easy and key question team members need to ask is, "**How will we know** whether and how much progress the child is making toward this goal?" Only when this question is answered to the satisfaction of all have the essentials of both law and good practice been fulfilled.

Parents have a right and perhaps even a responsibility to recognize that genuine progress can be measured, and to insist that the measurement/reporting scheme be as clear and understandable as weight loss, number of words read per minute, or number of widgets manufactured per week. Sometimes the jargon that professionals use in proposing goals and PLOPs can be intimidating. This ridiculous goal actually appeared on an IEP:

> The student will comprehend and use written language more effectively as determined by her use of written language during cognitive skills retaining [sic] activities as an Individual

Educational Plan goal, as implemented by the Speech and Language Therapist, starting 1/11/2004, enabling progress and addressing her needs, in a small group setting, with visual and verbal assistance, using materials at her skill level, with 5% current achievement, with evaluation every quarter, with 80% target achievement completed by 9/15/2005.

In dealing with children's progress there is no need, ever, to accept vague, unclear, overly technical, or otherwise silly language.

An Iowa ALJ spoke to the importance of objective assessment of progress:

> The progress monitoring data presented by the school district is vague for certain IEP components and nonexistent for others. Few meaningful data are available to help an IEP team review progress or confidentially [sic] convince this ALJ that the programs offered to Michael were calculated to provide meaningful benefit. In lieu of progress monitoring data for IEP goals, the [district] could have submitted teacher made tests, teacher observation, report cards, student handouts, and student portfolios as evidence of progress . . . , but no such evidence was offered. Instead, subjective judgments that Michael was "happy" or that he "loved his work experience program" were substituted for objective evidence of progress.[53]

And finally, the essential relationship between having measured objectives and PLOPs, and being able to assess progress, was emphasized by a hearing review officer:

> Parents [met] their burden of demonstrating that the progress reports which were provided— simple checkmarks indicating progress rather than regression or achievement of the Student's goals—did not meet the requirement that the report include an analysis of Student's progress toward IEP goals and an analysis of the extent to which Student's progress would enable him to reach his annual goals. It is difficult to imagine how a report meeting IDEA requirements could have been developed in the absence of a statement of current levels of performance and measurable goals and objectives.

> This failure to provide progress reports constitutes a violation of the IDEA's progress report requirement.[54]

Behavioral Plan

Whenever a student's behavior impedes his or her own learning or that of others, a behavior plan should be developed. Whenever discipline constituting a change in placement (typically a suspension of more than 10 days) occurs, a functional assessment of behavior must be conducted, and a behavioral plan developed. If this has previously been done and included in the IEP, the plan must be reevaluated and revised. Very simply, one must now deal programmatically, not just punitively, with inappropriate conduct, and this should be shown in the IEP.[55] However, courts have split on whether a behavior plan that is actually implemented needs to be in the IEP. The child's actual or potential regular education teacher who is now a mandated member of the IEP team should, to the extent appropriate, assist in the team's determination of the positive behavioral interventions and strategies for a child whose behavior interferes with learning.

As more and more districts adopt schoolwide positive behavior support systems, an issue arises as to whether the schoolwide plan is sufficient for an individual student on an IEP. Generally speaking, the question arises only when the system has not been effective for a given student. Therefore, it is relatively easy to conclude that an individualized behavior plan is essential, and this is the conclusion of the cases so far.

English as a Second Language (ESL) Needs

While a child may not be identified as disabled just because English is his or her second language (ESL), some children who are disabled also have special needs arising from their ESL status. These needs must be considered and addressed, as they relate to the rest of the IEP.

Braille

In recent years many children who need to be proficient in Braille have not been taught this skill. The explicit requirement of the IDEA is that the IEP team evaluate the child's reading and writing skills and needs, present and future, and provide Braille instruction unless it is not appropriate. The presumption that Braille is appropriate can only be rebutted by careful analysis showing it is not appropriate for a particular student.[56]

Communication Needs

Many lawsuits have arisen when parents of a deaf child wanted a different language mode for their child than the school was prepared to offer prior to 2004. The typical judicial resolution was to say this is an issue of methodology, and therefore the school may do whatever it chooses, regardless of the family's or child's needs or preference status. However, IDEA now requires the IEP team to "consider the child's language and communication needs, opportunities for direct communications with peers and professional personnel in the child's language and communication mode, academic level, and full range of needs, including opportunities for direct instruction in the child's language and communication mode."[57]

Children who are deaf and hard of hearing are not the only children who have unique communication needs. Special consideration also must be given, e.g., to the needs of nonverbal children who have autism, possibly for signing or a picture-based language system.

Assistive Technology

Assistive technology must be included in the IEP and provided to a student when it is a necessary part of his or her special education or related services, or supplementary aids and services. Districts need not provide assistive technology if the device or service is required regardless of whether the student attends school. This exclusion does not apply, however, if the device or service is necessary to allow the student to receive FAPE and is part of the student's special education, related services, or supplementary aids and services.[58]

An assistive technology device is broadly defined in the IDEA as:

. . . any item, piece of equipment, or product system, whether acquired commercially off the shelf, modified, or customized, that is used to increase, maintain, or improve the functional capabilities of a child with a disability . . . [excluding] a medical device that is surgically implanted, or the replacement of such a device.[59]

An assistive technology service means:

. . . any service that directly assists a child with a disability in the selection, acquisition, or use of an assistive technology device. The term includes

(a) The evaluation of the needs of a child with a disability, including a functional evaluation of the child in the child's customary environment;

(b) Purchasing, leasing, or otherwise providing for the acquisition of assistive technology devices by children with disabilities;

(c) Selecting, designing, fitting, customizing, adapting, applying, maintaining, repairing, or replacing assistive technology devices;

(d) Coordinating and using other therapies, interventions, or services with assistive technology devices, such as those associated with existing education and rehabilitation plans and programs;

(e) Training or technical assistance for a child with a disability or, if appropriate, that child's family; and

(f) Training or technical assistance for professionals (including individuals providing education or rehabilitation services), employers, or other individuals who provide services to, employ, or are otherwise substantially involved in the major life functions of that child.[60]

As potentially important as assistive technology devices and services are, relatively few cases about them have been reported.

One rather astonishing exception to the low profile of assistive technology cases comes from Connecticut. A three-year old was born without a left arm below the elbow. At 14 months of age she was fitted with a myoelectric prosthetic arm. The prosthetic arm was found to be assistive

technology (AT) and the Birth-to-Three program paid for it after losing at a hearing. In the pre-school program, however, the parents were once again forced to use due process to establish that the arm was AT and must be paid for by the district. The decision that the arm was **not** AT was based on the prosthetic not being necessary for the student to receive FAPE. The school board admitted the prosthetic arm improved the student's functional capabilities. The parents obtained the arm from a prosthetist without a prescription, so believed it was not a medical device. However, their insurance company demanded the prosthetist obtain an after-the-fact prescription from a physician. Based on those facts, the prosthetic arm was held to be a "medical device" for which the district need not pay. The fact that without the prosthetic, the youngster's balance, agility, and two-handed function in all activities was impaired was deemed irrelevant.[61]

IEP FORMS, COMPUTERS AND TIPS

In too many IEP meetings someone asks at least once, "Where do we put this on the form?" Forms by their nature interfere significantly with true individualization. The fewer lines and preshaped spaces a form has, the more likely one can readily use the form. That is the primary reason we recommend one of the IEP "Non-Forms." (More will be said about these forms and their use in **Chapter Five.**) It is important to reiterate that a proper form will contain all the required elements in the simplest way possible, allowing for the most flexibility and individualization. If a state or district has come to require more on the IEP form than IDEA requires, it would be best to go back to the basics. This is definitely a time and place where simpler is better. Shorter is also better. An IEP of 20, 30, 40 or more pages is so unwieldy, it cannot be, and is not, useful. We suggest that as a rule of thumb, much over five pages suggests something should be rethought. If we carefully delineate the child's most important unique needs and perhaps prioritize them, we'll frequently find up to six or seven needs that require a PLOP, progress markers and a goal.

Perhaps above all else, we need to remember what IEP stands for, especially the "I." The IEP is intended to be an **individualized** special education document—not a version of the entire general education curriculum. (See **Chapter 6** on standards-based IEPs.) The IEP indeed must address what the child needs in order to access the general curriculum (e.g., appropriate classroom behavior, better reading comprehension, ability to work cooperatively in a small group, etc.); but it need not and should not contain the general curriculum itself.

And finally, the IEP itself and the processes by which it is developed, reviewed and revised must be totally parent-friendly. Computers and certain software can play havoc with this, as has been noted by OCR when they investigated a complaint about a district computer print-out IEP:

> OCR interviewed five parent witnesses with respect to whether they understood the IEP process used by the district. All . . . indicated they felt intimidated by the process. . . . They indicated that they did not think the [computer-generated print out] format provided sufficient information to enable them to ask questions.[62]

In spite of obvious drawbacks, computers are being used ever more widely to assist in the "paperwork" of IEPs. In the two rulings located, computer generation of the IEP was found to result in a failure of individualization, and therefore it violated FAPE.[63,64]

The use of computers for management of IEPs, review dates, etc. is clearly appropriate, and is not to be confused with their more questionable use to generate descriptions of "unique" needs, present levels of performance, services, and goals and objectives. It is the latter use that raises serious questions about true individualization. The supporters of the use of computers suggest that the writing of behavioral objectives can be difficult. So, they reason, if the need, the services, and the annual goal have been selected for that child, is it not then appropriate to also use a computerized

bank of objectives for that goal? Perhaps, but not necessarily. First, remember that only two or three objectives are anticipated for each goal. Second, doesn't one expect different children to progress at different rates? Shouldn't the answer to the question of "How far, by when?" be as individualized as all the rest?

The short answer to the computer issue may be that if "it" can be efficiently generated by computer, "it" may not need to be on the IEP. Remember, too, that IEPs are to be developed by teachers, a parent, an evaluation expert, and a district representative who often has no special education expertise. One must think ever so carefully about what the IEP is supposed to be and do.

A closely related issue is that of preprinted IEP objectives. Here is the clear and simple conclusion of one hearing officer about them:

> The 1995–96 IEP is in violation of regulations. The goals and objectives in reading, writing, and spelling are a series of pre-printed statements which were, as related by the special education teacher's testimony, used for all students in the group with J. They were not designed to meet J's individual needs.[65]

Of all the "mass production" IEP form problems, few are as revealing of nonindividualization as short-term objective statements requiring that a blank be filled in with a percentage of mastery, e.g., "the student will do long division with ___% accuracy." This is vague and not truly individualized. Furthermore—if one examined either that student's prior IEP or examples of that teacher's current IEPs for other students—a safe bet would be that the percentage would barely vary. Eighty percent is a favorite, regardless of the task, e.g., "the student will interact appropriately 80% of the time." Sometimes the same preprinted goals and objectives will be used year after year with only the percentage of mastery changing. Typically they start at 70% and increase five percent per year, regardless of how nonsensical that may be. Mass-produced IEP goals and objectives are not responsive to students' **unique** educational needs, by definition. Nor are they legal, useful, or appropriate. Other than that . . .

The placement decision is not technically part of the IEP, but the placement form is usually included in the IEP. The Fourth Circuit Court has ruled that FAPE is denied if the district fails to name a specific school as the placement when that information is necessary for the parents to evaluate the program.[66] On the other hand, the Second Circuit Court ruled that the IEP need not include a specific school, based on the argument that "educational placement" refers to type of program, not location.[67]

CONFIDENTIALITY OF IEPS

In the past, many teachers, especially at the secondary level, reported they had no idea which of their students, if any, had IEPs, and that they never saw the IEP even when they were informed that a student had one. Teachers have every right and duty to see the IEPs of their students.

By its very nature a good IEP is always helpful and often essential in providing an appropriate program for the student. Rarely is a student's disability so mild or limited that he or she requires no modification or accommodations in regular classes. The IEP is the vehicle that allows all the student's teachers to know what they need to know and do.

When the practice of not allowing teachers access to IEPs was questioned, the common reason cited was that confidentiality would be violated if IEPs were shared. While it is true IEPs are education records and must be treated as such, the Family Educational Rights and Privacy Act (FERPA) has an exception which is pertinent. Under the FERPA regulations, an educational agency **may** disclose personally identifiable information from the education records of a student without written consent of the parents ". . . if the disclosure is to other school officials, including teachers, within the educational institution or local educational agency who have been determined by the agency or institution to have legitimate educational interests" in that information.[68]

In the unlikely event there is a state or district confidentiality requirement that appears to prohibit the sharing of IEPs, there are at least two solutions. The first is simply to obtain parental permission to do so. Parents should insist that all teachers have copies of their children's IEPs, even if they have to provide them themselves. The second is to recognize that superseding federal law requires the distribution of IEPs. Of course, it should go without saying that the IEP should not contain any information beyond what is required. It would not be appropriate, for example, to include the student's category of disability or intelligence test score.

THE IEP BIG PICTURE AND BOTTOM LINE

At least five general principles clearly emerge from a review of the many thousands of past IEP rulings from agencies and courts:

All of the student's **unique** needs arising from the disability must be addressed, not just his or her academic needs.[69]

However, in a minority view, the Tenth Circuit Court ruled that the district did not deny FAPE when it failed to provide needed speech therapy. The court reasoned that IDEA is to "open the door," not to provide every needed service.[70] This same court has also ruled, as has the Eleventh Circuit Court, that generalization across settings is not required to show educational benefit, i.e., to provide FAPE.[71]

The availability of services may not be considered in writing the IEP. If a service is needed to provide FAPE, it must be written on the IEP, and if the district does not have it available, it must be provided by another agency. One of the earliest of all the agency rulings mandated that availability of services be disregarded in writing the IEP.[75] This legal principle has been reiterated repeatedly for 30 years, but is still virtually ignored by many school districts.

The IEP is a firm, **legally binding commitment** of resources. The district must make available the services described, or the IEP must be amended.[76]

IEPs must be **individualized.** They must be developed to fit the unique needs of the child, not to describe an existing program or practices. The same amounts of therapy on many IEPs (e.g., every child who receives speech therapy in a particular building receives 30 minutes daily) is one common sign of a violation of this individualization requirement.[77]

All of the **components** of the IEP must be present as required, including measurable goals, a statement of the specific special education and related services, and a statement of how progress will be measured.

If, in addition to honoring these five principles, one also ensures the procedural essentials of IEP development are followed the result will be an IEP that provides FAPE to the child. The law requires no more and no less—an IEP that is legally correct and educationally useful.

Now that we've looked at the legal requirements within which the IEP process must operate we can move on, in the next chapter, to talk about how **not** to write IEPs.

References

Shaywitz, S. (2003). *Overcoming Dyslexia.* New York, NY: Alfred Knopf.

Notes

1. *Cobb Co. Sch. Dist.*, 26 IDELR 229 (SEA GA 1997).
2. *W.G. v. Target Range Sch. Dist.*, 960 F.2d 1479 (9th Cir. 1992).
3. *Smith v. Henson*, 786 F. Supp 43 (D DC 1992).
4. *Doe v. Defendant*, 898 F.2d 1186 (6th Cir. 1990).
5. *Deal v. Hamilton*, 392 F.3d 840 (6th Cir. 2004).
6. 20 USC §1414(d)(1)(A); 34 CFR 300.320.
7. 20 USC §1414(d)(3)(A); 34 CFR 300.324(a)(1).
8. 20 USC §1414(d)(3)(B); 34 CFR 300.324(a)(2).
9. 34 CFR 300, Appendix C, Question 36 (1981).
10. 34 CFR 300, Appendix A, Question 1 (1999).
11. *Rio Rancho Pub. Sch.*, 40 IDELR 140 (SEA NM 2003).
12. 34 CFR 300, Appendix A, Question 1 (1999).
13. 34 CFR 300, Appendix A, Question 4 (1999).
14. *Letter to Hayden*, 22 IDELR 501 (OSEP 1994).
15. 34 CFR 300.347, Note 3.
16. 20 USC §1414(d)(1)(A)(i)(IV); 34 CFR 300.320(a)(4).
17. www.wrightslaw.com
18. *J.L. v. Mercer Island Sch. Dist.*, 592 F.3d 938 (9th Cir. 2010).
19. 34 CFR, Appendix A, Question 28 (1999).
20. 20 USC §1402(10); 34 CFR 300.18.
21. 34 CFR 200.58.
22. *Hendrick Hudson Bd. of Ed. v. Rowley*, 102 S.Ct. 3034, 458 US 176 (1982).
23. *Letter to Ackron*, 17 EHLR 287 (OSEP 1990).
24. *Rockford (IL). Comm. Sch. Dist. #205*, 352 IDELR 465 (OCR 1987).
25. *Sch. Dist. of Beloit*, 25 IDELR 109 (SEA WI 1996).
26. *Doe v. Withers*, 20 IDELR 422 (WV Cir. Ct. 1993).
27. The authors are indebted to Jim Gerl for his excellent presentation on the topic of service animals at the 10th National IDEA Academy for Administrative Law Judges and Impartial Hearing Officers, Seattle, July 2010.
28. 28 CFR 35.104.
29. 28 CFR 35.136.
30. *Collier Co. Sch. Dist.*, 110 LRP 7471 (SEA FL 2009).
31. *Bakersfield City Sch. Dist.*, 51 IDELR 142 (SEA CA 2008).
32. *Gallia Co. Local Sch. Dist.*, 36 IDELR 205 (SEA OH 2002).
33. 104 S.Ct. 3371, 468 US 883 (1984).
34. 820 F.2d 587 (2nd Cir. 1987).
35. 666 F.Supp. 71 (WD PA 1987).
36. 715 F.Supp. 824 (ED Mich. 1989).
37. *Garrett F. v. Cedar Rapids Comm. Sch. Dist.*, 119 S.Ct. 992, 526 US 66 (1999).
38. *Clovis Unified Sch. Dist. v. Cal. Office of Admin. Hearings*, 903 F.2d 635 (9th Cir. 1990).
39. *Armstrong v. Kline*, 513 F.Supp. 425 (ED PA 1980).
40. 872 F.Supp. 1421 (D MD 1994).
41. *US Dept. of Ed. Commentary in IDEA Regulations*, 64 FR 12551 (Mar 12 1999).
42. 34 CFR 300.324(a)(3).
43. 34 CFR 300.43.
44. 20 USC §1414(34).
45. 34 CFR 300.520(a).

46. 34 CFR 300.324(c)(1).

47. 34 CFR 300, Appendix A, Question 12 (1999).

48. *Mason City Comm. Sch. Dist.*, 21 IDELR 241 (SEA IA 1994).

49. *Mason City Comm. Sch. Dist.*, 21 IDELR 248 (SEA IA 1994).

50. *Yankton v. Schramm*, 900 F.Supp. 1182 (D SD 1995).

51. *Yankton v. Schramm*, 900 F.Supp. 1182 (D SD 1995).

52. 34 CFR 300.320(a)(5).

53. *Linn-Mar Comm. Sch. Dist. and Grant Wood Ed. Agency*, 41 IDELR 24 (SEA 2004).

54. *Rio Rancho Pub. Sch.*, 40 IDELR 140 (SEA NM 2003).

55. 20 USC §1415(k)(1)(F).

56. 34 CFR 300.324(a)(2)(iii).

57. 34 CFR 300.324(a)(2)(iv).

58. *Letter to Anonymous*, 24 IDELR 388 (OSEP 1996).

59. 34 CFR 300.5.

60. 34 CFR 300.6.

61. *J.C. v. New Fairfield Bd. of Ed.*, 56 IDELR 207 (D Conn. 2011).

62. *Rockford (IL) Comm. Sch. Dist. #205*, 352 IDELR 465 (OCR 1987).

63. See n.62.

64. *Aaron S. v. Westford Pub. Sch.*, EHLR 509:122 (SEA MA 1989).

65. *Schoodic Comm. Sch. Dist.*, 26 IDELR 219 (SEA ME 1997).

66. *A.K. v. Alexandria City Sch. Bd.*, 484 F.3d 672 (4th Cir. 2007).

67. *T.Y. v. New York City Dept. of Ed., Reg. 4*, 584 F.3d 412 (2nd Cir. 2009).

68. 34 CFR 99.31(a).

69. *Russell v. Jefferson Sch. Dist.*, 609 F. Supp. 605 (ND CA 1985).

70. *Abrahamson v. Hershman*, 701 F.2d 223 (1st Cir. 1993).

71. *Maine Sch. Admin. Dist. #56 v. Ms. W.*, 47 IDELR 219 (D ME 2007).

72. *North Reading Sch. Comm. v. Bureau of Spec. Ed. Appeals*, 480 F. Supp. 2d 479 (D Mass. 2007).

73. *N.C. v. Utah State Bd. of Ed.*, 125 F. App'x 252 (10th Cir. 2005).

74. *Thompson R2-J Sch. Dist. v. Luke P.*, 540 F.3d 1143 (10th Cir. 2008).

75. *Letter to Leconte*, 211 IDELR 146 (OSEP 1979).

76. *Letter to Beck*, 211 IDELR 145 (OSEP 1979).

77. *Tucson, AZ Unified Sch. Dist.*, 352 IDELR 547 (OCR 1987).

CHAPTER FOUR

Not-the-right-way IEPs

Sadly, many IEPs are horrendously burdensome to teachers and other professionals and nearly useless to parents and children. Far from being a creative, flexible, data-based and individualized application of the best of educational interventions to a child with unique needs, the typical IEP is "empty," devoid of description of specific services to be provided. Its goals are typically not measured, nor is progress toward them. The IEP says what the IEP team hopes the student will be able to accomplish, but very little about the special education interventions and the related services or classroom modifications that will enable him or her to reach those goals.

Typically, the IEP team begins and ends its efforts with goals and objectives for the student to accomplish. For example, one IEP said merely, "Tim will improve his behavior 75% of the time." Apart from the other problems inherent in this slaughtering of behavioral language and concepts, we see the "empty IEP"—nothing is said about **what the district will do** to teach Tim to change his behavior for the better. All the responsibility is on Tim. Clearly, there is no intention of taking this goal seriously, that is, of using it to evaluate how well the program is working. Many, if not most, goals and objectives couldn't be measured if one tried, and all too often no effort is made to actually assess the child's progress toward them.

THE REAL WORLD

The real world of public school IEPs, teachers, students and their parents seems nearly untouched by the academic world of educational interventions. Parents are busy struggling, for example, to get districts to grant graduation credit for resource room or basic English; to include decoding goals on the IEP even though the school uses whole-language reading methodology; to obtain individual language therapy instead of group speech therapy; to prevent the student's threatened or impending expulsion; to ensure the IEP is implemented once it is written; to get the regular teachers to accept the need for shorter spelling lists and for oral reports and tests; and to get keyboarding instruction instead of bare computer time written into the IEP.

Special educators also struggle. They want to know, for example, how to cut down on paperwork, if it is legally correct to bring a completed IEP to the meeting, what happens if they tell the parent the child really does need a tutor, how to get the regular teacher to come to the IEP meeting, and if a caseload of 70 resource room students is legal.

The IEPs themselves often reflect currently available and ongoing instructional programs and packages, rather than the individual students' needs. They reflect available services, not needed services. They are not individualized and they are often not taken seriously. Some are never looked at, many are only partially implemented, and most are not distributed to all the teachers who work with the students.

How did it come about that IEPs are often such a far cry from what they could be? It began with the practice of the last many decades in which the basic special education procedure was to identify the child by category of disability (e.g., intellectual disability), and then place the child strictly by that disability category, i.e., place him or her in a program for intellectually disabled children. The assumption was that appropriate programs had been developed for each type of disability, and that those appropriate programs were implemented in placements designated by disability category. Barsch (1968) described this decades ago:

> Educators of the deaf, blind, physically handicapped, emotionally disturbed, trainable and educable mentally retarded [sic] have spent many years developing specifically defined curricula to meet the educational needs of these different groups of children. These curricula have a well-established rationale and, for the most part, are enacted by teachers in a high degree of comfort. A great deal is known about effective teaching methods and techniques for each of these groups. (p. 15)

When the IDEA (then called the Education of All Handicapped Children Act) went into effect in 1977, educators did the predictable human thing and changed their practices as little as possible. They added IEPs to "business as usual." They labeled a child eligible, decided on placement, made the teacher write up one more version of the ongoing program in that placement and called it an IEP. This basic erroneous and illegal framework has been fostered and upheld by a network of other questionable and/or illegal practices such as: computer generation of stock IEPs; failure to include needed regular class modifications on the IEP; failure to base related services on children's needs rather than on cost or availability, failure to base placement decisions on completed IEPs; failure to include a qualified district representative on every IEP team; failure to ensure full, equal, and meaningful parental participation on every IEP team; failure to address all the child's unique characteristics/needs and instead focusing almost exclusively on academic goals; failure to specify and describe the services to be provided; predetermination of placement or amount of services without serious consideration of parental input; and the list goes on and on.

When educators tried to incorporate IEPs into their old familiar framework, they did it by a sequential process:

▶ They labeled the eligible child by disability category, e.g., Amy is orthopedically impaired.

▶ They placed Amy into a program and placement designed for children with that disability.

▶ They required that the teacher write one more rendition of the ongoing program and they called it Amy's IEP, even though the program went on as it was, whether Amy was in it or not.

What the law has actually required since 1977 is also a three-step process, but with critical differences. The mandated, correct sequence is:

▶ We **must** determine whether the child is eligible for an IEP and if so, determine all the child's unique educational needs.

▶ We **must** carefully examine these needs and determine the services to be provided to address each need and the goals the child will reach if the services are effective. In other words, we must develop the IEP.

▶ We **must** place the child in the least restrictive environment in which an appropriate program can be provided to that child and in which that child's education can be achieved satisfactorily.

Graphically, the old way looks like that shown in Figure 4.1. And the IDEA way looks like that shown in Figure 4.2.

It was more than understandable that educators would attempt to implement the then-new law with as little change in practice as possible. It was downright predictable, human nature being as it is. One can only wonder whether the change-over should have taken the 35 years that have since elapsed.

Fully recognizing the differences between the old way and the IDEA way is crucial to improving IEPs. For many, the old way is deeply ingrained and it seems practical. And so, once more, and for almost the last time, we look at the wrong way: One who has maintained the old ways says, for example, "Joe is learning disabled, so we'll put him in the resource room for learning disabled students, and then have the resource teacher write up a copy of the ongoing program in that room and call it the IEP." Instead, one should say, "Joe is eligible, Joe's individual needs are X, Y, Z, and can be met by services A, B, C (his IEP), which we can implement in placement P." Districts try to fit children into existing programs, just as has long been done, rather than flexibly and creatively designing new programs, **one child at a time,** to fit the individual needs of each child.

A very trendy version of the old, wrong way is to say, for example, "Jim is eligible and he has to be in a regular class (no, he doesn't, but that's another story) and we use a consultation model so that's what his IEP will say." Jim's unique needs have been overlooked and the existing delivery system has been the tail that wagged the dog, again.

And now, not for the last time, what the IDEA requires is: (1) the evaluation and identification of an eligible student; (2) the development of a truly individualized education program (IEP), without regard to the category of disability or the availability of services; and (3) an individual placement decision based upon the child's IEP, not on the disability or on administrative convenience.

Before we leave the real world and head toward better IEPs, we'll take one further glance at some frequently occurring problems in the old-style IEPs.

COMMON PROBLEMS IN REAL-WORLD IEPS

Is there really any point in looking at not-so-perfect IEPs or parts of IEPs? Absolutely! Doing so provides an opportunity to demonstrate how common practices go astray from the letter and spirit of the law. We will examine some typical IEP problems. Each illustrates misconceptions or practices that must be reevaluated before one can start over on the road to better IEPs.

Problematic Statements of Needs and Present Levels of Performance

All the child's unique educational needs resulting from the disability must be spelled out. Whether or not a clear, precise, explicit listing of needs on the IEP is a legal requirement, it is surely a best practice. Since 1997, and even more so now, IDEA has mandated that the team which determines eligibility must also determine **all** of the child's unique academic, functional and developmental needs. These become the starting point for the IEP, the purpose of which is to address these unique needs and show how progress in meeting them will be assessed and reported.

The IDEA also expressly requires a description of how the disability affects the child's involvement and progress in the general curriculum. Too many IEPs contain little or no specification of needs. The fear is that if a need is mentioned in the IEP, it will have to be addressed. Right! It will, and it must. If Barry, for example, needs one-to-one tutoring in a quiet room, that need must be on the IEP, and the corresponding services must be provided. Remember, when an ostrich "hides" with its head on the sand its tail end is more than a little vulnerable. (An ostrich in hiding puts its head **on,** not **in** the sand, true.)

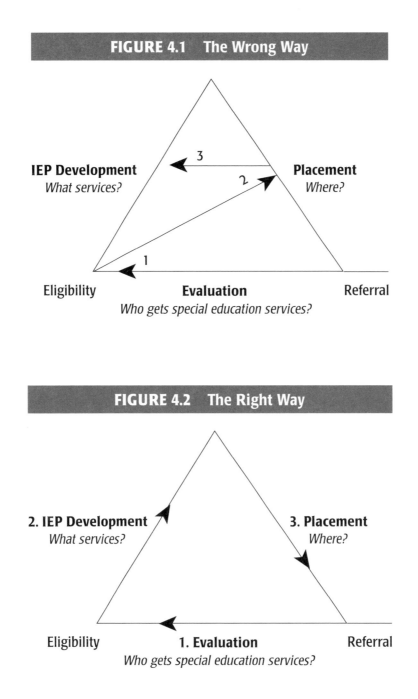

FIGURE 4.1   The Wrong Way

IEP Development
What services?

Placement
Where?

Eligibility

Evaluation
Who gets special education services?

Referral

FIGURE 4.2   The Right Way

2. IEP Development
What services?

3. Placement
Where?

Eligibility

1. Evaluation
Who gets special education services?

Referral

Present levels of performance (PLOPs) are the beginning point from which the child's progress must be measured. Every annual goal must itself be measurable, and the PLOP is the measured starting point on the journey toward the goal. There must be a measured PLOP; without it, progress toward the goal cannot be measured.

In a program for weight change, the program begins only when the client's entering weight has been measured. That measurement is **current,**

accurate and objective, i.e. it is the PLOP—the **present** level of performance. Suppose a professor of special education is going to take a year-long sabbatical leave for the purpose of publishing more. In the two years before the leave, she published six articles in refereed journals, a PLOP of three journal articles per year. This objectively assessed starting point is obviously an essential ingredient in determining, retrospectively, whether the sabbatical leave did or did not result in an increase in published writing.

A PLOP, measured recently (within a few weeks) and objectively (as well as reliably and validly) is an **absolutely essential** component of the IEP. A PLOP is required for every measurable annual goal **(Remember: Progress toward a goal can only be measured and reported if the starting point is known.)**

However, many IEP teams include extensive information in the PLOPs, beyond what is relevant to particular goals. This practice is **not** required and may not be helpful to the IEP process, but it may be useful for other purposes. Legally, the IEP need **not** contain anything not specifically required. Most certainly it is not appropriate to copy paragraphs or even sentences, let alone pages of material, from the most recent evaluations onto the PLOPs section of the IEP. All the information from evaluations can be "incorporated by reference," i.e. legally included in and made a part of the IEP simply by writing at the beginning of the PLOP section, for example, "the evaluation reports of Dr. Smith (10-8-11) and Dr. Jones (6-7-11) are hereby included in this document."

The bottom line is that all of the child's unique needs must be addressed by an accommodation or a service. The present level of performance and a goal must be specified for all instructional services. Pitfalls to be avoided include:

► Omitting a critical need, e.g., failing to state that Pamela is highly allergic to scents and therefore failing to provide the needed accommodation of a scent-free environment.

► Using the category of eligibility as a PLOP, e.g., "Todd has a learning disability in reading and language."

► Stating only a vague PLOP, such as "Jenna is deficient in keyboarding," rather than stating it in measured terms. When instruction is the needed service, as here, a measured PLOP and measurable goal are required.

► Including so much information in the PLOPs section of the IEP that the specific PLOPs related to the child's priority goals are lost in the verbiage.

Problematic Statements of Special Services and Modifications

Sins of omission prevail in the vital portion of the IEP specifying the services for the child. Not only does the law require a **statement** of the special education and related services, supplementary aids and services, program modifications, and personnel support the child needs, but it also requires a beginning date, frequency, location and duration for each. The services to be provided should be described in sufficient detail that a parent can truly determine, given the right to observe the services and the child, whether the services (so stated and described) are being provided.

IEPs commonly have omitted such statements altogether and have instead provided only a check mark and no descriptive statement, or a statement so vague as to prevent one from determining whether the needed service was or was not provided. Here are examples of typical, **too vague** or **too general** service descriptions: reading remediation, community trips for independent living skills, tutoring in math, modification of the curriculum, special education teacher/aide, social skill training, a crisis management plan, daily academic instruction, an educational assistant will provide training, the school counselor will assist in exploring college options, the teacher will work with the student on the computer, etc. Vague and general as these are, they are one tiny step above a printed list of services waiting for a check mark.

Complete descriptions of services that allow meaningful determination of when the service is being provided, and that therefore constitute an enforceable commitment of district resources, will appear in **Chapter Four.** For now, here is one example of an acceptable statement of services: "One-to-one direct instruction in color, shape and spatial concepts by the classroom teacher for 15 minutes per day in the classroom beginning Sept. 1, 2009 until Sept. 1, 2010." An unacceptable but common example is "90 minutes of special education per day." How would a parent know if what was being observed was or was not "special education"?

Problematic Goals and Progress Markers

Several common problems in writing annual goals and progress markers are presented next. Unfortunately there are more problems than these, but these examples do serve to illustrate several critical points.

IDEA presently places strong emphasis on the measurability of student progress and on the overall effectiveness of programs. It is crucial that IEP goals be measurable and that the child's performance be measured. Lack of measurability is the largest problem in goals, so we present several examples:

Not-So-Wonderful Goals: Not Measurable

1. Jason will increase his social skills with no more than one prompt in 4 consecutive recording periods.

Comment: This goal is not measurable because (1) "Increase in social skills" is vague; (2) there is no baseline from which to measure an increase; and (3) there are no criteria by which to judge the sufficiency of whatever level of social skills he has reached. The problem with vague language like "social skills" is that to make them measurable, we have to guess at what behaviors the goal writer might have meant. For example, one possibility might be "Jason will initiate 3 positive peer interactions daily for three of four consecutive days."

2. Jason will demonstrate age appropriate life skills and behaviors to foster independent living in 4 of 5 opportunities.

Comment: This goal is totally vague. "Life skills and behavior" and "independent living" are so broad they are useless as goals. However, there is an even worse hidden problem in this goal—in the words "age appropriate." Jason is 10 years old, but he is functioning at a two- to three-year old level. It is difficult to envision he will accomplish the goal of "age appropriate" in one year. That would require a gain of over eight years of functioning level in one year, which is all but impossible, especially for one whose cognitive ability is

severely deficient. A more reasonable statement might be "Will dress himself independently except for buttoning and tying in no more than three minutes when his clothes are preselected for him."

3. Jesse will improve her language by using/listening to complete sentences 80% of the time.

Comment: This goal is indecipherable and not measurable. What does it mean that Jesse is to do? And even if we knew what is meant, how does one do something 80% of the time? Eighty percent of what time?

4. Jen will increase her ability to fluently read grade appropriate texts within one year.

Comment: This goal lacks measurability because no criteria are given for "fluently," it fails to specify oral or silent reading, and no baseline is given from which progress could be measured. Furthermore, Jen now reads at a kindergarten level. Is it reasonable to suggest that she can improve to a fifth grade level in one year, given that her cognitive ability is below the first percentile? Perhaps a real goal for her might be to read 50 sight words correctly from the XYZ list in one minute.

A Not-So-Wonderful Annual Goal: Insufficient Progress Projected

1. By one year from today, Jerry will improve his reading score by six months on a standardized reading test such as the Woodcock-Johnson (W-J).

Comment: Six months' (or even a year's) gain would not begin to get a learning disabled student caught up to his ability level, assuming he is substantially behind. There is a most troublesome trend now whereby some professionals confuse learning disabilities with intellectual disability. Many children who need reading goals on their IEPs are learning disabled, not intellectually disabled. By definition, research and experience, it is known that learning disabled children **can** learn to read at or near their ability level, i.e., they can catch up if they are taught effectively. For almost all children who have learning disabilities, a systematic, highly structured, synthetic phonics-based method of teaching reading is essential (Shaywitz, 2003). Among such reading programs are Direct Instruction, Orton-Gillingham, Slingerland, Read Well, Herman, Wilson, Spalding, Lindamood-Bell, and Alphabetic Phonics. All these and all other highly effective reading programs require specific and thorough teacher training to a defined level of expertise. Perhaps that is why some schools resist these programs and prefer the "mix children with print and stir lightly," osmotic and other noninstructional approaches to teaching reading.

To define a proper annual goal in reading for a learning disabled student, given an appropriate and effective methodology, first determine how long it would take a skilled teacher to get the student to grade level and then project progress on a fairly straight-line basis. Let us say, for example, one has a sixth grade student with average intellectual ability who reads at a third grade level. The teacher says that in two years the student can be at grade level. That is, by eighth grade, he'll be at eighth grade level. He has five years of work to make up in two years, so the projection would be about two or two-and-a-half years' gain in sixth grade.

Not-So-Wonderful Goals: Misuse of Percentages

1. Karen will improve her handwriting by 80%.

Comment: One gets the general idea readily—Karen has a need for better writing and total perfection is not expected immediately. However, writing IEPs isn't playing horseshoes and this just doesn't get close enough. Percentages seem to be worshiped unduly, although they have some legitimate uses in goals and objectives. For example, to strive for 90% of spelling words to be written correctly on the first weekly test might be quite appropriate. However, to accept only 90% of the words in a reading passage to be decoded accurately is to accept an error rate which interferes with comprehension. Similarly, if 80% of the words in an essay were legible, one of five would **not** be legible. That is not an acceptable target.

Even more glaring is the misuse of percentages in goals related to behavior. One memorable IEP from a small town in western Oregon projected that, "Levi will have acceptable behavior 80% of the time." Can you imagine what it would be like to be around someone whose behavior was unacceptable 20% of the time? And to think that was the goal! Bad enough if it had been Levi's present level of performance.

2. Given a short paragraph, James will be able to identify the main idea with 95% accuracy.

Comment: Exactly how does one identify a main idea with 95% accuracy? Does this mean that if James were given 100 short paragraphs he would correctly identify the main idea in 95 of them? Or that given one paragraph he would almost accurately (but not quite) identify the main idea? The old rule of editing applies here—if in doubt, delete. Better to say that James will be able to identify the main idea in a short paragraph at his reading level.

A Not-So-Wonderful Goal: The Student Will "Choose"

1. Joshua will choose to be responsible for his own behavior. If he fails to do this, his parents will be called to remove him for the remainder of the day.

Comment: If the only specific special education and related services to be provided are check marks on the IEP face sheet, this "choose" language is especially apt to sound empty. Of course, this particular goal/objective statement is also too vague. People who frame objectives in terms of "the student will choose" to do or not do usually have a strong philosophical reason for choosing that language. However, that language poses the "empty IEP" problem in that it appears as if the district's sole contribution to the improved behavior may be its expectation that Joshua will choose to do better.

If a student provided an IEP has behavioral-social-emotional needs, they must be addressed by services on the IEP. Any time it is known or there is reason to suspect a child will need it, a behavioral intervention plan (BIP) should be included. It is not the case that only children who are labeled seriously emotionally disturbed or emotionally or behaviorally disabled, etc., should have behavior plans in their IEP. Behavior intervention plans (BIPs) vary greatly in complexity and sophistication. IDEA specifies only that positive strategies should be included. One source for guidance in preparing simple but effective behavior plans is *Why Johnny Doesn't Behave* (Bateman & Golly, 2003).

Too often, parents will be requested or pressured to accept some responsibility through the IEP. This may range from providing a study space to removing the child from school. There is no authority or power in the IEP process to require the parents to provide services. This part of the law is about what the district must do, not what parents must do. Parental cooperation is helpful in the extreme, beyond any doubt. The point is just that the IEP is not the place to formalize that cooperative working relationship.

The particular parental involvement suggested in Joshua's goal (coming to school and removing him) is a transparent and legally unacceptable way to avoid calling suspension what it is. The law has placed stringent limitations on the extent and manner of suspensions, and it is impossible to evade these by pretending that suspension isn't suspension.

The whole area of discipline of students who have disabilities is complicated and difficult. A major principle that emerges from case law is that educators are expected to treat inappropriate behavior in a programmatic way, not just by exclusion from school. Another very important principle is that it is not appropriate to punish a student for behavior caused by the disability. If a deaf student fails to hear a teacher's request, or if a blind kindergartner accidentally knocks down another child's blocks, punishment is not even considered as the proper response. The appropriate response is less clear when a student diagnosed as severely emotionally disturbed because of violent, unprovoked aggression and hostility then continues that same pattern.

A determination must be made by the IEP team as to **whether the misconduct was caused by the disability.** If it is, the IDEA requires a program change and/or change in placement rather than discipline per se.

While an in-depth examination of the issue involved in disciplining special education students is beyond our discussion, Figure 1.3 (p. 18) does provide a helpful flow chart and overview of the basic discipline procedures required by the IDEA.

A Not-So-Wonderful Goal: It Is Unnecessary

1. Given a blank outline map, Pat will label the continents and the major oceans with 90% accuracy.

Comment: Many goal or objective statements are similar to this one. They immediately trigger the question of whether they are really special education. Does such a goal/objective, legitimate as it may be, need to be on the IEP? If one recalls that **only** special education need be dealt with on the IEP, that by definition special education is specially designed instruction to meet a student's unique needs, and that it must be delivered by certified special educators or by aides working under direct supervision, it seems likely that this social studies goal need not be included. If the student were blind and the map was a relief map labeled in Braille, perhaps this goal would be closer to being special education. If the student were 21 years old and doing this exercise as part of a "travel in the community" unit preparatory to learning to ride the bus, perhaps it would be addressing a unique need. However, even that leaves the question of whether it would be "specially designed instruction."

The very same questions can be raised about objectives such as, "Given 10 fraction problems with mixed fractions, Pat will be able to add, subtract, multiply and divide correctly nine out of 10 times."

Here is what one hearing officer said about various IEP goals prepared for a special education student:

. . . [E]ach of [the] student's IEPs were so general that it would be difficult to believe the goals were even written for a special education student. For example:

. . . will improve math assignments . . . will be able to complete story problems . . . will identify the process to use in solving word problems correctly . . . will complete lessons dealing with algebra and geometry . . . will complete grade level math assignments, but at her own pace . . . will complete grade level math tests . . . will bring all materials needed to study periods . . . will develop a positive, hardworking attitude to understand the relationship between forces, motion, and energy . . . to understand American history from 1790–1865 . . .

These IEP examples clearly do not meet the *Rowley* threshold of providing personalized instruction to permit a child to benefit educationally.[1]

A Not-So-Wonderful Goal: Vague, Meaningless and/or Not Measurable

1. Rebecca will increase her active listening skills.

Comment: Other inadequate goals from the same IEP include ". . . [she] will increase auditory sequencing skills, auditory memory skills, active communication skills with peers, organizational skills, and written expression skills."[2] Goals must include an expected ending level so that an observer can readily determine whether that level was or was not reached. If one says, for example, by the end of the year Zack will weigh no more than 140 pounds, the observer can readily determine success. But if the goal were simply to "lose weight," the observer would be unable, without more information, to ascertain whether the goal had been accomplished.

The following five common problems in IEP goals are frequently intertwined: **(1) vague, meaningless and/or not measurable goals; (2) insufficient progress projected; (3) misuse of percentages; (4) "student will choose" language;** and **(5) including regular curriculum goals instead of special education goals**. One

needs to avoid each and every one. The following IEPs further illustrate these and other problems.

REAL-WORLD PROBLEMATIC IEPS

The following IEPs and partial IEPs are all real. They come from schools in several states, so the formats differ from one another. Our focus is **only** on the essentials of the IEP—the PLOPs, the services and the goals/progress markers—and the closeness of the sequential fit among them, moving from PLOP to service to goals.

Tammy

Tammy is an 11th grader who has cerebral palsy. She functions academically at a third to sixth grade equivalent level. Her speech is about 65 percent intelligible; she responds with one- or two-word phrases, or by pointing. She presents no behavioral problems, is quiet in class and responds to some humor by smiling. Her IEP consisted of 10 pages of content area objectives in English, study skills, consumer education, math and state history. Three selected pages are shown in Figure 4.3.

Needs and Present Levels of Performance

In addition to the descriptive information just given, an evaluation attached to Tammy's IEP mentioned that she would benefit from a vocational skills training program, that her low motivation is an ongoing problem, and that she needs orally presented instruction that is short, concrete and step-by-step. Additional detail was also given about her academic levels.

Services

No services were specified beyond her enrollment in one study skills class. Her extreme need for speech and language therapy was ignored, as were her needs for vocational programming, and for specific oral instruction. Based on Tammy's performance levels, a truly individualized program

FIGURE 4.3 Tammy's IEP

INDIVIDUALIZED EDUCATION PROGRAM

Name _Tammy_   Monitoring teacher _____

Subject area/related service _English Phase III_   ☐ Diploma   ☐ Certificate

Method of evaluation
1 Tests
2 Observation, records
3 Daily work
4 Other _____

Evaluation code
N/P No progress: No gains or improvement
P Progressing: Shows gains in learning the objective
M Mastered: Has learned the skills for the objective
NA Not applicable: Objective not yet covered

Annual goal number _____	Short-term objective(s)	Method of eval.	Evaluation				Comments
			1QT	2QT			
1c To improve literature awareness	1. Given a short story in American literature in VHS presentation form, Tammy will identify the conflict, state how it is resolved, and justify her statements by citing from the tape with at least 75% accuracy.	2, 3					Summer School 1c
1d To improve language study skills	1. Given 2 examples of personal views, Tammy will read or listen to the language used and explain what cultural beliefs, values, and/or interests are being reflected, and support her answer by citing from the examples given with 75% accuracy.	2, 3					Summer School 1d
1e To improve oral communication	1. Tammy will use complete sentences and explain her ideas in logical sequence (without pointing) with at least 80% accuracy, 75% of the time.	2, 3					Summer School 1e

(Cont'd next page)

would have a large speech/language therapy component. Since low motivation is also a major concern, the IEP should address this directly and squarely. A source such as Thomas Lovitt's *Preventing School Dropouts* (1991) is invaluable for developing IEP components for high school students' motivation, social behaviors, attendance, compliance, self-concepts and much more.

Goals and Objectives

Tammy's goals are totally vague and absolutely unmeasurable. Her one goal for study skills is a classic: "to improve basic and other life skills." Not only is that goal not measurable, but it is

evident from the objectives, and even more so from the "methods of evaluation," that no one ever, for even one moment, intended to measure Tammy's progress!

Discussion

Tammy's IEP, like so many, deals only with academics. It denies FAPE in several ways. Neither speech therapy nor vocational training was offered even though both were needed. The excerpts from her IEP illustrate a fairly common practice of pretending to "individualize" by filling in blanks with a percentage. For example, for the consumer education component there are

FIGURE 4.3—Continued

INDIVIDUALIZED EDUCATION PROGRAM

Name *Tammy*

Subject area/related service *Study Skills*   ☐ Diploma ☐ Certificate

Method of evaluation
1 Tests
2 Observation, records
3 Daily work
4 Other _____

Evaluation code
N/P No progress: No gains or improvement
P   Progressing: Shows gains in learning the objective
M   Mastered: Has learned the skills for the objective
NA   Not applicable: Objective not yet covered

Annual goal number _____	Short-term objective(s)	Method of eval.	Evaluation				Comments
a To improve basic and other life skills	Given activities and exercises in the following workbook-text, *Getting Smarter: The Study Skills Improvement Program,* Tammy will in written form or oral evaluation, establish, or demonstrate the following objectives:	1, 2, 3 1, 2, 3					Summer School 2d
	1. Tammy will improve her current study habits using her workbook texts with 75% accuracy.	1, 2, 3					
	2. Tammy will improve her organizational skills by giving 6 examples pertinent to organizing her work, assignments, and homework with 75% accuracy.	1, 2, 3 1, 2, 3					
	3. Tammy will give 7 affective examples of how to budget a given time period, including 6 steps on designing her own schedule with 75% accuracy.	1, 2, 3					
	4. Tammy will examine priorities and goals and list 3 examples of long-term, short-term, weekly, and daily goals with 75% accuracy.						
	5. Tammy will improve her reading comprehension within an instructional range of 3.0 to 5.0 reading levels with 75% accuracy.						
	6. Tammy will improve note-taking skills using a given outline format, identifying the main ideas with 75% accuracy.						
	7. To improve testing techniques, Tammy will state the 2 steps for test preparation.						

(Cont'd next page)

FIGURE 4.3–Continued

INDIVIDUALIZED EDUCATION PROGRAM

Name _Tammy_

Subject area/related service _Consumer Education_   ☐ Diploma   ☐ Certificate

Method of evaluation

1 Tests
2 Observation, records
3 Daily work
4 Other _____

Evaluation code

N/P No progress: No gains or improvement
P   Progressing: Shows gains in learning the objective
M   Mastered: Has learned the skills for the objective
NA   Not applicable: Objective not yet covered

Annual goal number _____	Short term objective(s)	Method of eval.	Evaluation				Comments
To understand the value of money and the importance of money	1. Tammy will create a sound budget when given a hypothetical financial situation with 75% accuracy.	1, 2, 3					Summer School 2d
	2. Tammy will spell, define, and use 10 vocabulary words per chapter/unit, pertinent to banking and money management with 75% accuracy.	1, 2, 3					

objectives of creating a budget with 75% accuracy and using 10 banking and money management vocabulary words with 75% accuracy. One can only wonder whether the latter means 7½ words will be used correctly, or that each of the 10 words will be used ¾ correctly. Her math skills do not include multiplication, or division, or fractions, or decimals. The skills she does have will be extended by preparing a budget, even though it need be only 75% accurate, whatever that may mean.

The English objective requires Tammy to explain the cultural beliefs or values being reflected in a personal view with 75% accuracy. This may be slightly difficult for a young woman who responds orally with only one or two words or by pointing. And one can only wonder how it was decided that Tammy was a "75%" person. The odds are very high that all students with disabilities in these classes have identical IEPs except, perhaps, for the percentages. In addition to denying needed services, not being the least bit individualized, and having meaningless and unmeasurable goals and objectives, Tammy's IEP also illustrates the "no-

no" of being nothing more than excerpts from an ongoing regular curriculum. (See **Chapter Six** on standards-based IEPs.) The evaluation method and code are also dead give-aways that no meaningful or real progress assessment was ever undertaken.

J.R.

J.R. is a student who has a speech impairment. Selected portions of his IEPs from third, fourth and fifth grades are shown in Figure 4.4. They speak for themselves. When a service has not been effective, something needs to change! And decreasing the amount of the same service is not an appropriate response. These excerpts are strong evidence of the failure of the district's program to rise to the level of legally appropriate. The parents could well consider obtaining private therapy and requesting the district to pay. The parents would probably prevail if the district refused.

This IEP also reveals yet another misuse of percentages. An "r" sound said with 90% accuracy is an "r" sound misarticulated, is it not? Surely

FIGURE 4.4   Selected Portions of J.R.'s IEPs

THIRD GRADE

Annual goal(s)	Special education related services	Date signed Person(s) responsible for implementation	Hours/week	Evaluation criteria
J.R. will say correct "r" sounds with 90% accuracy in conversation	Speech therapy		40 min. (2 or 3 15-min. sessions per week)	• Picture test for articulation • Teacher-made criterion test • Sample of conversation

FOURTH GRADE

Annual goal(s)	Special education related services	Date signed Person(s) responsible for implementation	Hours/week	Evaluation criteria
J.R. will say correct "r" sounds with 90% accuracy in conversation	Speech therapy		40 min.	• Picture test for articulation • Teacher-made criterion test • Sample of conversation

FIFTH GRADE

Annual goal(s)	Special education related services	Date signed Person(s) responsible for implementation	Hours/week	Evaluation criteria
J.R. will say correct "r" sounds with 90% accuracy in conversation	Speech therapy		30 min. (two 15-min. sessions per week)	• Picture test for articulation (annual) • Teacher-made criterion test • Sample of conversation • Classroom teacher's observation

the intent was to say that 90% of J.R.'s "r" sounds would be articulated clearly. Even so, why 90%? Why not 100%?

Kevin

Kevin's IEP (see Figure 4.5) illustrates yet another abuse of percentages combined with questionable evaluation methods. Is it really believable that once per quarter a resource room teacher and/ or assistant will determine whether Kevin has

decreased his inappropriate remarks to other students 90% of the time? Exactly how would one do that if one were truly trying to do so? Would that be practical? Reducing inappropriate remarks is clearly a good thing to do, but just to attach a number to it does **not** make it measurable. Many goal writers seem to mistakenly believe that inserting a number is all that is required, even though the number attached makes no sense, as here.

FIGURE 4.5 Kevin's IEP

GOALS AND OBJECTIVES
(Primary Service Provider)

Status key C—Completed
D—Dropped
R—Revised
N—Parent notified

Student's name _Kevin_   Date _March 8_

Present level of performance in _Socialization skills and behavior are below average according to checklists filled out by_ _parents and teachers_

Annual goal statement _Kevin will demonstrate improved socialization skills and behavior by March_

Short-term objectives	Criteria	Evaluation method	Scheduled evaluation	Position responsible	Status	Date
1. Kevin will improve attention during teacher-directed lesson	80% of the time	Teacher observation	Quarterly	ERC teacher & assistants		
2. Kevin will improve requested standard behaviors from one class to the next including: Standing in line, walking and following directions	85% of the time	Teacher observation	Ongoing	ERC teacher & assistants		
3. Kevin will decrease inappropriate remarks to other students	90% of the time	Teacher observation	Quarterly	ERC teacher & assistants		
4. Kevin will react appropriately when adult gives corrections	90% of the time	Teacher observation	Weekly	ERC teacher & assistants		
5. Kevin will increase eye contact with adults and peers	85% of the time	Teacher observation	Weekly	ERC teacher & assistants		

Kevin's behaviors are reasonably well targeted. However, social behaviors can sometimes be quite difficult to convert to appropriate IEP components. Sugai and Colvin's (1990) tips for writing goals and objectives for social behaviors are presented in **Chapter Four.** These would have been very helpful to the people writing Kevin's IEP. Notice that his annual goal is 100% not measurable.

School personnel have become so accustomed to certain ways of writing IEPs that it would be helpful to sometimes stop and ask if a given component makes any sense. For example, what does it mean that Kevin will increase eye contact 85% of the time? Will this be checked once per week? How will that work? What data will the teacher actually collect? How? When? It is obvious that many IEPs like this one were never intended to be taken seriously, never intended to serve as an objective monitor for the efficacy of the services provided.

This IEP specifies no services. What will the **district do** to enable Kevin to improve attention, decrease his inappropriate remarks and so on? Or is Kevin to "choose" these behavioral changes on his own? This kind of disconnectedness between PLOPs and goals and objectives is too common, because IEPs like this one focus only on what the student

FIGURE 4.6 Andy's IEP

GOALS AND OBJECTIVES
(Primary Service Provider)

Status key C—Completed
D—Dropped
R—Revised
N—Parent notified

Student's name _Andy_   Date _11/20_

Present level of performance in _Reading ability—2.3; achievement 1.0 (3-1) according to Woodcock-Johnson Psycho-_
Educational Battery

Annual goal statement _Andy will make six mo. to 1 year gain in reading by Nov. as measured by Woodcock- Johnson Psycho-_
Educational Battery

Short-term objectives	Criteria	Evaluation method	Scheduled evaluation	Position responsible	Status	Date
Andy will know and say letter names	100%	Commercial	Semester	ERC	C	Nov
Andy will know and say letter sounds	100%	Commercial	Semester	ERC	C	Nov
Andy will read sight words on a 1.5 to 2.0 grade level	85%	Commercial	Semester	ERC	Continue	Nov
Andy will read sentences and short stories on a 1.5 to 2.0 grade level	85%	Commercial	Semester	ERC	C	Nov
Andy will answer literal comprehension questions	85%	Commercial	Semester	ERC	C	Nov

will do, not on what the district will provide. A further serious problem is the total reliance on teacher observation, with no objective progress assessment.

Andy

Andy was a nonreader after three years in school. Then his parents independently found a private clinic that successfully taught Andy using the Lindamood-Bell program. They went to hearing and won all their expenses, including transportation time as well as mileage and all tutoring costs. Additionally, they won all legal fees related to the hearing. The legal issue at hearing was whether the school's IEP (see Figure 4.6) provided FAPE to Andy.

The hearing officer pointed out, among many other serious problems, that Andy's teacher had completed the IEP before the meeting. It is evident there was no parental input. The total reliance on the Woodcock-Johnson (W-J) test is apparent when one recognizes that each objective reflects a W-J subtest. Andy's district was shown at hearing to rely totally and solely on the W-J for identification of students as learning disabled, for determining present levels of performance, for establishing goals and objectives, and for evaluation of progress.

These "objectives" are all projected to be completed in a year. They are not the "how far, by when" progress markers toward goals that objectives are expected to be. It is also unrealistic to believe the W-J (the "commercial" evaluation

FIGURE 4.7 Ryan's Third Grade IEP

GOALS AND OBJECTIVES
(Primary Service Provider)

Student's name _Ryan_ Date _1/23_

Present level of performance in _Reading letter identification—4.3; word ident.—1.9; word attack—1.6; word comprehension—1.4; passage comprehension—2.3; total—2.1, as measured by Woodcock Reading Mastery Test_

Annual goal statement _Ryan will make 1 year's gain in reading by Jan. as measured by Woodcock-Johnson Reading Test_

Short-term objectives	Criteria	Evaluation method	Scheduled evaluation	Position responsible
1. Ryan will read sight words on a 2.9 grade level	85%	Commercial	Semester	ERC
2. Ryan will use decoding skills for unknown words	85%	Commercial	Semester	ERC
3. Ryan will complete analogies on a 2d-grade level	85%	Commercial	Semester	ERC
4. Ryan will read short stories on a 3d-grade level	85%	Commercial	Semester	ERC
5. Ryan will answer literal and inferential comprehension questions	85%	Commercial	Semester	ERC

FIGURE 4.8 Ryan's Sixth Grade IEP

GOALS AND OBJECTIVES
(Primary Service Provider)

Student's name _Ryan_ Date _11/9_

Present level of performance in _Reading achievement is 3.3 as measured by the Woodcock-Johnson_

Annual goal statement _Ryan will make 6 month's to 1 year's gain in reading achievement by November as measured by Woodcock-Johnson Psychoeducational Battery_

Short-term objectives	Criteria	Evaluation method	Scheduled evaluation	Position responsible
1. Ryan's progress in reading will be monitored in the regular classroom.	Passing grade	Grades and teacher observation	Monthly	Regular classroom teacher and resource teacher

method) is actually going to be given each semester every year. Nor should it be.

Finally, a projected gain of six months to one year in the annual goal is totally inadequate to allow Andy to catch up.

Ryan

Ryan is Andy's older brother. His third and sixth grade IEPs are both presented (see Figures 4.7 and 4.8). The district wisely settled his case without going to hearing. They paid for his private tutoring, transportation and legal expenses just as they were ordered to do with Andy. Ryan's third grade IEP and Andy's IEP were written almost four years apart. The minor differences are related to different levels on the W-J. Three years later, now in the sixth grade, Ryan was still reading at a third grade level, having gained only one year during three years, and fallen that much further behind.

The district's response was to do nothing, i.e., to "monitor" Ryan in the regular classroom. One has to wonder how, if at all, this sixth grade IEP meets the requirements for: (1) specification of special education and related services (delivered by qualified/certified special education personnel) and (2) measurable behavioral goals. These "monitoring" or "consulting" IEPs are becoming common as more children with disabilities are educated full-time in regular classrooms. If the student no longer needs special education, his or her IDEA eligibility should be reevaluated. If a legitimate monitoring period is part of that determination one would expect the IEP to contain specific classroom modifications and very precise criteria and evaluation procedures. Too few "monitoring" or "consulting" IEPs contain these provisions.

All three of Andy's and Ryan's IEPs reveal a built-in "behindedness" and a total lack of individualization. They all project a totally inadequate annual gain of six months to a year. Worse yet, the actual reading programs provided the boys were as bad or worse than the IEPs! The district personnel obviously had a procedure for writing IEPs, and that procedure did not in any way include looking at the individual student. Rather, only the W-J test was considered.

A SUMMARY OF IEP SINS

The sins we've highlighted in these real IEPs (see Figure 4.9) are common and they occur in varying degrees of "wrongness." A district's entire program for a child may be declared a denial of FAPE if sins in the IEP render it so. Among the worst of these are the failure to individualize (often revealed in computer generation and in misuse of

percentages); failure to address all needs; failure to specify services adequately; and writing vague, meaningless and unmeasurable PLOPs, objectives and goals.

Sadly, it is easy to describe goals and objectives that are unusable, illogical and downright silly; we have a plethora of readily available, not-so-good real IEPs to use. The next chapter takes up the challenge of describing how to write IEP goals that make sense, lend themselves to measurement and address students needs.

FIGURE 4.9   IEP Sins

▶ Failure to individualize the program to fit the student
▶ Failure to address all the student's needs
▶ Failure to sufficiently describe and specify all necessary services
▶ Failure to write clear, objective, meaningful, and reasonable PLOPs, progress markers and goals.

References

Barsch, R.H. (1968). Perspectives on learning disabilities: The vectors of a new convergence. *Journal of Learning Disabilities, 1,* 7–23.

Bateman, B., & Golly, A. (2003). *Why Johnny doesn't behave: Twenty tips and measurable BIPs.* Verona, WI: Attainment Co.

Lovitt, T.C. (1991). *Preventing school dropouts.* Austin, TX: PRO-ED

Shaywitz, S. (2003). *Overcoming dyslexia.* New York, NY: Alfred Knopf

Sugai, G., & Colvin, G. (1990). From assessment to development: Writing Behavior IEPs. *The Oregon Conference Monograph,* 125–179. Eugene, OR: University of Oregon.

Notes

1. *Independent Sch. Dist. #204 Kasson-Mantorville,* 22 IDELR 380 (SEA MN 1994).

2. *Independent Sch. Dist. #283 St. Louis Park,* 22 IDELR 47 (SEA MN 1994).

CHAPTER FIVE

Educationally useful IEPs

In **Chapter Three,** we described the development of legally correct IEPs, and in **Chapter Four** we analyzed some of the many ways IEPs can go astray. Now we will turn our attention to describing a better way of writing IEPs that prescribe effective services for students who have disabilities and provide useful guidance to the teachers who work with them.

It bears repeating that IEPs must focus on the student's **unique needs,** arising from the disability, that affect his or her ability to participate and progress in the **general curriculum,** as appropriate. For this reason, the IEP team includes a **regular educator** on the IEP team for any student who may participate in a regular education environment. Except for the fraction of students who have moderate or severe disabilities, most special education-eligible students spend much of their school time in regular classes, so it is more than ever necessary for IEPs to spell out the **supplementary aids, services and accommodations** they will need in those settings as well as needed **supports for staff** who will implement the IEP. We will demonstrate how to include these and other important features in IEPs.

The essence of better IEP development is a three-fold inquiry: (1) What are this child's unique educational characteristics and needs that must be taken into account in a truly individualized education program? (2) What will the district do or provide in response to each of these characteristics and needs? (3) If the services are effective, what goals and objectives will the child reach? In other words, what accomplishments will tell us the services are on the right track?

Good IEPs begin with good planning, so let's prepare for IEP development.

GATHER INFORMATION

In order to fashion a legally correct and educationally useful IEP, the team must first gather information about the student. We will not discuss evaluation and assessment in detail here; that topic deserves a book of its own. However, initial evaluation, periodic reevaluations and ongoing formal and informal assessments yield crucial data needed to configure an IEP geared to the needs of an individual student, so a brief survey is appropriate here.

The school's preparation for the IEP meeting includes a review of the student's files, progress reports and any new data and relevant materials that will inform IEP development. Teachers often prepare a draft IEP or a portion of the IEP to take to the meeting. At the first IEP meeting, especially, this might improperly convey to the parent that IEP meetings are one more "school tells parent" situation, rather than the desired message of full and equal partnership. It is important to let the parents know that such a document is only a starting point, and that the team may subtract from and add to it. The primary concern is with the parents' opportunity to participate. Any IEP participant, including the parents, can come to the meeting with prepared notes. However, it is both illegal and counterproductive to complete the entire IEP and simply present it to the parent.

As with all other phases of the IEP process, parents are participants. Parents offer rich knowledge of their children's strengths and weaknesses, schooling history, habits, disposition and other characteristics that might not be readily apparent to educators who have limited opportunities to observe and learn about students. It would be foolish (and contrary to IDEA) to neglect parents as both partners and data mines.

Of equal importance with including parents is the need to draw on a variety of assessment sources and strategies. Initial evaluation happens once, and reevaluations generally happen several years apart—formerly every three years—and now an indeterminate period of time can elapse between formal evaluations. Of course, these intermittent evaluations cannot provide current information to identify needs and articulate the present levels of performance (PLOPs). These well-articulated PLOPs mark the starting point for selecting services and designing an educational plan on an annual basis, or more frequently when necessary. Especially important for instructional purposes are materials directly connected to the student's

performance in the classroom, such as work samples, classroom tests and staff observations.

After all the assessment reports and other materials are compiled, it will be time to meet. In most situations, it is probably not necessary to hold a meeting just to wade through all the information, as IEP teams can normally review this information as part of the IEP meeting.

DEVELOPING THE IEP

The IEP Non-Form

Ideally, no more structured or detailed form than the recommended IEP Non-Form (see Figure 5.1, pp. 91–93) would be allowed in the meeting. Some commonly used forms interfere with creative, flexible individualization. The form is interfering whenever the team concerns itself with fitting information into the right slot rather than with the substance and appropriateness of the information.

Do we hear protests that state education agencies or school districts recommend or even require the use of a standard form? Yes, we know. School personnel are understandably skittish about compliance with the IDEA, and mandated standard forms exist in an effort to ensure compliance. The finalized IEP will be on whatever form your district uses. However, using the Non-Form at IEP meetings encourages the creation of strong, individualized, substantively compliant IEPs, and the information is easily transferable to the standard form later.

Form need not and should not prevail over substance. The Non-Form is a generic representation of current IDEA requirements for IEP content that could be used in any school in any state. Stop a moment and get to know the Non-Form. It can become your best friend. The first and second pages of the Non-Form are self-explanatory; while we believe they are more simple and straightforward than many standard forms, they are not the key to IEP success. The third page contains the **critical components of the IEP**—the three-part sequence of needs → services → goals. In its essence, this crucial part of the Non-Form is

Student's name _____ IEP meeting date _____

Date of birth _____ Grade _____ Case manager _____

Copies of this IEP will circulate among staff members who are working with this student. Please observe the federal and state laws that protect the student's right to confidentiality of education records. Do not share with unauthorized persons, and do not include such sensitive information as disability category or IQ.

Special factors to consider	Participation in statewide or other large-scale assessments
For all students, consider: ☐ The student's strengths ☐ Concerns of the parent(s) for enhancing the student's education ☐ Need for assistive technology devices and services ☐ Communication needs	The following individual, appropriate accommodations are necessary to measure the student's academic achievement and functional performance on state and districtwide assessments:
If behavior impedes learning of student or others, consider: ☐ Positive behavioral interventions and support strategies, including positive behavioral interventions ☐ Other strategies to address behavior	The IEP Team has determined that the student should take an alternative assessment because:
If student has limited English proficiency, consider: ☐ Language needs as they relate to student's IEP	
If student is blind or visually impaired, consider: ☐ Instruction in use of Braille (unless IEP team decides that instruction in Braille is not appropriate)	The IEP Team has determined that the student should take the following alternative assessment:
If a student is deaf or hard of hearing, consider: ☐ Opportunities for direct communication with peers and professionals in student's language and communication mode ☐ Opportunities for direct instruction in student's language and communication mode	

Additional comments about this student relevant to developing an appropriate IEP:

(Cont'd next page)

nothing more than a sheet of paper divided into three columns.

Also remember that the IDEA requires explicit description of the means for assessing progress toward goals. This is more important than ever! Without clear guidance to specify the ongoing measurement of progress, it is impossible for the IEP team to know if the services prescribed in the IEP are effective and thus providing FAPE. Best practice is to include the progress assessment means in the behavioral objectives. If these objectives do not include the progress assessment

means, they would have to be added. In addition to describing how progress will be assessed, it must **actually be measured** at least every grading period. The IEP must also include the amount, location, beginning date, and duration of related services to be provided.

IEP Process

"Repetition is the mother of learning," says a Russian adage, so accordingly we repeat here that the heart of effective IEP development is the team's

FIGURE 5.1–Continued

Transition services

The IEP team has developed a Transition Plan because

☐ although the student will not yet be 16 during the effective period of this IEP, the Team has determined that transition planning is appropriate at this time,

☐ the student will be 16 during the effective period of this IEP, or

☐ the student has reached the age of 16.

Transition services must address the student's individual needs, taking into account his/her strengths, preferences, and interests as described here:

Based on these factors, this IEP includes services & appropriate measurable postsecondary goals on page _____, that draw upon age-appropriate transition assessments related to training, education, employment, and, where appropriate, independent living skills.

The transition services, including the course of study needed to assist the student in reaching those goals includes:

☐ Instruction

☐ Related services

☐ Community experiences

☐ The development of employment and other post-school adult living objectives

☐ If appropriate, acquisition of daily living skills and functional vocational evaluation

The student has been informed of the IDEA rights that will transfer to him/her upon reaching the age of majority.

_____
Student's signature

Progress report

Parents will receive reports on the student's progress toward annual goals through:

☐ IEP progress report completed per the report card schedule on these dates:

_____ _____ _____ _____

☐ Other progress reporting system as follows:

Progress toward each annual goal must be measured through the criteria and evaluation measures established for each goal.

Participation with nondisabled students

Explanation of extent to which the student will **not** participate with nondisabled children:

(a) In regular classes:

(b) In special education services:

IEP team members

Signature	Position

(Cont'd next page)

three-fold inquiry: (1) What are this child's unique educational characteristics and needs that must be taken into account in a truly individualized education program? (2) What will the district do or provide in response to each of these characteristics and needs? (3) If the services are effective, what goals and objectives will the child reach? In other words, what student accomplishments will tell us the services are on the right track?

Before beginning, make sure the legally required team members are present, especially those who know the child well. Remember that someone who has expertise in the instructional implications of evaluation must be there, as well as a qualified district representative authorized to allocate district resources and guarantee that no administrative veto of the IEP team decisions will occur. After brief greetings, introductions and amenities, IEP development is ready to begin.

FIGURE 5.1—Continued

Unique educational needs, characteristics, and measured present levels of academic achievement and functional performance (PLOPs)	Special education, related services and supplemental aids and services (based on peer-reviewed research to the extent practicable); assistive technology and modifications or personnel support	Measurable annual goals and short-term objectives (progress markers),* including academic and functional goals to enable students to be involved in and make progress in the general curriculum and to meet other needs resulting from the disability
(Including how the disability affects student's ability to participate and progress in the general curriculum)	(Including anticipated starting date, frequency, duration and location for each)	(Including progress measurement method for each goal)

*For students who take an alternative assessment and are assessed against other than grade level standards, the IEP **must** include short-term objectives (progress markers). For other students, the IEP **may** include short-term objectives. The IEP **must** for all students clearly articulate how the student's progress will be measured, and that progress must be reported to parents at designated intervals.

THE CORE SEQUENCE

The usefulness of an IEP hinges on clear, accurate and comprehensive articulation of the student's unique educational needs. The team must appropriately address every **need** of the student that arises from the disability by providing some combination of **specially designed instruction, related services, supplementary supports, program modifications,** or **supports for staff** responsible in one way or another for implementing the IEP. Finally, the team identifies **measurable annual goals** and describes how the student's **progress toward the goals** will be measured.

The Student's Unique Characteristics, Needs and PLOPs

The IEP team must describe the student's present levels of academic achievement and functional performance. The student herself should be visible in the IEP through detailed description of individual characteristics and needs. How does the disability manifest itself in educational settings? What compensatory strategies has the student developed? What interventions have the staff used in the past, and how has the student responded to them? How does the student behave upon encountering an obstacle related to the disability? One helpful way to learn to think in terms of these essential characteristics is to imagine that you are describing the student to a new volunteer who is going to take her or him to outdoor education camp for a week. What would the volunteer need to know about **this** student that couldn't be predicted from her age and sex alone?

Describing Students' Needs

Identified needs must include those related to the student's ability to participate and make progress in the general curriculum. It is not enough to describe achievement and performance solely in terms of test scores, as this does not adequately describe the individual student's characteristics. The law requires that all evaluations include information which **leads directly to educational planning.** Test scores and other quantitative measures, along with narrative descriptions using information from parents and staff, round out the picture and lead the team toward selection of attainable goals and a description of necessary, specially designed instruction and services.

Judges and hearing officers have described learning disabled students' needs in these words taken verbatim from cases:

> ▶ The student needs reteaching and repetition, small classes, flexible programming, computer access and training.[1]
> ▶ This student needs a highly structured environment, small campus, small classes, frequent teacher feedback, clear commands, individualized attention and consistent behavior management.[2]
> ▶ This student needs daily multisensory reading, spelling and writing, needs never to hear "if only he worked harder" and he needs to be with other dyslexics.[3]
> ▶ He needs full-time learning support and extended school year, as well as help with organization and attention.[4]

Smith and Strick (1997) have listed these 10 needs common to many students who have learning disabilities:

1. Manageable class size (below 25)
2. Limited distractions
3. An active, guiding teacher who monitors, keeps the students on task, models respect and offers encouragement
4. A noncompetitive atmosphere
5. An orderly, structured, on-task approach to learning;
6. A focus on basic skills
7. Instructional flexibility, including peer tutors, study partners, etc.;
8. Clear expectations for achievement;
9. Effective, data-based monitoring of pupil performance;
10. Ample positive feedback.

At least some of these, as they fit the individual student, should appear on the IEPs of many learning disabled students.

Too often we have tended to think of needs only in terms of "she needs 45 minutes a day in the resource room." That vague statement does not describe what the student needs. By contrast, the examples above, from cases and a textbook, illustrate a style of thinking about needs that leads directly to educational services.

Notice that children's unique needs are of two types: (a) needs for **certain conditions for learning,** such as limited distractions and positive feedback, and (b) needs for **improved performance,** such as better keyboarding skills or better decoding. The needs for certain learning conditions are addressed by modifications or accommodations, while improved performance needs are addressed by PLOPs, services and goals.

Characteristics/needs of the child will often "cluster." The team may well decide in the next stage that one service will address more than one characteristic or need. However, at this point it is important to just brainstorm and list all the unique characteristics that require individualized attention. Sometimes the natural flow seems to work "across" the third page of the IEP Non-

Form, i.e., when a characteristic or need has been identified, the team next moves to what service or accommodation will address it and then, when the service is instructional, moves on to the goals for that service. Other times it may feel better to list all the characteristics, then move to services, and then to goals. Either way, or a combination of both, is perfectly okay.

Present Levels of Performance

The law requires that the student's present level of performance (PLOP) be indicated in a readily understandable way that is sufficiently precise to let us measure progress. Sometimes the PLOP is contained in the characteristic itself (e.g., has **no** friends, **always** plays alone at recess, **never** volunteers in class, was absent **80 of 175 days,** is tardy to class **at least once daily**). Other times it can best be presented as the beginning point in a sequence of PLOP → objectives → goal. For example, suppose the characteristic is slow, inaccurate decoding, and the present level of performance is 15–20 correct words per minute (CWPM) in second grade material. The first objective might be 25–35 CWPM, the second objective 50 CWPM, and the goal 80 CWPM in second grade material.

Thus the PLOP may be an elaboration of the characteristic (need) and the beginning point in the succession of PLOP → objectives → goal. The PLOP is now, the objectives are next, and the annual goal is where the student is projected to be in a year. Figure 5.2 illustrates the PLOP as a quantified characteristic, and Figure 5.3 shows the PLOP as a beginning point for the goal.

Sometimes a present level of performance is best described by a work sample, which can be attached to the IEP. A picture can speak very loudly, as in the handwriting sample shown in Figure 5.4. Notice how the quality of the content of the writing can be seen in spite of the near illegibility. Transcripts or recordings of oral reading of a few sentences of unfamiliar material can also be very useful.

The following examples of unique characteristics/needs in academic areas reveal how some do, and some don't, need further refinement to become a measured PLOP:

▶ Handwriting slow, labored, "drawn," and nearly illegible due to improper size and spacing of letters and words. (PLOP: writes legibly at a rate of five letters per minute.)

▶ Lacks understanding of place value and regrouping in both addition and subtraction.

FIGURE 5.2 Illustrative Sequence: PLOP as Measurable Characteristic

Characteristics/needs/PLOPs	Service	Goal/objective
1. Terri's handwriting is very slow, awkward and poor. **PLOP:** 10 letters copied per minute with 2–4 illegible.	1. Two 2-minute probes daily with number of legible letters copied per minute graphed and rewarded by a point system or by self-charting.	1. **Annual goal:** Copy/generate 40 letters per minute with 40 legible. **Obj. 1:** 20 letters with <2 illegible, by Dec 1.

FIGURE 5.3 Illustrative Sequence: PLOP as Part of PLOP/Objective/Goal

Characteristics/needs/PLOPs	Service	PLOP/Goal/objective
1. Terri's handwriting is very slow, awkward and poor.	1. Two 2-minute probes daily with number of legible letters copied per minute graphed and rewarded by a point system or by self-charting.	**PLOP:** 10 letters copied per minute with 2–4 illegible. **Obj. 1:** 20 letters with <2 illegible, by Dec 1. **Goal:** Copy/generate 40 letters per minute with 40 legible.

FIGURE 5.4   Work Sample as a PLOP

(No PLOP needed, as a zero rate can be assumed.)

▶ Attributes literal, concrete meaning to everything he hears and reads. (No PLOP needed.)

▶ Understands spoken language and decodes words accurately but does not comprehend material read independently. Oral reading reveals severe lack of expression and no attention to punctuation. (PLOP: comprehension score of 3.1 grade equivalent on the XYZ test; decoding appropriately 5th–6th grade level.)

▶ Works very slowly, becomes upset if he makes a mistake, quits, and refuses to continue if paper is "messy." (No PLOP needed, or could elect to state an approximate rate of occurrence, e.g., twice daily.)

▶ Answers before thinking, in both oral and written work; work is impulsive; many "careless" errors. (No PLOP needed, or could elect to state approximate rate of occurrence, e.g., 10–15 times daily.)

▶ Gets arithmetic problems "messed up" and copies them incorrectly off board and out of book. Lines up problems incorrectly and also lines up answers wrong in multiplication and division. (PLOP: More than half of his arithmetic problems are wrong due to these errors.)

Some examples of unique characteristics/needs in social-emotional-behavioral areas would be:

▶ Shy, no friends, never volunteers in class, never initiates social contact with other children.

▶ Bully, doesn't know how to play with other children.

▶ Overreacts and has temper outbursts, is noncompliant, pouts and whines, is sullen and negative when suggestions are made.

▶ Short attention span, easily distracted by sounds.

Social behaviors such as these can be converted into IEP components, as shown by Sugai and Colvin (1990) in a series of steps. They recommend more than is required to be on the IEP, but the steps are helpful:

1. **Problem Behavior:** Behavior displayed by student that is observed and determined to be problematic (e.g., student does not follow adult directions the first time).

2. **Problem Context:** Setting(s) or condition(s) in which behavior is most problematic (e.g., when in 45-minute, large group math or reading lessons).

3. **Desired Behavior:** Replacement behavior selected for the problem behavior (e.g., student follows adult directions within five seconds without comment or inappropriate facial expression).

4. **Current Level of Functioning:** How often or long occurrences of the problem and replacement behavior are desired (e.g., student follows teacher directions within five seconds in 45% of the opportunities).

5. **Desired Level of Functioning:** How often or long occurrences of the problem and replacement behavior are desired (e.g., student follows teacher directions within five seconds in 90% of the opportunities for five consecutive days).

6. **Intervention Strategies:** The names of possible strategies for achieving the desired level of functioning (e.g., behavioral contract, token economy, self-recording sheet, peer tutor).

7. **Evaluation Measurement:** Type of measurement strategy for assessing student progress and intervention effectiveness (e.g., frequency counts of following and not following teacher directions).

8. **Evaluation Schedule:** Schedule for how often measurements should be conducted (e.g., frequency counts will be daily for 45 minutes during math and reading groups).

Those elements that are mandated to be on the IEP are shown on T's fictitious partial IEP (see Figure 5.5), which uses the Sugai and Colvin

FIGURE 5.5   T's IEP

Unique educational needs, characteristics, and measured present levels of academic achievement and functional performance (PLOPs)	Special education, related services and supplemental aids and services (based on peer-reviewed research to the extent practicable); assistive technology and modifications or personnel support	Measurable annual goals and short-term objectives (progress markers),* including academic and functional goals to enable students to be involved in and make progress in the general curriculum and to meet other needs resulting from the disability
(Including how the disability affects student's ability to participate and progress in the general curriculum)	(Including anticipated starting date, frequency, duration and location for each)	(Including progress measurement method for each goal)
T. does not follow adult directions the first time. **PLOP:** Follows adult directions within 5 seconds about 45% of the time.	Token economy; behavioral contract. Services begin 1/21 and continue for 2 months, in all classrooms. Aides and regular teachers will receive one hour training and handouts on the classroom use of a token economy (by 12/5).	**Goal:** Follow appropriate adult directions within 5 seconds without negative comment or facial expression Obj. 1: Will do so in 75% of the opportunities for 3 consecutive days by 2/15 Obj. 2: Will do so in 90% of the opportunities for 5 consecutive days by 3/15 (PLOP could also be in this column)

*For students who take an alternative assessment and are assessed against other than grade level standards, the IEP **must** include short-term objectives (progress markers). For other students, the IEP **may** include short-term objectives. The IEP **must** for all students clearly articulate how the student's progress will be measured, and that progress must be reported to parents at designated intervals.

procedure. This IEP also illustrates how the PLOP may be either part of the characteristic/need or the beginning point in the PLOP to objective to goal sequence. Other examples appear in the sample IEPs later in this chapter. At the end of the chapter, we will discuss functional behavioral assessment and behavioral intervention plans.

Special Education and Related Services

The second essential inquiry in the IEP process asks "What will the district do in response to the child's needs?" These "District Do's" include special education, related services, regular class modifications, personnel support and other creative, flexible, innovative and often inexpensive ways to meet needs. This listing of services becomes the "Special Education and Related Services" which the law requires be specified on the IEP. Too often this is omitted or simply perverted into a mere placement check mark or a percentage of time in special education. The amount of related services, such as speech therapy or physical therapy, must be shown, along with the beginning date, location, and anticipated duration of the service.

When a legal dispute arises, the central issue is often whether the services provided addressed all the child's special needs—those special needs that must be specified in the first stage of IEP development, and be based on the evaluation. It is difficult to imagine how one could either attack or defend the services offered to meet a child's unique needs if the IEP or the evaluation describes the needs in vague terms.

Services to Allow Access to the General Curriculum

IDEA emphasizes the provision of services needed to allow the student access to the general curriculum. We must make a critical distinction between services which **allow the student to access the curriculum** (such as following teacher direction, reading at grade level, etc.) versus **incorporating the general curriculum itself** into the IEP, which is not appropriate. Special education services are necessary to allow some students

to progress in the general curriculum. It is these special services, not the general curriculum, that are to be in the IEP. The question for the IEP team to ask is: "What does Kim need in order to access and progress in the general curriculum?" The answer might include: intensive, effective remedial reading services, supplemented initially by texts on tape; or a peer tutor; or oral reports rather than written reports, etc. These are special services, supports and accommodations that need to be on the IEP. The IEP must deal with special education and with any needed changes in regular education, not with the regular education curriculum itself. All persons concerned must understand this point, so that IEPs don't become mere restatements of the regular education curriculum. **Chapter Six** on standards-based IEPs discusses this issue further.

Methodology

One of the interesting issues about services is the question of whether methodology need be specified. If, for example, the service is remedial reading, must the method be spelled out? In its 1999 commentary to the IDEA regulations, the US Department of Education explained:

> Case law recognizes that instructional methodology can be an important consideration in the context of what constitutes an appropriate education for a child with a disability. At the same time, these courts have indicated that they will not substitute a parentally-preferred methodology for sound educational programs developed by school personnel in accordance with the procedural requirements of the IDEA to meet the educational needs of an individual child with a disability. In light of the legislative history and case law, it is clear that in developing an individualized education there are circumstances in which the particular teaching methodology that will be used is an integral part of what is "individualized" about a student's education and, in those circumstances will need to be discussed at the IEP meeting and incorporated into the student's IEP. For example, for a child with a learning disability who has not learned to read using traditional instructional methods, an appropriate education may require some other instructional strategy.[5]

Methodology becomes a source of conflict when parents are convinced their child will receive benefit from a particular method and will not benefit from the method the district wants to use. The most frequently sought methods are a particular method of communication for children who are deaf, a highly structured applied behavioral analysis (ABA, Lovaas) method of teaching children who have autism, and/or intensive, systematic, phonics-based reading programs for children who are dyslexic or otherwise learning disabled.

Much case law supports the authority of schools to select methods. However, in a few cases parents have been able to show that a particular method is necessary to allow the IEP to be "reasonably calculated" to allow benefit. Many of the successful cases involve children who have autism. A few cases have been won when the judge understood that a dyslexic student required an intensive phonics program.[6,7,8] It is extremely important to note that when the US Supreme Court said methodology should be left to the state, it said so in the context of its belief that schools have and employ expertise in relevant, effective methods.[9] This, of course, is not always the case. *Rowley* also supposes that hearing officers and administrative law judges have expertise in special education methodology. Some do.

It is possible courts will understand that the new emphasis in IDEA on the use of scientific, research-based instruction and services indicates congressional intent to ensure that schools use demonstrably effective methods. However, most cases to date do not so indicate.

In-service Training for Staff

A common and interesting question related to these "District Do" services is that of inservice training for teachers. Suppose, for example, Rob has Tourette Syndrome and needs teachers who are knowledgeable about how his symptoms are affected by stress. The agreed-upon service to be provided by the district is inservice training by the local physician for all the school staff. Does that "District Do" belong on Rob's IEP? Absolutely! The

IDEA names **personnel support** as a mandated service when it is needed. Although delivered indirectly, it is a service to meet Rob's unique need. One concern is that such a service doesn't lend itself directly to a goal formulated in terms of Rob's behavior. This concern is easily addressed by looking to what we hope to see in Rob's behavior as a result of having informed, empathic teachers who assist him in avoiding unnecessary stress. One obvious answer is improved academic performance. Other outcomes (goals) could be a direct decrease in frequency and severity of his symptoms, and an increase in attendance.

Modifications in the Classroom

For many years some districts resisted including on IEPs the modifications needed in the regular classroom. However, it is well-settled law that they must be included. A checklist of types of modifications (e.g., in grading, discipline, assignments, texts, tests, etc.) can be helpful to insure that all necessary modifications are addressed (see Figure 5.6).

Remember, however, that needed modifications may be unique and may not appear on the checklist. They are also essential.

Measurable Annual Goals

For all instructional services, the IEP will include **measurable annual goals** and possibly short-term objectives. The goal must relate directly to the PLOP and identify a learning gain that the IEP team thinks reasonable for the student to achieve, given the instruction and services he or she will receive. One way to write IEPs, which makes this connection obvious, is to move from present level of performance to the needed service, and then to the goal and objective. For example, an IEP writing sequence for a child who has a reading disability might be as follows:

1. **Present level of performance:** Reads first grade material at 20–30 words correct per minute and guesses at all unknown words.

2. **Service to be provided:** One-to-one tutoring in highly structured reading program; five sessions

FIGURE 5.6   Classroom Modifications Checklist

To be part of _____'s IEP   _____ (initial by participant)

Date _____   _____ (initial by participant)

                                                       _____ (initial by participant)

                                                       _____ (initial by participant)

Directions: Write "all" if a modification is required in **all** classes where applicable. If it is needed only in a particular class, specify accordingly.

Modifications related to input of information

Teacher talk

_____ Directions restated; short, clear sequence of steps

_____ Seating near teacher; near chalkboard

_____ Slow, careful speech

_____ Simple vocabulary; check for student comprehension; use synonyms

_____ Allow student to tape class

_____ Tape particularly important information, directions for student

_____ Interpreter

_____ Other _____

_____ Other _____

Texts, handouts

_____ Different text at student's reading level

_____ Provide highlighted texts; teach student to highlight

_____ Provide second copy of texts for student to keep at home

_____ Issue clear, readable photocopies

_____ Highlight worksheets and handouts

_____ Provide reader

_____ Provide tapes of text

_____ Other _____

_____ Other _____

Tests

_____ Administered orally by aide, teacher, peer tutor

_____ Untimed

_____ Other _____

_____ Other _____

(Cont'd next page)

---

weekly; 45 minutes each; provided in private, quiet area of resource room.

3. **Annual goal:** Given a 500-word story at second grade reading level, student will read orally 80–100 correct words per minute.

The same relationship between present level of performance and goals can be seen in a non-academic area:

1. **Present level of performance:** Five to ten times daily student draws or talks inappropriately about blood, killing and torture.

2. **Services provided:** Behavior-contingency plan with student selected reward and response cost. Teacher-monitored chart that allows student to record incidents of inappropriate talk or drawings about blood, killing and torture and to observe progress in reducing this behavior.

FIGURE 5.6–Continued

Modifications related to output of information

Tests

_____ Tape responses instead of written
_____ Shortened
_____ Single word or phrase answers rather than complete sentences
_____ Objective rather than essay
_____ Other _____
_____ Other _____

Assignments

_____ Shortened with full credit _____ partial credit _____
_____ Taped rather than written
_____ Manuscript rather than cursive
_____ Demonstrations, drawings, models, etc., rather than writing
_____ Additional time for work in class _____ out of class _____
_____ Peer editing
_____ Other _____
_____ Other _____

Aids

_____ Calculator on assignments _____ on tests _____
_____ Franklin speller on assignments _____ on tests _____
_____ Advance info on questions teacher will ask and material student will recite
_____ Special paper, overlays, etc. (describe) _____
_____
_____

Grades

_____ Pass/fail with credit toward regular diploma
_____ Pass/fail with no credit toward regular diploma
_____ Based on effort and so indicated on transcript _____ not so indicated _____
_____ Based on shortened assignments and reduced amount of work but held to same
quality standard as other students
_____ Other (describe fully) _____
_____
_____
_____
_____
_____

3. **Annual goal:** Beginning immediately, the rate of inappropriate talk or drawings about blood, killing and torture will reduce and will reach zero.

   a. **Progress marker 1:** By February 1, fewer than 2 such inappropriate drawings or speech per week.

   b. **Progress marker 2:** By April 15 maintain fewer than 2 such inappropriate drawings or speech per month.

The last step, after a characteristic or need/PLOP and the appropriate services to meet it or them have been specified, is to write an annual goal and two or three objectives. Writing goals and objectives begins with asking, "If the service we're providing is effective, what will we see in Todd's behavior that tells us so?" The purpose of the mandated goals and objectives is to evaluate the service. We need to know when or if it is necessary to change the service we are providing. As long as we're on track and the child is making reasonable progress we just keep going. That's why the objectives we use for tracking are to be statements of **how far** the student will progress toward the annual goal (12-month objective) **by when.**

It is not at all clear how even the most conscientious teacher could determine in December (or any other time during the term of the IEP) whether the current rate of progress would enable the student to reach the annual goal by June, without objectives or progress markers. Again, we strongly encourage IEP teams to specify progress markers to help teachers keep students on track toward their goals.

Sometimes one goal can evaluate a cluster of several services. For example, think of a secondary student who has a severe learning disability affecting his written expression. He might need several services, including keyboarding instruction, tutoring in writing, modifications in test taking and length of written assignments, substitution of oral presentations for some term papers, and modified grading. The entire service cluster could be reasonably evaluated in terms of his improved rates of successful course completion and attendance. Other goals could also be appropriate. The point is just that as characteristics or needs often cluster to require one service, so services sometimes cluster and can be assessed by a common, single goal.

One of the common and major problems with goals and objectives is that they are not taken seriously by their writers, who have no intention of actually checking whether the student has reached them or not. It is as if we never understood the most basic tenet of the IEP—that we are going to try the listed services and **see if they work** for that student. The goals and objectives are to be **real.** They are not just legal requirements to be completed and filed. They are to be used

to evaluate program effectiveness. Figure 5.7 illustrates the contrast between real goals and "pretend" goals.

Goals are measurable statements of what we believe the student can do in a year if the service we provide is effective. Therefore it is only logical to look at where we are starting (PLOP), where we'll be in a bit (Objective) and where we are headed in a year (Goal). These examples illustrate the sequence.

ANITA

PLOP	Anita averages 10 unexcused absences/tardies per month.
Objective 1	By Feb. 1 she will have fewer than 5 unexcused absences/tardies per month.
Objective 2	By April 2 she will have fewer than 2 unexcused absences/tardies per month.
Goal	From April through June 1 she will average fewer than ½ unexcused absence/tardies per month.

JEREMY

PLOP	Jeremy submits fewer than half his homework assignments.
Objective 1	By Nov. 15 he will have submitted 75% of all homework assignments.
Objective 2	By Jan. 15 he will have submitted 85% of all homework assignments.
Goal	By the end of the year he will regularly submit all assigned homework on time.

JILL

PLOP	Jill orally reads 6th grade material at a rate of 50–75 words per minute and correctly answers 30–40% of factual comprehension questions asked orally.
Objective 1	By Dec. 1 Jill will read 6th grade material orally at 75–100 words per minute with 0–2 errors and correctly answer 60% of factual comprehension questions.
Objective 2	By March 1 Jill will read 6th grade material orally at 100–125 words per minute with 0–2 errors and correctly answer more than 70% of factual questions.
Goal	By June 15 Jill will orally read 7th grade material at 75–100 words per

FIGURE 5.7 Examples of Annual Goals	
Not real goal	**Real goal**
▶ Joe will have a better attitude toward school 80% of the time. ▶ Sara will make wise choices in her use of leisure time. ▶ Max will be 75% successful in the mainstream. ▶ Beth will show an appropriate level of upper body strength.	▶ Joe will have no more than 5 unexcused absences/tardies this year. ▶ Sara will participate weekly in a supervised extracurricular activity. ▶ Max will maintain a C+ average in his regular classes. ▶ Beth will pass upper body strength items on the ABC fitness test.

minute with 0–2 errors and correctly answer 90–100% of factual questions.

The usefulness of annual goals and objectives in evaluating the service provided is, in large part, a function of how well those goals and objectives are written. Although we've provided many examples, a detailed description of developing useful goals and objectives is beyond the scope of this book. The reader can find detailed discussions in the classic how-to-do-it *Preparing Instructional Objectives* (Mager, 1997), in *Writing Measurable IEP Goals and Objectives, 2nd ed.* (Bateman & Herr, 2006), and in *From Gobbledygook to Clearly Written Annual IEP Goals* (Bateman, 2007).

THE TRANSITION COMPONENT OF THE IEP

The transition component of the IEP is just that, one portion of the student's regular IEP. It is not a parallel document, a separate entity, or a "transition IEP." All the IEP development requirements and procedures discussed previously apply to the transition component. The legal significance of transition being but one aspect of the IEP process is substantial. A student is entitled only to those transition services which, for that student, are either special education or related services necessary to enable the student to benefit from special education. The period of "benefit" to be considered has arguably been lengthened beyond school and into adult life, but the substantive entitlement is still only to special

education and related services, not to those **plus** transition services.

Transition planning is no longer a new IEP component, but districts continue to struggle to understand what is required. IDEA provides that IEP teams must include **appropriate measurable postsecondary goals** based upon age appropriate **transition assessments** related to training, education, employment, and, where appropriate, independent living skills and must specify the transition services (including courses of study) needed to assist the child in reaching those goals.[10] A student's transition plan is to be based on his or her individual needs, taking into account the student's strengths, preferences and interests.[11]

One way to approach student transition needs is to envision the future, for example, a typical weekday and a typical weekend after secondary school. Is the student still living in his or her parent's home? Has she gotten an apartment? Does he know how to find apartment ads in the classifieds? How to respond to an ad? How to locate the address? What about social contacts? Is she attending any sort of post-secondary schooling? This kind of questioning will help the team focus on the individual student's situation and needs.

The exact process the IEP team goes through in looking into and planning for a student's post-school future will differ from student to student, as it should. The essential elements which should not vary include student and family participation and the willingness of the IEP team to address all the areas of need—intensive and effective basic skills instruction (not just exposure and not just repetitive practice), explicit survival skills, graduation requirements and transition.

One logical beginning point for the transition component itself is with the team reaching agreement about the individual student's needs with regard to the mandated areas: (1) instruction; (2) related services; (3) community experiences; and (4) employment and other post-school living objectives; and, (5) when appropriate, acquisition of daily living skills and functional vocational assessment. If the team deems it inappropriate to address an area, presumably because the student presents no unique needs, the IEP must include the basis for that determination. The student's needs, taking into account interests and preferences, can be explored prior to the meeting and substantial input should also be sought from the parent. Questionnaires are one appropriate way to start the student and parent input process.

Self-advocacy is one of the most important transition skills for many students who have disabilities. The student's presentation of his or her needs at the IEP meeting may itself provide one opportunity to assess and discuss self-advocacy skills. Another concern for some students with learning disabilities is passing the examinations required to obtain a driver's license. We can use the same basic three-step inquiry process used in the rest of the IEP for Jim's needs for self-advocacy and obtaining a driver's license. Figure 5.8 illustrates the inclusion of these transition services on his IEP.

BEHAVIOR INTERVENTION PLAN (BIP)

Districts must provide a Behavior Intervention Plan (BIP) for any student with a disability who is excluded from school for more than ten days for disciplinary reasons. If a BIP already exists, the team must review its effectiveness and revise it as necessary to address the behavior that led to the removal from school. Otherwise the team must develop a new BIP.

The point of a BIP is to teach and support appropriate behaviors as well as to eliminate misbehavior. In order to achieve this, a Functional

Behavior Assessment (FBA) may be necessary to discover the conditions that trigger or reinforce the behavior. Children who misbehave do so for reasons that are identifiable and remediable.

IDEA does not define either BIP or FBA. The omission has caused some consternation among school personnel, but IEP teams are not without resources. Since these provisions first appeared in IDEA in 1997, a wealth of credible material on BIPs and FBAs has made its way to the internet, to textbooks, and to professional development opportunities (see Resources, pg. 163).

A functional behavior assessment may require collecting data across settings on the events that precede (antecedents) and those that follow (consequences) the behavior of concern, so that interventions can be developed to change the form or rate of the behavior or to teach alternative behaviors. In addition, the team examines data from other sources, including the student's behavioral file and interviews with persons familiar with the student and the behavior in question.

BIPs should draw upon the FBA data for each student and be individualized plans rather than boilerplate restatements of classroom or school behavioral expectations and lists of consequences for failing to comply. The BIP must include positive behavioral interventions, strategies and supports to address behaviors that interfere with learning, as appropriate for the individual student. BIPs may specify needed changes in the school environment, instruction, counseling and other services and accommodations needed to support the student's efforts to meet behavioral expectations. Regular education teachers may assist in determining these positive interventions, strategies and services.

The key portions of the BIP are: (1) the specification of targeted behaviors to be increased, e.g., time on task, or decreased talking out without permission and (2) the intervention strategies (including positive strategies) to be used, based on the analysis of what elicits and/or maintains the problem behavior and the techniques such as modeling or role playing to be used to teach the appropriate replacement behavior (Bateman & Golly, 2003).

FIGURE 5.8   Jim's IEP: Transition Components

Unique educational needs, characteristics, and measured present levels of academic achievement and functional performance (PLOPs)	Special education, related services and supplemental aids and services (based on peer-reviewed research to the extent practicable); assistive technology and modifications or personnel support	Measurable annual goals and short-term objectives (progress markers),* including academic and functional goals to enable students to be involved in and make progress in the general curriculum and to meet other needs resulting from the disability
(Including how the disability affects student's ability to participate and progress in the general curriculum)	(Including anticipated starting date, frequency, duration and location for each)	(Including progress measurement method for each goal)

Instruction
 	
Self-advocacy PLOP: Jim is unaware of his legal rights under §504 & ADA, and he is unable to request appropriate accommodations he would need in given situations, such as a large lecture class. He becomes embarrassed and anxious when discussing his disability and its affects on his school performance, and he becomes angry or tries to change the subject.
 	
Community
 	
Driver's License PLOP: Jim has been driving for a year on a learner's permit and is concerned that he cannot pass the written test required for his license, although he is confident of all his driving and related skills except map reading.
 	
Employment and other
 	
Not needed at this time. Jim intends to enroll in the computer network support program at Leland Community College (LCC) and is on track for a regular diploma. He is a tech lab assistant this year and is doing very well.
	1. Small group instruction from Special Ed teacher in relevant rights, procedures, and remedies under §504, ADA, & IDEA
	  • Role playing in describing needed accommodations to employers, professors, and other adult life figures of authority.
	  • Services to begin Tuesday, Sept. 15; two 30-minute sessions weekly until goals are met.
	  • (L&R) Protection & Advocacy will assist teacher and provide materials at no cost. (Verified by phone—M. Adams)
	  • LCC Office of Disability Services will meet with Jim to set up an accommodation plan. (Verified by phone—S. Holvey)
	
	2. Within two weeks from the date of this IEP, the driver training instructor will inform Jim about accommodations available in the state, if any, for licensing persons with reading disabilities. Then she and Jim will develop a plan to follow through and that plan will be added to this IEP no later than Oct. 10.
	  • (L&R) DMV will assist instructor and will provide information on test accommodations. (Verified by phone—J. Hill)
	  • Instruction in map reading and route highlighting.
		Goal 1: Given a 25-item objective test over basic rights and procedures under §504 & ADA, Jim will pass with a score of 75% or better.
		
		Goal 2: In hypothetical role-play scenarios of disability-based discrimination, Jim will calmly and accurately explain to an employer, professor or other representative of the post-school world his rights and remedies under §504 and ADA.
		
		Goal 3: Given a real world meeting with the Director of Disability Services at LCC, Jim will describe the effect of his disability in a school situation and will explain what accommodations help him to meet expectations.
		
		Goal 4: Jim will become a competent driver in Jefferson state and will take the licensing exam on March 15. By March 1, given a practice exam administered under real world conditions, Jim will score at least 70%.
		
		Goal 5: Given a city map, Jim will accurately highlight 6 common routes he routinely follows and 4 routes he will use next year, when he is attending LCC, e.g. from his home to the mall, from his home to LCC, etc.

*For students who take an alternative assessment and are assessed against other than grade level standards, the IEP **must** include short-term objectives (progress markers). For other students, the IEP **may** include short-term objectives. The IEP **must** for all students clearly articulate how the student's progress will be measured, and that progress must be reported to parents at designated intervals.

In addition to creating BIPs for students who have been suspended, expelled, or removed to an interim alternative educational setting (IAES), IEP teams must consider behavior support for every disabled student whose behavior impedes his or her learning or that of others. Does this mean that IEPs for these children include BIPs? Unfortunately, IDEA does not explain what it looks like to "consider" behavior interventions. Some have even argued that behavior plans do not need to become part of the students' IEPs. This is not consistent with the overall design of IDEA. It makes no sense to interpret that language to mean that the team needs only to talk about the behavior but need not devise a plan to remediate it. It also makes no sense to assume that an IEP team could somehow address a student's problem behavior without including this in the IEP. Given the requirement that IEPs address all of a student's needs, we can imagine no basis for believing that the behavior plan would not become part of the IEP.

We recommend that teams prepare BIPs for any student whose behavior does not improve through the consistent implementation of school-wide behavior support systems. The BIP should explicitly describe the behaviors of concern and present levels of performance, behavioral goals the team expects the student to achieve, and the instruction and other services that will enable the student progress toward the goals.

The Texas law firm of Walsh, Anderson, Brown, Schulze and Aldridge, P.C. (1997) has developed a menu of positive strategies and consequences (Figure 5.9) that IEP teams might find useful in writing BIPs. Their list offers a useful shortcut for BIP writing, but teams should be careful not to pick and choose items from it at random or in accordance with a generic pattern. Look to the FBA for guidance, and select only those strategies that relate to the behavior of the individual student. If an intervention is not effective as shown by a measured increase or decrease within a few weeks, another intervention should be implemented.

THE THREE-STAGE IEP PROCESS ILLUSTRATED

Mike's case illustrates the three-stage IEP process. Mike is a seven-year-old who has average intelligence and is legally blind. First, his unique characteristics/needs were described as follows:

1. Makes inappropriate gestures (e.g., hands clasped in air over head, shaking arms) dozens of times per hour;

2. Calls children names, speaks very negatively to others (e.g., "You're dumb," "You stink") and uses inappropriate vulgar and sexual vocabulary many times daily;

3. Is noncompliant with reasonable requests and suggestions from peers and adults several times daily; and

4. Has a progressive visual condition which currently requires the use of Braille and ongoing mobility training.

The IEP team quickly agreed that they could cluster characteristics 1–3 together and that the appropriate district service was a behavior change plan using some combination of reinforcement of incompatible behaviors and perhaps response cost. The team agreed that the behavior expert who serves Mike's building would develop such a plan within one week, and it would be put into his IEP. The goal for the behavior plan was to bring all three kinds of behavior to an acceptable level by mid-year. The group agreed that within two weeks Mike would be participating in a fully implemented plan and that within one month all undesirable behaviors would be decreased by more than half. And so on.

The team agreed that Mike needed Braille instruction, and the IEP also provided for a volunteer back-up person to Braille his materials and for an itinerant specialist who would make daily visits to Mike's class. The goal was that Mike would continue to perform in all academic content areas at an average level. Objectives for that goal

FIGURE 5.9 Positive Behavior Strategies and Consequences

Positive behavior strategies for increasing prosocial behaviors

Consequences reasonably calculated to improve behavior and enable student to receive instruction

A. Remove distractors

B. Provide a structured environment

C. Set well-defined limits, rules, and task expectations

D. Establish consistent routine

E. Simplify activities

F. Allow enough time to process information

G. Use visual cues and supports

H. Offer choices

I. Set easily attainable daily goals

J. Premack principle (if you do your work task, you may have computer time)

K. Earn activities/privileges

L. Planned ignoring of minor inappropriate behavior

M. Provide frequent feedback concerning appropriateness of behavior

N. Verbal reminder

O. Stand near the student

P. Provide nonverbal signal for appropriate behavior

Q. Positive reinforcers
   (List:_____)

R. Point system

S. Use home-school reward system

T. Use behavior graphs

U. Coach in problem-solving situations

V. Role play consequences of behavior

W. Teach alternative behaviors

X. Contract for appropriate behavior

Y. Teach social skills—direct instructions in prosocial behaviors

Z. Set up and reinforce social interaction

AA. Praise behaviorally appropriate students

BB. Work completion contracts

CC. Use timer for self-monitoring of on-task behavior

DD. Direct overactivity into productive tasks within or outside the classroom (errands, performance tasks)

EE. Frequent verbal reinforcement for appropriate behavior

FF. Help student to use language (communication system) to label and communicate feelings

GG. Permit student to remain in a quiet, non-threatening, non-stimulating place in order to regain control when upset (a safe area)

HH. Permit student to engage in physical activities

Other: _____

Other: _____

Consequences should be determined based upon the functioning level of the student and the severity of behaviors exhibited.

A. Review consequences before behavior escalates

B. Signal nonverbal disapproval

C. Ask student to practice appropriate response

D. Allow for peer pressure

E. Withhold earned activities/privileges

F. Response Cost Contracting

G. Offer student choice of changing behavior or going to cooling off area

H. Teacher-initiated cooling off period

I. Physical escort

J. Principal/student conference

K. Administrative behavior contract

L. Use conflict management and mediation steps

M. Referral to counselor for Anger Control/ Replacement Training

N. After school detention

O. Lunch detention

P. In-school suspension for _____ period

Q. In-school suspension for _____ days

R. Call parent

S. In-school suspension up to 10 school days

T. Suspension for up to 3 consecutive days

U. Placement of student in AEP for up to 10 school days

Other: _____

Other: _____

specified a timeline for increasing the speed and accuracy of his Braille reading and writing.

Daily mobility training was agreed to with a goal of independent travel within the school. The first objective was for Mike to learn the layout of his new school building in one month. Sub-objectives (not required by law, but sometimes useful) were to learn the route from the school bus stop to the office, to his classroom, to the restroom and back to the classroom within two weeks.

In the best of worlds, all IEP teams would see as clearly and agree as professionally as Mike's did.

EXAMPLES OF EDUCATIONALLY USEFUL IEPS

Several excerpts from IEPs follow (all put on our IEP Non-Form). Because these are all from real IEPs, their contents vary, and none are perfect. Nevertheless, they illustrate acceptable, instructionally useful IEPs. These excerpts are intended to show only the core substantive components of the IEP—the needs, services and goals. The IEP excerpts also include short-term objectives or progress markers as appropriate. It is conceivable—though not necessarily simpler, more efficient, or more effective—to rewrite some of these to eliminate short-term objectives by writing much more detailed goals.

Joe

Joe (see Figure 5.10) earned no credits in ninth grade except in weightlifting. Even though he has above average intelligence, he has severe academic problems related to ADD and learning disabilities. The school told him to leave since he never handed in work and had failed all his classes. After staying out for three years, he is now returning to school. His rural high school has only seven teachers, very limited access to specialists, and fewer than 40 students. Joe's IEP reflects his real school world.

Curt

Curt (see Figure 5.11) is a ninth grade low achiever who was considered by the district to be a poorly motivated disciplinary problem student with a "bad attitude." His parents recognized him as a very discouraged, frustrated student who had learning disabilities, especially in language arts.

Aaron

Aaron (see Figure 5.12) is a third grader with some troubling behavior, poor reading comprehension and very poor handwriting.

Megan

Megan (see Figure 5.13 is a ten-year old child who functions cognitively at about a four-year old level. She has Down syndrome and is being educated in a regular class at her parents' insistence. These few components are but a small fraction of those in her complete IEP. Note that this is an IEP for which short-term objectives are mandatory, not optional!

Timothy

Timothy (see Figure 5.14) is a very friendly, likable ten-year old who has Asperger's Syndrome. His IEP, like many others, gives Timothy's present levels of performance in narrative description rather than measured quantified skill levels. These PLOPs do, nevertheless, give a fairly clear picture of how he functions.

Note that Timothy's writing goal is about effectively using skills he already possesses. His IEP would look quite different if he needed to learn to write a paragraph, punctuate a sentence, or complete any of the other tasks involved in producing written work. Under those circumstances, the services provided would include instruction in those skills. Timothy needs only instruction in the use of computer technology to refine his writing.

These IEPs aren't perfect. But they are better, and that's what we want—better IEPs.

FIGURE 5.10 Joe's IEP

Unique educational needs, characteristics, and measured present levels of academic achievement and functional performance (PLOPs)	Special education, related services and supplemental aids and services (based on peer-reviewed research to the extent practicable); assistive technology and modifications or personnel support	Measurable annual goals and short-term objectives (progress markers), including academic and functional goals to enable students to be involved in and make progress in the general curriculum and to meet other needs resulting from the disability
1. Joe needs more time to complete written assignments. **PLOP:** Joe has been out of school for three years. Completed virtually no assignments during 9th grade and is failing all classes.	1. Adjust amount of work required (e.g., selected questions, page limits) and/or extend time for completion (e.g., for essays and content area assignments). *Services begin immediately and continue throughout the year.*	**Goal:** Joe will complete classroom assignments satisfactorily and earn a "C" or better in all classes. **Progress markers:** 1. Within one month, Joe will complete 50% of his assignments with grade of "C" or better. 2. Within three months, Joe will complete 80% or more of his assignments with a "C" or better. 3. For the remainder of the year, Joe will maintain a "C" or better in all classes.
2. Because of his attention deficits and difficulties, Joe needs frequent access to a low-distraction environment. See modifications* 2.1–2.3.	2.1. Provide in-classroom seating away from high distractions. 2.2. Provide an alternative workplace for independent work (e.g., study hall, library, resource room). *Services begin immediately and continue throughout the year.* 2.3. Provide in-service to all teachers on Attention Deficit Disorder (by Oct. 3).	
3. Joe needs assistance with oral and written directions. See supplemental service* 3.2.	3.1. Provide Joe with tape, tape recorder, and headphones, and instruct him in using this equipment unobtrusively in any classroom setting (by Oct. 3). 3.2. Classroom teachers will condense lengthy directions into steps and will write directions and assignments on chalkboard, wall chart, overhead transparency, handout, etc. *Services begin immediately and continue throughout the year.*	

*Some educational needs require a PLOP (number 1). Others require supplemental aids, modifications or accommodation (numbers 2 and 3).

(Cont'd next page)

MORE NEEDS (PLOPS), SERVICES AND GOALS

Academic (Figure 5.15) and non-academic (Figure 5.16) components from several quasi-fictional students' IEPs show a range of characteristics, services and goals and different ways of presenting them. The student's profiles are all based on well-known lawsuits and depict the actual students' needs as described in the courts' decisions. For each, the remainder of the IEP indicates either what the court actually required, or what we believe it should have, or a combination of the two. Note that each row is for a different student.

Maria—A Case Study in Needs and Goals

The case study of Maria will illustrate one of the most complex, challenging situations one might encounter. This 16-year-old is an

FIGURE 5.10—Continued

Unique educational needs, characteristics, and measured present levels of academic achievement and functional performance (PLOPs)	Special education, related services and supplemental aids and services (based on peer-reviewed research to the extent practicable); assistive technology and modifications or personnel support	Measurable annual goals and short-term objectives (progress markers), including academic and functional goals to enable students to be involved in and make progress in the general curriculum and to meet other needs resulting from the disability
4. Joe doesn't know how to approach teachers to seek assistance. **PLOP:** Joe never approaches teachers.	4. Provide direct instruction in teacher approach behaviors. *Services begin Sept. 5 and continue through Nov. 15.*	**Goal:** Joe will always seek needed assistance appropriately from teachers. **Progress markers:** 1. Within one month, Joe and two of his teachers will agree he is interacting more, and more appropriately, with teachers. 2. Within three months, Joe and four of his teachers will agree he is "appropriate" in his interactions with teachers.
5. Joe is very disorganized, does not keep track of due dates, assignments, etc. See services** (5).	5. Provide appropriate materials and specific instruction in establishment and maintenance of an organizational system that includes a notebook and a calendar/checklist system. *Services 10 minutes/day, Sept. 5–10.*	**Goal:** Joe will successfully use organizing aids such as a notebook and calendar, i.e., to the satisfaction of a staff person. **Progress markers:** 1. Within one week, Joe will physically organize a notebook with dividers for each class and use a calendar to track assignments, due dates, etc. Joe will check these daily with staff person. 2. By six months, Joe will independently use organized notebook and calendar list.
6. Joe needs to learn to deal with peers who tease him. **PLOP:** Once or twice daily, Joe reacts inappropriately to peer teasing.	6. Provide instruction using appropriate assertive behaviors when teased. *Services one hour weekly, Sept. 5–Nov. 15.*	**Goal:** Joe will react appropriately to peers who tease him, 10 out of 10 times. **Progress markers:** 1. Within two weeks, in role-playing situations, Joe will respond appropriately to staged teasing. 2. Within six weeks, Joe will respond successfully in confrontations with peers 50% of the time (self-monitoring). 3. Within six months, Joe will respond successfully in confrontations with peers 100% of the time (self-monitoring), and the confrontations will be much less frequent.

**Some educational needs require PLOP (e.g., numbers 4 and 6). Others require accommodation (e.g., number 5).

FIGURE 5.11   Curt's IEP

Unique educational needs, characteristics, and measured present levels of academic achievement and functional performance (PLOPs)	Special education, related services and supplemental aids and services (based on peer-reviewed research to the extent practicable); assistive technology and modifications or personnel support	Measurable annual goals and short-term objectives (progress markers), including academic and functional goals to enable students to be involved in and make progress in the general curriculum and to meet other needs resulting from the disability
Present level of social skills: Curt lashes out violently when not able to complete work, uses profanity, and refuses to follow further directions from adults.* **Social needs:** • To learn anger management skills, especially regarding swearing • To learn to comply with requests	1. Teacher and/or counselor consult with behavior specialist regarding techniques and programs for teaching skills, especially anger management. 2. Provide anger management for Curt. *Services 3 times/week, 30 minutes.* 3. Establish a peer group which involves role playing, etc., so Curt can see positive role models and practice newly learned anger management skills. *Services 2 times/week, 30 minutes.* 4. Develop a behavior plan for Curt which gives him responsibility for charting his own behavior. 5. Provide a teacher or some other adult mentor to spend time with Curt (talking, game playing, physical activity, etc.). *Services 2 times/week, 30 minutes.* 6. Provide training for the mentor regarding Curt's needs/goals.	**Goal:** During the last quarter of the academic year, Curt will have 2 or fewer detentions for any reason. **Obj. 1:** At the end of the 1st quarter, Curt will have had 10 or fewer detentions. **Obj. 2:** At the end of the 2nd quarter, Curt will have had 7 or fewer detentions. **Obj. 3:** At the end of the 3rd quarter, Curt will have had 4 or fewer detentions. **Goal:** Curt will manage his behavior and language in an acceptable manner as reported by all of his teachers. **Obj. 1:** At 2 weeks, asked at the end of class if Curt's behavior and language were acceptable or unacceptable, 3 out of 6 teachers will say "acceptable." **Obj. 2:** At 6 weeks, asked the same question, 4 out of 6 teachers will say "acceptable." **Obj. 3:** At 12 weeks, asked the same question, 6 out of 6 teachers will say "acceptable."

*This PLOP would be more useful if it were quantified, e.g., more than 4 times daily.

(Cont'd next page)

unusually attractive young woman, pleasant and accomplished. Until about 7th grade, she was a gifted high achiever, a fine musician and dancer, and a socially popular student. However, from 7th grade through 10th grade, her performance slipped markedly in all areas—academic, social, linguistic, and even physical, as she began falling asleep at inappropriate times. Early on, some blamed puberty, others thought she was rebelling against high expectations, and some saw no real problems at all. In 9th grade she was diagnosed with Obsessive Compulsive disorder (OCD) and Attention Deficit Disorder (ADD), and a sad saga of medications and reactions to them began, which complicated the diagnostic picture.

Additionally, two specialists agreed she had early onset Bipolar Disorder. The medications changed and continued with no good results. That same year, the school found her to be Other Health Impaired. Recently, it was discovered and verified that she actually has Primary Generalized Epilepsy, Intractable (predominantly bi-frontal) and she was experiencing the sequelae of the seizure activity. A month of residence and diagnostic teaching in an outstanding neuropsychological clinic followed and her areas of need were systematically

FIGURE 5.11–Continued

Unique educational needs, characteristics, and measured present levels of academic achievement and functional performance (PLOPs)	Special education, related services and supplemental aids and services (based on peer-reviewed research to the extent practicable); assistive technology and modifications or personnel support	Measurable annual goals and short-term objectives (progress markers), including academic and functional goals to enable students to be involved in and make progress in the general curriculum and to meet other needs resulting from the disability

Study skills/organizational needs:
• How to read text
• Note taking
• How to study notes
• Memory work
• Be prepared for class, with materials
• Lengthen and improve attention span and on-task behavior
 	
Present level: Curt currently lacks skills in all these areas.
	1. Speech/lang. therapist, resource room teacher, and content area teachers will provide Curt with direct and specific teaching of study skills, i.e.,
	  • Note taking from lectures
	  • Note taking while reading text
	  • How to study notes for a test
	  • Memorization hints
	  • Strategies for reading text to retain information
	2. Assign a "study buddy" for Curt in each content area class.
	3. Prepare a motivation system for Curt to be prepared for class with all necessary materials.
	4. Develop a motivational plan to encourage Curt to lengthen his attention span and time on task.
	5. Provide aide to monitor on-task behaviors in first month or so of plan and teach Curt self-monitoring techniques.
	6. Provide motivational system and self-recording form for completion of academic tasks in each class.
		Goal: At the end of academic year, Curt will have better grades and, by his own report, will have learned new study skills.
		
		Obj. 1: Given a 20–30 min lecture/oral lesson, Curt will take appropriate notes as judged by that teacher.
		Obj. 2: Given 10–15 pgs. of text to read, Curt will employ an appropriate strategy for retaining info., i.e. mapping, webbing, outlining, notes, etc. as judged by the teacher.
		Obj. 3: Given notes to study for a test, Curt will do so successfully as evidenced by his test score.

(Cont'd next page)

identified. Only then could a meaningful IEP be developed.

Her needs, as shown in Figure 5.17 were categorized under the headings: (a) cognitive training; (b) language; and (c) social skills, coping and stress reduction. In addition to the clinic's data, parent and teacher observations were very important in delineating her needs. The following goals were written to address specific deficiencies noted in the needs data. Therefore, these goals may be narrower and more specific than many we see.

Maria's Goals

1. Given 5 sets of material (e.g., grocery lists, friends to call, historical events, characters in a novel) with 3 to 7 units of information in each, Maria will select and use at least 3 different mnemonic strategies to recall the sets, with no more than one omission in each.

2. Given 5 topics of interest, Maria will choose and use a different graphic organizer appropriate to generate and organize content for each, with a minimum of six components for each topic.

3. Given a topic of interest, Maria will: (a) independently write a 400 word (minimum) paper to include an introduction, body and conclusion, and (b) two days later will edit the paper. The edited paper will contain no more

FIGURE 5.11—Continued

Unique educational needs, characteristics, and measured present levels of academic achievement and functional performance (PLOPs)	Special education, related services and supplemental aids and services (based on peer-reviewed research to the extent practicable); assistive technology and modifications or personnel support	Measurable annual goals and short-term objectives (progress markers), including academic and functional goals to enable students to be involved in and make progress in the general curriculum and to meet other needs resulting from the disability
Academic needs/written language: Curt needs strong remedial help in spelling, punctuation, capitalization, and usage. **Present level:** Curt is approximately 2 grade levels behind his peers in these skills.	1. Provide direct instruction in written language skills (punctuation, capitalization, usage, spelling) by using a highly structured, well-sequenced program. *Services provided in small group of no more than four students in the resource room, 50 minutes/day.* 2. Build in continuous and cumulative review to help with short-term rote memory difficulty. 3. Develop a list of commonly used words in student writing (or use one of many published lists) for Curt's spellling program. *Adaptations to regular program:* • In all classes, Curt should sit near the front of the class. • Curt should be called on often to keep him involved and on task. • All teachers should help Curt with study skills as trained by spelling/language specialist and resource room teacher. • Teachers should monitor Curt's work closely in the beginning weeks/months of his program.	**Goal:** Within one academic year, Curt will improve his written language skills by 1.5 or 2 full grade levels to a 6.0 grade level as measured by a standardized test. Obj. 1: Given 10 sentences of dictation at his current level of instruction, Curt will punctuate and capitalize with 90% accuracy (checked at the end of each unit taught). Obj. 2: Given 30 sentences with choices of usage, at his current instructional level, Curt will make the correct choice in 28 or more sentences. Obj. 3: Given a list of 150 commonly used words in 6th grade writing, Curt will spell 95% of the words correctly.

than 2 errors and will score a 3 or higher on the writing rubric used in her high school.

4. When Maria has a word retrieval problem with an adult who knows of her difficulty in this area she will acknowledge the difficulty and apply a learned retrieval strategy on 3 consecutive observed occasions. Success is in applying the strategy, not necessarily in retrieving the word.

5. Given 20 words whose meanings she has studied one week earlier, Maria will give the meaning of each word and use it correctly in a sentence, oral or written.

6. Given 20 definitions or descriptions of known words, Maria will provide the word being defined, e.g., "unusual clothing you could wear to a party where everyone dresses in strange clothes," with no errors.

7. Maria and a willing peer will record several of their ordinary conversations. Given 10 minute excerpts of these recordings, Maria will identify and correct any of her word usage or pragmatic errors, with no more than one undetected or uncorrected error in each 10 minute segment.

8. Maria's friend will model and role play with her how Maria can respond when communication problems (e.g., word retrieval, word usage, undue concreteness, getting 'stuck', failure to track the conversation, etc.) occur and are

FIGURE 5.12   Aaron's IEP

Unique educational needs, characteristics, and measured present levels of academic achievement and functional performance (PLOPs)	Special education, related services and supplemental aids and services (based on peer-reviewed research to the extent practicable); assistive technology and modifications or personnel support	Measurable annual goals and short-term objectives (progress markers), including academic and functional goals to enable students to be involved in and make progress in the general curriculum and to meet other needs resulting from the disability
1. Aaron draws and talks inappropriately about weapons, torture, blood, etc. **PLOP:** 10–20 times daily.	1. Behavioral intervention, including: • Behavior contract—to be implemented immediately. • Social skills program—one hour weekly for three months, beginning 9/20. • In-room display of appropriate work	**Goal:** No inppropriate talking or drawing about weapons, torture, blood, or related topics of violence. Obj. 1: No more than twice daily by 10/1 Obj. 2: No more than once weekly by 10/15
2. Aaron makes many errors in reading and doesn't seem to recognize that the errors interfere with proper comprehension. **PLOP:** Reads 3rd grade material at 80–100 WPM with 5–12 errors and 30% accuracy on factual questions.	2. Remedial reading with emphasis on accuracy of decoding and monitoring comprehension: • 30 minutes daily, beginning 9/15	**Goal:** Grade level decoding and comprehension. Obj. 1: Reduce errors to 0–2 at 50–80 WPM by 11/1. Obj. 2: Read 3rd grade material at 80–100 WPM with 0–2 errors by 12/15 with 70% accuracy on factual questions.
3. Aaron has great difficulty in cursive writing. **PLOP:** 8–10 legible manuscript letters per minute.	3. Timed manuscript probes—only legible letters to be counted—self-selected contingencies: • Minimum two 1-minute probes daily. • Implemented immediately and continuing throughout the school year.	**Goal:** 35 per minute by 6/1 Obj. 1: 15–20 per minute by 11/15 Obj. 2: 20–25 per minute by 3/15

noted by peers. Given three actual instances, Maria will respond as she practiced, report to her therapist what happened, how she handled it, and how she felt. Success is responding as practiced on three consecutive occurrences.

9. Given three ordinary conversational questions such as "What are you wearing tomorrow?" or "Did you like that movie?" Maria will reply with at least three specifics and with no grammatical errors. Maria will then ask a similar question, listen to the answer and repeat the gist of the answer, recalling major specifics without error.

10. Given a list of common foods, Maria will select three appropriate breakfasts, 3 lunches and 3 dinners. She will identify the foods or food combinations she must avoid. She will state and provide examples of 3 strategies for managing sugar highs/lows.

11. Given ordinary conversations among peers or adults, Maria will be able to paraphrase the main ideas expressed by the others within the past 5 minutes.

12. Maria will recognize 5 instances when she needs immediate stress reduction and demonstrate at least three different strategies which are appropriate to deal with these situations, e.g., quietly excusing herself, briefly explaining that she needs to rest immediately, or putting on earphones with calming music.

FIGURE 5.13 Megan's IEP

Unique educational needs, characteristics, and measured present levels of academic achievement and functional performance (PLOPs)	Special education, related services and supplemental aids and services (based on peer-reviewed research to the extent practicable); assistive technology and modifications or personnel support	Measurable annual goals and short-term objectives (progress markers), including academic and functional goals to enable students to be involved in and make progress in the general curriculum and to meet other needs resulting from the disability
Present level: Megan needs constant attention and reminders to complete tasks. She has difficulty remembering important daily routines:	Provide the following services and accommodations, and give direct instruction on how to use them.	
1. Lunch (remembering hot or cold), taking medication, notes from home	Design a daily routine pocket board: • Lunch pocket—blue for cold, red for hot. • Note pocket for notes from home. • Medication pocket to put card into when she has taken medication. • Reward pocket for notes from teacher and reward tickets to be traded for prize from menu.	**Goal:** Independently use the daily routine board within one month Obj. 1: Each day for one week, Megan will use the board with teacher's assistance. Obj. 2: Each day for the second week, Megan will use the routine board with only one reminder.
2. Has difficulty finding her books and locating the correct page.	• Color code Megan's books so she can easily identify them. • Put a marker in Megan's book before class so she can find her place.	**Goal:** Megan will locate her own books and find her place without any assistance in one week.
3. Gets lost in the building.	• Make a game of finding her way from one location to another—teacher visual clues. • Have Megan to mark on a map all the paths she has mastered.	**Goal:** Megan will find her way to any point in the building within six months. Obj. Megan will learn to find her way from one given point to another each week. Examples: Classroom to bathroom, playground to classroom, lunchroom to classroom, etc.

13. Given a daily planner with hour or half hour spaces, Maria will write detailed plans for the next day and execute them with no more than 30 minutes of avoidable deviation. She will do this on 10 separate days, including three days that differ in their activities, such as a weekend day, a school day and a special occasion.

14. Given a schoolwork planner for all assignments, due dates, etc., Maria will independently complete it to the satisfaction of a daily monitor.

15. Given a list of at least 50 specifics from 10 categories (such as titles, logos, movies, people, furniture, etc)., Maria will classify them by general category. Given categories such as holidays, rock stars, clothing, etc., Maria will generate at least 5 specifics for that category. She will do these tasks without error.

16. Given 20 slang terms, common figures of speech, and words with more than one meaning, Maria will explain the meaning of the slang and figures of speech and give at least two meanings for the multiple meaning words.

17. Given 10 recipes or other instructions of varying length and complexity Maria will copy the ingredients or instructions and

Unique educational needs, characteristics, and measured present levels of academic achievement and functional performance (PLOPs)	Special education, related services and supplemental aids and services (based on peer-reviewed research to the extent practicable); assistive technology and modifications or personnel support	Measurable annual goals and short-term objectives (progress markers), including academic and functional goals to enable students to be involved in and make progress in the general curriculum and to meet other needs resulting from the disability
1. Timothy communicates well with adults, but lacks conversational skills in his peer relationships. He often misinterprets social situations and may need adult help in problem solving.	Social skills curriculum implemented by a trained person in a small group (N = <6) one hour per week; 8 hours per week in ESY.	**Goal 1:** In four instructional settings, over 40 min. of observation, Timothy will do the following approximately 4 times more frequently than he fails to perform or does it inappropriately: • Initiate conversations on topics of interest to others • Listen to and respond appropriately to other's point of view • Use questions appropriately to maintain conversations with peers • Make comments appropriately to maintain conversations with peers • Change topics in conversation appropriately • Express feelings and point of view appropriately **Progress markers:** Grade period one—2x in 2 settings Grade period two—3x in 3 settings Grade period three—3x in 4 settings Grade period four—See Goal 1
2. Timothy has excellent verbal skills. He has made good progress in using word processing skills to express his ideas in writing, but there continues to be a discrepancy between his verbal skills and his ideas as written. He sometimes chooses to dictate his ideas to a scribe to avoid writing them himself. He can independently open the appropriate application, title his working files, save his writing, and print his document with no teacher prompts.	Keyboarding 30 min. week Word Processing 40 min. week	**Goal 2:** Timothy will use a spell checker and edit his work. He will generate appropriate ideas for the assigned task and type his assignments in paragraphs including grammatically correct sentence structure using supporting details, capitalization, and end punctuation, with 100% accuracy in 4 of 5 trials with no more than 2 teacher prompts. **Progress markers:** Grade period one—90% accuracy with 4 teacher prompts Grade period two—95% accuracy with 3 teacher prompts Grade period three—95% accuracy with 2 teacher prompts Grade period four—See Goal 2

Unique educational needs, characteristics, and measured present levels of academic achievement and functional performance (PLOPs)	Special education, related services and supplemental aids and services (based on peer-reviewed research to the extent practicable); assistive technology and modifications or personnel support	Measurable annual goals and short-term objectives (progress markers), including academic and functional goals to enable students to be involved in and make progress in the general curriculum and to meet other needs resulting from the disability
James James is a very bright 16 year old who is functionally illiterate, i.e., cannot distinguish "ladies" from "gentlemen" on doors. By shrewd guessing and a few sight words he can score from 1st to high 2nd grade on comprehension tests. His word attack skills are few, random and ineffective.	Intensive, systematic, synthetic phonics reading instruction, 1:1 or small group (no more than 4) with a teacher or aide trained in the methodology used. Minimum one hour daily, plus same methodology to be used in all language arts areas consistently. Resource room and classroom.	End 1st 9 weeks: James will be able to decode all regular CVC words at 50 WPM w/ 0 errors. End 2nd 9 weeks: James will write and read the Dolch 220. End 3rd 9 weeks: James will read from 3rd grade material at 60 WPM w/ 0–2 errors. End 4th 9 weeks: James will score above 3.5 grade equivalent on 2 standardized reading tests.
Rafael Rafael is a 9 year old who has Down Syndrome and whose IQ is about 50. He lacks understanding of the alphabetic principle and is unable to associate any letters, other than t and m, with their sounds. He is easily distracted from any task by sound or movement.	1:1 tutoring in a multisensory sound-symbol association method 15 minutes twice daily before noon in a small, quiet, distraction-free room.	**Goal:** Given alphabet flash cards, R will be able to produce the main, regular sound for all short vowels, consonants & digraphs with 100% accuracy, and when given each sound by the teacher, R will be able to print the corresponding letter(s) legibly. Obj. 1: By Nov. 1 R will demonstrate s-s, as above, for f,m,s,r,t,a,i,l. Obj. 2: By Jan 15 R will (ditto) b,c,p,h,k,n, and o, wh, ch. Obj. 3: By Mar. 15 R will (ditto) remainder, including e and u.
Jeremy Jeremy lacks understanding of the processes of multiplication and division and does not know the multiplication facts beyond x2. **PLOP:** Jeremy scored 10 correct problems out of 100 on the district comprehensive test of multiplication and division.	1. 20 minutes per school day, small group (< 5) instruction with remedial math specialist in the resource room. 2. Computerized drill and practice in multiplication and division for 15 minutes each school day.	**Goal:** By the end of the school year, Jeremy will be able to complete 85% of multiplication and division problems correctly, on the district math test. Obj. 1: By Nov. 15 Jeremy will be able to complete a test of two-digit multiplication with at least 22 out of 25 score. Obj. 2: By Feb. 15 Jeremy will be able to complete a test of simple division with at least a 22 out of 25 score.

(Cont'd next page)

FIGURE 5.15–Continued

Unique educational needs, characteristics, and measured present levels of academic achievement and functional performance (PLOPs)	Special education, related services and supplemental aids and services (based on peer-reviewed research to the extent practicable); assistive technology and modifications or personnel support	Measurable annual goals and short-term objectives (progress markers), including academic and functional goals to enable students to be involved in and make progress in the general curriculum and to meet other needs resulting from the disability
Tarah Tarah's expressive language skills are underdeveloped although she scores in the average range on non-language measures of intelligence. She doesn't initiate conversation and answers questions with 1 or 2 word sentences. She has a spoken vocabulary of approximately 50–100 words. Her articulation is only slightly delayed (r, l not yet perfect) at the age of 7.	One-on-one direct instruction in vocabulary provided by a speech and language pathologist (SLP) three times a week/20 min. a session. Small group, SLP-led discussions with same-age peers twice a week/20 min. a session.	**Goal:** Tarah will initiate conversation with peers at least twice a day. 1. By November, Tarah will initiate a conversation with peers or with an adult on at least one occasion per week as monitored by teacher, instructional assistants, parent volunteers, recess teachers, special ed. teacher, or SLP. 2. By March, Tarah will initiate conversation with same-age peers during speech class, or during work or play activities at least once a day.
RS RS needs a quiet structured learning environment with minimal distractions. He currently can spell an average of 3 words from a 3rd grade list of 50 selected words.	Provide a quiet, structured learning environment with minimal distractions. Provide 1:1 direct instruction in spelling 5 days a week for 15 minutes each day.	**Goal:** RS will spell 45 of 50 selected 3rd grade words by end the of the year. *Short-term:* • By the end of the first quarter, RS will correctly spell 15 of 50 words. • By the end of the second quarter, RS will correctly spell 30 of 50 words.

(Cont'd next page)

will paraphrase the directions with no significant errors.

18. Given 20 pages of 10th grade level text in a content area, Maria will highlight the topic sentence or main idea in each paragraph with no more than one error per ten paragraphs. She will then accurately paraphrase each highlighted sentence.

19. Maria will identify at least three areas of challenge for her such as word retrieval, memory, etc. She will then locate and use at least 5 relevant web sites which address these areas. From each website she will locate a strategy or suggestion to try. She will apply it and write a brief report of what happened when she tried it and evaluate how helpful, if at all, it was to her. The report will be at least 150 words long for each website and will

contain no more than random error of the sort a proficient adult might make.

The specificity of her needs and goal statements directly related to the effects of the seizures on her cognitive functioning. The goals were written to address these needs in the most functional way possible. After they were written, the goals were analyzed to determine which needs each addressed. IDEA does not require this step, but it helped the team to understand the inter-relatedness of Maria's needs and the desirability of getting the most coverage possible from each goal. The Team knew that Maria's performance lagged relative to each goal and knew what level of performance they deemed appropriate but were unable to determine her present levels of performance until after writing the goals. The sequence is unusual, but this is an unusual case in almost every respect. The goals themselves pointed

FIGURE 5.15–Continued

Unique educational needs, characteristics, and measured present levels of academic achievement and functional performance (PLOPs)	Special education, related services and supplemental aids and services (based on peer-reviewed research to the extent practicable); assistive technology and modifications or personnel support	Measurable annual goals and short-term objectives (progress markers), including academic and functional goals to enable students to be involved in and make progress in the general curriculum and to meet other needs resulting from the disability	
Todd Todd's reading level is between the 4th and 5th grade level. His oral reading fluency rate is 70 words per minute with 5–6 errors, in 4th grade material.	Small group instruction from a reading specialist 30 minutes per day in a resource room beginning 11/24.	**Goal:**	In 3 one-minute timed passages, Todd will increase his oral reading fluency to 150 words/minute with 0–1 error by 11/24.
		STO 1:	In 3 one-minute timed passages, Todd will increase his oral reading fluency to 90 words/minute with 2–3 errors by 4/24.
		STO 2:	In 3 one-minute timed passages, Todd will increase his oral reading fluency to 110 words/minute with 1–2 errors by 9/24.
Daniel Daniel recognizes one color by name (red). Daniel recognizes one shape by name (circle). Daniel recognizes the words for two spatial concepts (on, under).	One-on-one direct instruction in color, shape & spatial concepts by the classroom aide for 10 minutes per day in the classroom, beginning September 1.	**Goal:**	Daniel will follow directions, answer questions or identify objects to demonstrate understanding of 21 new concepts without error.
		STO 1:	Daniel will point on request to brown, white, orange, purple, yellow, blue, green, black by 4/24 with no errors.
		STO 2:	Daniel will point on request to diamond, oval, square, star, heart by 6/13.
		STO 3:	Daniel will demonstrate an understanding of near, far, above, next to, in front of behind, beside, by 11/23 without errors.

to the specific assessments needed to identify to Maria's present levels of performance.

IEPS FOR SECTION 504 STUDENTS?

Section 504 of the Rehabilitation Act of 1973 prohibits discrimination against persons solely on the basis of disability. Confusion abounds about what kind of IEP or IEP-like document, if any, students are entitled to when they are eligible for Section 504 (of the Rehabilitation Act of 1973) but not for IDEA. Many schools treat some students who have been diagnosed as having ADD (Attention Deficit Disorder) or ADHD (with hyperactivity) as though they are eligible only under Section 504. Other Section 504-eligible, but not IDEA-eligible students could include students who have a mental or physical disability which substantially limits a major life activity, such as diabetes, epilepsy, asthma, etc., but who do

FIGURE 5.16 Partial IEP Nonacademic Examples

Unique educational needs, characteristics, and measured present levels of academic achievement and functional performance (PLOPs)	Special education, related services and supplemental aids and services (based on peer-reviewed research to the extent practicable); assistive technology and modifications or personnel support	Measurable annual goals and short-term objectives (progress markers), including academic and functional goals to enable students to be involved in and make progress in the general curriculum and to meet other needs resulting from the disability
Jeff 10–15 violent or near violent outbursts weekly, lasting for 10–15 min. each.	Response cost contract in all classes.	**Goal:** Zero inappropriate outbursts by end of year Obj. 1: By Dec. < 3 for 5 minutes weekly Obj. 2: By Mar. < 1 monthly
Jed Jed talks to and interrupts other students during study time an average of 10 times per half-hour.	Lunch detention after 5 interruptions.	**Goal:** By the end of the school year, Jed will not talk to other students during quiet work times. Obj. 1: By Jan. 15, Jed will interrupt others no more than 5 times per half hour. Obj. 2: By March 15, Jed will interrupt other students no more than 2 times per half hour.
Rafael Has outbursts in the classroom. These outbursts consist of yelling, biting, and kicking. Outbursts occur at least twice a day for a duration of approximately 20 min. **PLOP:** When Rafael is asked to follow teacher directions that he perceives as difficult, the tantrum behavior is observed. Rafael follows teacher directions, without tantrum, within 5 seconds no more than 35% of the time.	Physical escort to cooling-off area.	**Goal:** Rafael will follow teacher directions within 5 seconds without verbal and physical tantrums. Obj. 1: Rafael will follow teacher directions without tantrums in 70% of the opportunities for 3 consecutive days by 11/14. Obj. 2: Rafael will follow teacher directions without tantrums in 90% of the opportunities for 5 consecutive days by 1/15.

(Cont'd next page)

not need special education. Please note that if a student has a disability which necessitates special education, he or she may be eligible under both IDEA and Section 504.

The basic educational entitlement under Section 504 is to

> . . . regular or special education and related aids and services that (i) are designed to meet the individual educational needs of handicapped persons as adequately as the needs of nonhandicapped persons are met and (ii) are based upon adherence to procedures. . . .[12]

An IDEA IEP is one legally recognized way to meet this Section 504 requirement. A school might choose this option just because it is familiar. That is a perfectly okay way to proceed.

A widespread and deeply held misconception is that Section 504-eligible students are entitled only to "reasonable accommodations." How and why this misconception arose is outside the scope of this discussion—suffice it to say it was and is an erroneous reading of Section 504. In fact, the Section 504 entitlement is exactly as quoted above, i.e., to education and services that meet the needs of the disabled student as well as the needs

FIGURE 5.16—Continued

Unique educational needs, characteristics, and measured present levels of academic achievement and functional performance (PLOPs)	Special education, related services and supplemental aids and services (based on peer-reviewed research to the extent practicable); assistive technology and modifications or personnel support	Measurable annual goals and short-term objectives (progress markers), including academic and functional goals to enable students to be involved in and make progress in the general curriculum and to meet other needs resulting from the disability
Daniel Doesn't know how to play with others. Grabs toys away from other children, has difficulty sharing. **PLOP:** During parallel play with a small group of peers Daniel grabs toys away from a classmate at least 6 times daily (twice in each of 3 ten minute periods.	A behavior plan (attached) that addresses cooperation and sharing. • Teach alternative behaviors. • Frequent verbal reinforcement for appropriate behavior.	**Goal:** When playing in a small group of peers, Daniel will ask his peers if he can borrow their toy and will not grab. Obj 1: When playing in a small group of peers, and verbally cued during play time, Daniel will ask his peers if he can borrow their toys half of the time by 1/15. Obj 2: When playing in a small group of peers, and hearing a verbal announcement about toy sharing before the play session began, Daniel will ask his peers if he can borrow their toys ¾ of the time for 5 consecutive days by 3/15.
RG RG worries excessively about his schoolwork. **PLOP:** RG asks to go to the school nurse at least once a day because of stress-related stomach pains or headaches.	In-school "stress-proof" group counseling once a week for ½ hour with school psychologist. Behavioral contract with self-selected reinforcements.	**Goal:** By the end of the school year, RG will not miss any school time because of stress. Obj 1: By 12/15, RG will ask to go to the nurse no more than 3x/week. Obj 2: By 2/28, RG will ask to go to the nurse no more than once/week.
Todd Todd is a social isolate at recess and lunch, seldom if ever seen interacting with other students.	• A volunteer "special buddy" will be assigned to draw Todd into socialization with others. • Playground & cafeteria monitors will comment favorably to Todd about his interactions after such are observed, at least once daily.	**Goal:** Todd will interact with peers at a rate not noticeably different from that of his peers. Obj. By Dec. 15 he will participate in at least 2 observed appropriate interactions during each recess and lunch. Obj. By Mar. 15 he will (ditto) at least 4 interactions.
WG WG has trouble staying in his seat during class. He gets up and wanders during both instruction and independent work time. Currently he leaves his seat an average of 10–15 times per day.	Place WG's desk where the teacher can monitor him. Give WG 3 cards per day that allow him to get out of his seat during independent work time only. A token economy will be used to increase uninterrupted seat time.	**Goal:** WG will get out of his seat <3 times/day during independent work. *Short-term:* • By 11/1, WG will decrease by half out of seat episodes. • By 3/1, WG will get out of his seat < 4x/day.

FIGURE 5.17 Maria's Needs Cross-Referenced to Goals

Needs	Goals
1. Cognitive training/rehabilitation	
► Memory: Mnemonics, graphic organizers, word retrieval	1, 2, 4, 19
► Classification/categorization	15
► Concept generation	2, 9, 15, 19
► Planning	13, 14, 19
2. Language	
► Written expression	2, 3, 18, 19
► Comprehension (listening and reading)	9, 11, 17, 18
► Paraphrasing	11, 17, 18
► Internet use	1, 2, 19
► Vocabulary	5, 6, 16
3. Social skills, coping, stress reduction	
► Conversational skills, pragmatics	4, 7, 8, 9, 11, 16
► Self-advocacy, self-help	1, 2, 4, 8, 10, 12, 19
► Coping with and avoiding stress	4, 7, 8, 10, 12

of the nondisabled students are met. That is what Section 504 is about—nondiscrimination on the basis of disability. And an appropriate education under Section 504 is one that meets the needs of the disabled student as well as the needs of nondisabled students.

Section 504 does not describe the process or document to be used in specifying the services required for nondiscrimination. Parents and school personnel should focus on the result of meeting needs and should use the simplest possible writing to document that result. Sometimes providing only "reasonable accommodation" would be sufficient to meet the "as adequately as non-disabled" standard. Oftentimes it would not.

One fascinating Section 504 case involves a student whose disability was a blood condition that could cause fatal bleeding from a minor injury. The student accidentally cut herself in art class and, in a fearful outburst, she uttered two expletives. The school expelled her for this misconduct. The student successfully sought an injunction to prevent the expulsion. The court found that the student's behavior was caused by her disability and concluded that, under these circumstances, Section 504 required leniency in applying the student conduct code. The court cautioned that "blind adherence to policies and standards resulting in a failure to accommodate a person with a disability is precisely what the Americans with Disabilities Act of 1990 and the Rehabilitation Act of 1973 are intended to prevent."[13]

In other words, Section 504 requires public and private schools that receive or benefit from federal monies to provide such services — including making accommodation, changes, or allowances—as to result in the student not being disadvantaged or discriminated against solely because of a disability.

In a powerful decision (2010) the Ninth Circuit Court held that monetary damages are available under Section 504 if a district, with deliberate indifference, fails to provide a disabled student with meaningful access to education.[14]

HOW MUCH WILL IEPS CHANGE?

The basic structure of IEPs remains as it has been for 35 years (see Figure 5.18), but Congress has made some significant changes that will impact IEP development for the foreseeable future.

Research-Based Services

IEPs must now include special education and other services that are based on peer-reviewed research to the extent practicable. Since education journals and recent textbooks are bulging with reports of peer-reviewed research on effective methods, especially in reading and behavior support but also in other curriculum areas, it would be difficult indeed for a district to successfully argue that it was not practicable to use research-validated methods. This is terrific news for students with disabilities, who have often stagnated in special education programs based more on habit and custom than demonstrated effectiveness. It is also good news for school districts. For the first time, Congress has issued an unmistakable directive to schools about the nature of required special education services. While it may be challenging to organize the staff development necessary to prepare teachers to learn the theory and practice of research based methods and services, this will also better equip schools to meet the requirements of No Child Left Behind (NCLB). When students with disabilities achieve at higher levels, the entire school benefits!

However, the majority of courts disregard this recent IDEA statutory emphasis on effective services and they still rely on the 1982 *Rowley* decision which arguably allows the district (state) to employ any methodology that provides some benefit, even if more effective methods are available.[15,16]

The Ninth Circuit made this position very clear when it acknowledged that in at least three places in the IDEA amendments Congress addressed improving educational outcomes for students with disabilities. In reversing the District court which had found that IDEA 1997 had created a higher FAPE standard than *Rowley*, the Ninth Circuit said that if Congress had intended to overrule *Rowley* it would have explicitly said so.[17]

But What About Short-Term Objectives?

In a move to reduce paperwork, Congress eliminated the requirement for short-term objectives or benchmarks in most IEPs. They are still required in the IEPs of students with disabilities who take alternate assessments aligned to alternate achievement standards.

The view of most special educators is that the use of short-term objectives remains good practice. They make it possible for teachers to continuously monitor whether the student is progressing at the anticipated rate and alert them to the need to revisit IEPs that do not provide adequate progress.

IEPs are required to contain a description of how the district will measure the student's progress toward annual goals as well as noting when parents will receive progress reports. Without such intermediate progress markers as short-term objectives, the how of measuring progress is more difficult. It is ironic that while IDEA 2004 emphasizes effectiveness in instruction and other services, it eliminates a linchpin of measurability.

If IEP teams choose to eliminate intermediate progress markers from IEPs, they will have to write much more detailed and precise measurable annual goals because measurability and progress monitoring will hinge entirely on them. In a dispute between parents and schools, the party that can most clearly document the student's progress (or lack of it) is likely to prevail. Districts that want to be in a position to demonstrate that they are providing FAPE should think twice before dropping short-term objectives.

References

Bateman, B. (2007). From gobbledygook to clearly written IEP goals. Verona, WI: Attainment Co.

Bateman, B., & Golly, A. (2003). *Why Johnny doesn't behave: Twenty tips and measurable BIPs*. Verona, WI: Attainment Co.

Bateman, B., & Herr, C. (2006). *Writing measurable IEP goals and objectives* (2nd ed). Verona, WI: Attainment Co.

Mager, R.F. (1997). *Preparing instructional objectives* (3rd ed.). Atlanta, GA: Center for Effective Performance.

Smith, C., & Strick, L. (1997). *Learning disabilities: A to Z*. New York, NY: Free Press.

Sugai, G., & Colvin, G. (1990). From assessment to development: Writing Behavior IEPs. *The Oregon Conference Monograph*, 125–179. Eugene, OR: University of Oregon.

Walsh, Anderson, Brown, Schulze, & Aldridge, P.C. (1997). *Positive behavioral strategies and consequences* [handout]. Austin, TX: 6300 La Calma, Ste. 200.

Notes

1. *Farmington Bd. of Ed.*, 24 IDELR 1067 (SEA Conn. 1996).

2. *Capistrano Unified Sch. Dist. v. Wartenburg*, 59 F.3d 884 (9th Cir. 1995).

3. *Evans v. Bd. of Rhinebeck Central Sch. Dist.*, 930 F. Supp. 83 (SD NY 1996).

4. *Western Wayne Sch. Dist.*, 25 IDELR 867 (SEA PA 1997).

5. *US Dept. of Ed. Commentary in IDEA Regulations*, 64 FR 12405 (Mar 12, 1999).

6. *Susquenita Sch. Dist. v. Raelee S.*, 25 IDELR 120 (MD PA 1996).

7. *Evans v. Bd. of Ed. of Rhinebeck Central Sch. Dist.*, 930 F. Supp. 83 (SD NY 1996).

8. *Hawaii Dept. of Ed. v. Tara H.*, Civ. No. 86-1161 (D HI 1987).

9. *Hendrick Hudson Bd. of Ed. v. Rowley*, 102 S.Ct. 3034, 458 US 176 (1982).

10. 34 CFR 300.320(b).

11. 34 CFR 300.321(b).

12. 34 CFR 104.33(b)(1).

13. *Thomas v. Davidson Academy*, 846 F. Supp. 611 (MD Tenn. 1994).

14. *Mark H. v. Hamamoto*, 620 F.3d 1090 (9th Cir. 2010).

15. *Carlson v. San Diego Unified Sch. Dist.*, 388 Fed. App'x 595 (9th Cir. 2010).

16. *D.G. v. Cooperstown Central Sch. Dist.*, 746 F. Supp. 2d 435 (ND NY 2010).

17. *J.L. v. Mercer Island Sch. Dist.*, 592 F.3d 938 (9th Cir. 2010).

CHAPTER SIX

Standards-based IEPs

"Standards-based IEPs" (S-B IEPs) do not appear in IDEA, but they are appearing more and more frequently in the professional literature and in schools. This chapter explores standards, what S-B IEPs are, where they came from and how they relate to IDEA IEPs, among other issues.

ABOUT STANDARDS

We know, intuitively, that standards can be good things. We often base our choice of a partner, college, or almost anything important on whether our "standards" are met. But what does that mean? In general, standards are established by some authority as a way to measure and evaluate a quantity or quality. A standard sets a target or criterion to be met.

Most of us believe the establishment of generally accepted models or criteria for assessing quality is positive and even necessary. Without standards, our food might be infested with more disease-causing organisms, the air might be filled with more toxic chemicals, and defectively designed cars might flip over more often on our highways. Standards allow buildings to withstand earthquakes, medical doctors to be board-certified, credit to be obtained and so much more.

We probably also agree that standards are critically important in schooling. Administrators must meet standards in leadership, supervision, evaluation, law, public relations and more. Teachers must meet standards relating to curriculum, instruction, assessment, and classroom management. The current wave of school reform, animated by a series of dramatic critiques[1] of American education, is all about establishing standards for student learning. Driving this investment in education standards is the need for public schools to be accountable to the tax-paying public, to parents, and to students.

We can intelligently discuss standards-based IEPs only if we first understand standards in the context of school reform. Over the past two decades, every state has adopted standards. (Such standards were mandated by the optimistic *No Child Left Behind* in 2001.) These standards are typically classified in two categories:

1. **Content Standards** which specify what students should know and be able to do. They define targets for student learning and focus curriculum and instruction on those targets.

2. **Achievement or Performance Standards** which specify criteria for students to reach on large-scale assessments which are aligned to the content standards.

Content standards identify general curriculum goals for specific grade levels. They may be broad or specific. The standards in any state and any content or skill area are necessarily a selective sample from the curriculum, not the entire content of it.

It is difficult to generalize or compare content standards across states because each state has its own content and organization. The following examples from two states are fairly representative.

Oregon fifth-grade social science standards relate to five topics: civics and government, economics, geography, history, and social science analysis. Under each topic is a set of Common Curriculum Goals (CCG), and under most CCGs are one or more standards. Figure 6.1 shows a typical CCG and standards.

Content standards address basic academic skills as well as academic content. Figure 6.2 shows an example from Pennsylvania first grade reading

---

FIGURE 6.1   Civics and Government

CCG: Understand how government is influenced and changed by support and dissent of individuals, groups, and international organizations.

> SS.05.CG.06 Identify and give examples of how individuals can influence the actions of government.
> SS.05.CG.06.01 Identify and give examples of actions citizens can take to influence government policy and decision making.

Available online at: http://www.ode.state.or.us/teachlearn/readl/standards/sbd.aspx

---

FIGURE 6.2   Standard Area 1.1: Reading Independently

Grade Level—1.1.1: Grade 1
1.1.1.A: Identify the author's purpose and type, using grade level text.
1.1.1.B: Demonstrate:
  • Phonological awareness through phoneme manipulation.
  • Knowledge of letter-sound correspondence (alphabetic principle) to decode and encode words.
1.1.1.C: Use increasingly robust vocabulary in oral and written language.
1.1.1.D: Demonstrate listening and reading comprehension / understanding before reading, during reading, and after reading through strategies such as think aloud, retelling, summarizing, connecting to prior knowledge, simple note-taking, and non-linguistic representations
1.1.1.E: Demonstrate accuracy and automaticity in decoding and oral reading of grade level text.

Available online at: http://www.pdesas.org/Standard/Views

---

standards for reading independently. Other standards address analyzing and interpreting text and literature.

The structure of achievement or performance standards varies from state to state, but in general, they are more specific than content standards and include performance criteria. For example, North Dakota math achievement standards are benchmarked at every grade level and include proficiency indicators for each standard. Figure 6.3 shows a typical example.

Although all states have content standards that cover more or less the same academic turf, they vary in breadth, depth, and taxonomy. The assessments that measure student achievement similarly vary in design and rigor. For this reason, the Council of Chief State School Officers (CCSSO) and the National Governors' Association (NGA) have joined forces to create Common Core State Standards.[2] Although content area standards may follow at some time in the future,[3] the Common Core Standards now address only math and language arts.

Within a year of the June 2010 publication of the Common Core Standards, 46 states had adopted them. They have become a major focus of many special educators who believe that IDEA requires IEPs to include the general curriculum rather than special education.

S-B IEPS IN THE CONTEXT OF IDEA

To examine S-B IEPs in a book about IEPs is, in a sense, to look at general education and special education in the context of each other. In an unpublished article, award-winning author James Kauffman (2010) described the current Zeitgeist of special education as disgraceful, in that so many special educators fail to recognize that "special education **has** to be different from general education." Among the most disgraceful ideas, he observes, are that general educators can and should provide special education, that full inclusion should be mandated, that all education should be special, and that S-B IEPs should be required, i.e., that all IEPs should be aligned with the general curriculum and universal standards of learning. To view S-B IEPs clearly, they must be seen in the context of the relationship between general education and special education.

An underlying premise of advocates of S-B IEPs is the belief that all students (except possibly 1%), can learn and achieve at age and grade level. Those who oppose S-B IEPs believe that differences in students' inherent ability, prior learning, language facility and other factors result in substantial variations in their educational needs, and in their ultimate performance levels.

A related premise of S-B IEP advocates is that state and/or Common Core academic standards

FIGURE 6.3 Performance Criteria—Math				
Benchmark expectation	**Proficiency descriptor**			
	Advanced proficient	**Proficient**	**Partially proficient**	**Novice**
Numeric and algebraic representations • Identify a variable in an expression	Students accurately identify a variable in an expression.	Students identify a variable in an expression with few errors.	Students identify a variable in an expression with some errors.	Students identify a variable in an expression with many errors.

Available online at: http://www.dpi.state.nd.us/standard/perform/index.shtm

embody priority goals for all students, including those who have a disability. Those who oppose S-B IEPs believe that for some students, daily living and functional skills may be more important than academics and should be the primary focus of their programs.

The most basic and divisive issue is the one that underlies all of these—whether special education, including its unique and individualized IDEA IEPs, should be merged into or subsumed under general education with the same S-B goals for all students, or whether special education should remain somewhat separate and specialized. Universal use of S-B IEPs would be a huge step on the journey of special education into oblivion—an end desired by some and feared by others.

A CLOSER LOOK AT S-B IEPS

In 2010, as a major step in the current standards-based reform movement in education, the Common Core State Standards in language arts and mathematics (2010) were released by the National Governor's Association and the State School Superintendents. These national standards fill hundreds of pages, two pages of which detail the application of these core standards to students with disabilities.[4] According to this source, all students, including IDEA-eligible students, must be "challenged to excel within the general curriculum and [be] prepared for success in their post-school lives, including college and/or careers."

Their IEPs must include "annual goals aligned with and chosen to facilitate the attainment of **grade-level** [emphasis added] academic standards." Any adjustments or extensions to the standards which are provided to students with significant intellectual impairments "must align with and retain the rigor and high expectations of the common core standards."

Some state departments of education, e.g., Hawaii, have space on each IEP form where the IEP team must write the state or common core general curriculum standard to which each of the student's goals is aligned, and from which the goal is derived.

In an S-B IEP the goals must address the content of the standards for the **grade** in which the student is enrolled or would **be enrolled based on age.** (See, e.g., the Alabama Department of Education's website.) Further, the goals must allow for the student to earn a high school diploma.

HOW S-B IEPS DIFFER FROM IDEA IEPS

The primary difference between S-B IEPs and IDEA IEPs begins with the determination of the annual goals for the student. IDEA requires that the IEP address the student's unique educational needs as determined in a full, individual **evaluation.** In stark contrast, the curriculum for general education students is the guiding force for S-B IEPs. Before exploring the ramifications of this basic difference, it is helpful to look more broadly at the basic differences between general education and special education. Zigmond and Kloo (2011) analyzed these fundamental differences, among others:

► General education is governed by states and local governments; special education by the federal government.

► Local boards of the state govern general education curriculum; the IEP governs the curriculum for IDEA students.

► General education focuses on the group; special education is about the individual.

► General education uses "differentiated instruction by classroom teachers" (although there is widespread doubt as to its actual implementation); special education is predicated on intensive, individually designed special instruction delivered by a specialist. This intensive instruction places far more emphasis than does general education on systematic, sequential, scaffolded tasks, and on direct instruction.

With these differences in mind, we can examine the implications of general curriculum-driven goals versus individual, unique needs-driven goals. IEP goals determine what will be taught to the student. What will be taught is at the heart of education—what is taught is the education received by a given student.

Suppose a 16-year-old is physically strong, a nonreader functioning academically below a first-grade level, socially immature and aggressive, verbally very limited, with a multitude of overt and inappropriate sexual behaviors. If a standards-based approach is used to develop goals for our student, we would have to generate an instructional goal aligned to a high school math standard such as this one from the Common Core Math Standards:

▶ Understand that vectors can be added end-to-end, component-wise or by the parallelogram rule; and/or

▶ Understand that a system of linear equations can be represented as a single matrix equation in a vector variable; and/or

▶ Use the unit circle to explain symmetry (odd and even) and periodicity of trigonometric functions.

If our high school-age student cannot make change for a purchase under $1.00, cannot add or subtract with regrouping, has no multiplication skills and cannot efficiently operate a calculator, we must wonder whether basing his goals on the common core standards above is more appropriate than basing them on his present levels of performance in this area of unique educational need. What appropriate grade level goal could possibly be derived from or aligned to the common core standards for this student?

In one more example, suppose a 15-year-old eighth grader functions academically at approximately a second-grade level in reading, writing and basic math skills. His verbal level and interactions are roughly like those of a first or second grader. His personal hygiene habits are severely deficient. He cannot tell time, has never worked or helped with household chores, used a microwave or made a sandwich. If he were in Hawaii, his S-B IEP would address this social studies standard: "Analyze major political systems of the world." That hardly seems an appropriate focus for him.

When the goals of an IEP are inappropriate and impossible for that student, the instruction becomes irrelevant, as does progress assessment. As has been stressed throughout this book, the heart of the IEP is a three-fold sequence identifying: (1) what are the students' unique educational needs; (2) what services must the district provide to address these unique needs; and (3) how will we assess whether the goal has been reached? If a student's unique educational needs do not currently touch on vectors, systems of linear equations or unit circles, why should the IEP team be required to do anything whatsoever about those matters? To waste time pretending or creating a presumed "alignment" between vectors and simple addition using a calculator seems highly inappropriate and frankly silly.

HOW DID WE GET FROM IEPS TO S-B IEPS?

A few years ago, the term standards-based IEP was never heard and had it been, it would have been considered a joke, an oxymoron. An IEP, by legal definition and by name, must be individualized. It cannot simultaneously be individualized and derived from and focused on group norms or standards. Nevertheless, Standards-Based IEPs are now encouraged and touted by a surprisingly large number of school districts and even some state departments of education.

How and why did some of us move from IEPs to S-B IEPs? At least two complex and intertwined factors can be identified in recent decades. These include: (1) a trifecta of the Regular Education Initiative (Will, 1984), the social philosophy of inclusion, including widespread misunderstanding of both "access" to the general curriculum and "least restrictive environment," and the *Brown v. Board of Education*[5] Supreme Court case ruling that racially segregated public education violates equal protection; and (2) more recently, some of the legal requirements of *No Child Left Behind* (2001) and IDEA related to assessment have been interpreted to support high (grade level) academic expectations for all students.

Regular Education Initiative, Inclusion, and Brown

The origins of inclusion go back at least to the 1960s when questions were raised about the efficacy of special education classes, which were separate or segregated from general education classes (e.g., Dunn, 1968). Soon, questions of civil rights violations were raised about special education. Some of those who raised civil rights questions believed that *Brown v. Board of Education,* banning racially segregated public education, also applied to separate facilities for children with disabilities. However, race is a "suspect" class (meaning that discrimination on that basis is suspect) and its justification therefore requires "strict scrutiny" by a court. Discrimination against a suspect class is permissible **only** if there is a finding that there is a **"compelling"** justification for it; however, disability is **not** a suspect class and, in *Cleburne v. Cleburne Living Center,*[6] the US Supreme Court has explicitly said it is not.

Discrimination (in this case, segregation) against a nonsuspect class such as disability can be justified if it has a merely **rational basis,** as contrasted to the **compelling interest** required to uphold discrimination against a suspect class. *Brown* simply did not and does not apply to separate or segregated education for children with disabilities. However, as the years have gone by many advocates, especially beginning in the early 1980s, mistakenly cloaked special education placements in the *Brown* garb of civil rights, and erroneously claimed that equal protection was violated by separate, specialized education for children who have disabilities.

Deno (1970) proposed a continuum, or cascade, of appropriate placements for special education students, which ranged from regular classes with resource or itinerant support, through special classes and schools, to hospitals, institutions and home-based instruction. Her point was that a range of services and placements was necessary in order to match the varying needs of individual students. In 1975 the federal special education law now known as IDEA included a requirement, still in the law, that every district must make available

this full continuum of placement options. The IDEA placement team decides which placement, or combinations of placements, on the continuum best matches the student's unique needs as shown on the IEP.

By the mid 1980s, Will (1984) and Stainback & Stainback (1984) were calling for special education to be merged into regular education, in what became known as the Regular Education Initiative (REI).

The Regular Education Initiative's (REI) push toward inclusion of special education students in general education, and the merging of special education administration and financing into regular education, went hand-in-hand with a rapidly spreading misunderstanding of the legal concept of "least restrictive environment" (LRE). LRE rapidly moved from meaning the placement on the continuum that was most appropriate for a particular child to being the regular classroom for every child.

Contemporary legal usage of LRE had its origin in mental health cases in the 1960s, in which state mental institutions were required to allow patients to have such freedom of movement and activity, e.g., community week-end passes or home visits, as they could safely and appropriately handle. These activities and settings were less restrictive than locked wards or isolation. The concept of LRE did not translate readily into public education settings, but that didn't slow it down. Full inclusion advocates succeeded in amending IDEA to create a rebuttable presumption that a regular education classroom is the appropriate placement for every child when education there can be achieved satisfactorily. Unfortunately, "achieved satisfactorily" is not defined in IDEA and now is the subject of much litigation.

The REI, the full-inclusion philosophy and the misunderstanding of LRE coalesced into a movement which has decreased the "approval ratings" of special education in favor of general education. This has been a major factor in the rise of S-B IEPs, which are derived from the general education curriculum at the expense of the child's unique special education needs. As special education became more like general education and partially subsumed by it, some individualized, special education IEPs became standards-based, general education curriculum plans.

Ten years later, Diamond (1993) wrote that "the current buzzwords . . . in special education are integration, least restrictive environment, mainstreaming, the regular education initiative, and, most recently, inclusion. . . . [T]he handwriting on the wall could not be clearer." (p. 3)

IDEA 1997, NCLB AND USDOE

Close on the heels of the REI-inclusion-misconstrued LRE push of special education into general education came another factor. It, too, was a conglomerate of several components: (a) the IDEA 1997 language referencing the general curriculum and requirements related to state and districtwide assessments, (b) the *No Child Left Behind Act of 2001* (NCLB), and (c) the current emphasis of the US Office of Education on assessment and higher academic standards for all.

The 1997 IDEA Amendments added the mantra, "enabling the child to be involved in and progress in the general curriculum," which many special educators have interpreted to mean that special education must all be tied directly to the general curriculum. Neither the language of the statute nor the legislative history support this interpretation. Included among several congressional findings enumerated in IDEA 97 was the following:

> Over 20 years of research and experience has demonstrated that the education of children with disabilities can be made more effective by—
> (A) having high expectations for such children and *ensuring their access in the general curriculum* to the maximum extent possible . . . [7]

The Senate Report accompanying IDEA 97 explained that:

> The new emphasis on participation in the general education curriculum is not intended by the committee to result in major expansions in the size of the IEP or dozens of pages of detailed goals and benchmarks or objectives in every

curricular content standard or skill. The new focus is intended to produce attention to the accommodations and adjustments necessary for disabled children to access the general education curriculum and the special services which may be necessary for appropriate participation in particular areas of the curriculum due to the nature of the disability.

It seems clear that Congress did not intend special education to replicate or incorporate the general curriculum but rather to remove barriers—including the barriers of low expectations or inferior curriculum—for students with disabilities and increase their access to the general curriculum. However, neither IDEA 97 nor IDEA 2004 indicate in any way that all students with disabilities are expected to achieve grade level standards. The individualization so fundamental to the IDEA since its enactment in 1975 remains firmly in place, including the need to identify and appropriately address each student's unique educational needs.

NCLB and IDEA together currently require that all special education students (except the 1% who have the most serious intellectual disabilities) must take state and districtwide assessments (perhaps with some accommodations which do not affect scores), and that their performance be judged by the same grade level standards as nondisabled students. NCLB holds districts accountable for the progress of four specific subgroups of students—low-income students, English language learners, racial and ethnic minorities, and special education students. NCLB imposes sanctions on the school if adequate yearly progress (AYP) is not met by each of the four groups.

Some have interpreted NCLB as substituting general education standards for the individualization requirements of IDEA. One need only note that enactment of the 2004 IDEA Amendments followed the enactment of NCLB by three years, and yet Congress retained all of the components of IDEA that involve comprehensive individual evaluation and program planning based on student-specific evaluation information. While the state assessment mandate of NCLB imposes a higher level of accountability on schools for improved instruction and achievement for all students, it does not nullify the IDEA.

In short, the unfortunate journey from IEPs to S-B IEPs was fueled first by the beliefs that special education is not necessary, that it is inferior to general education and ought to be subsumed by it or merged into it. Next, the path to S-B IEPs was paved by legal requirements which are either not fully understood (LRE) or should be modified (NCLB), or both.

Finally, Secretary of Education Arne Duncan has now made improved student academic achievement a primary focus of the US Department of Education. This emphasis on higher academic standards has not made exceptions for those students whose disabilities make traditional academic achievement a low priority, or altogether irrelevant.

As important as these legal and historical factors have been, yet another terminological misunderstanding also played a major role in moving us from special education IEPs to standards-based IEPs. IDEA requires that IEPs specify the specially designed instruction (i.e., the special education) necessary for the child to access the general curriculum.[8] This access requirement has been widely misconstrued to mean that the special education student must be taught the general curriculum. Accessing the general curriculum does **not** mean teaching the general curriculum. Accessing the general curriculum requires certain basic skills and behaviors which are expected in a regular classroom, but which are not necessarily taught there. This thinking error is further compounded by the false perception that the IEP is supposed to contain the child's entire education program, rather than just the special services needed to meet his or her unique individual needs, as IDEA requires.

The basic IDEA legal framework remains intact and strong. It requires that individualized education programs (IEPs) be developed to address the child's unique educational needs. There is no requirement, legal basis, or logical foundation for believing that general education curriculum or standards should appear on an individualized plan for a special education student.

EVALUATING STANDARD-BASED IEPS

Proponents view standards-based IEPs (S-B IEPs) as a message of equality for students with disabilities, and a mechanism for ensuring that students with disabilities can participate in the general curriculum. Of course, no one would want to argue against either equality or an appropriate curriculum for each student. The question is how best to achieve equality and access to that curriculum.

The IDEA answers that question. Students with disabilities are entitled to have IEPs when regular education is inadequate to meet the unique needs arising from their disabilities. An IEP is supposed to describe a student's **disability-related learning needs** and the **special education and related services** the school will provide to address those needs. IDEA IEPs focus on special education, not general education.

In 1997, Congress amended the IDEA to strengthen the benefits offered to students with disabilities, and to impose a higher level of accountability upon state departments of education and local school districts. Permeating the amendments was an emphasis on "enabling the child to be involved in and progress in the general curriculum." Neither logic nor language indicate Congressional intent to replace special education with general education. Rather, the clear purpose of these provisions was to require schools to identify and address—on an individual basis—barriers to general education participation, progress, and achievement.

Barriers are not the same for all students with disabilities, for all students in the same disability category, or for all those at the same grade level. If barriers are not the same, IEPs designed to address those barriers cannot be the same. Although barriers do differ from one student with a disability to another; they also tend to clump around certain predictable skills.

The most common skill deficit interfering with academic achievement is in reading, with writing close behind. This is true across grade levels and across disability categories. Students who struggle with literacy flounder in all content classes, because progress in all academic areas requires the efficient intake of information through reading, and the expression of understanding through writing. Filling an IEP with grade level standards for either literacy skills or content knowledge skirts obstacles rather than facing them head on. Each individual student's set of skill deficits is unique and requires a correspondingly unique set of interventions, which is exactly why special education consists of **specially designed** instruction to meet the unique needs of this student.

Conforming their behavior to the demands of school is another common obstacle for students with disabilities, spanning grade levels and disability categories. Some grade level standards related to behavior exist, but these vague descriptions of generally appropriate behaviors are not designed to define—and cannot define— the specially designed instructional needs of an individual. Therefore, holding some special education students to the general student conduct code may be a violation of IDEA.[9]

The assessments required by IDEA are closely related to the students' IEP but are different from what would be necessary to plan an S-B IEP. To be properly individualized, as the IDEA requires, it is necessary to assess the specific needs of each student with a disability through comprehensive assessment, and to develop an IEP that describes equally specific goals and interventions. However, since the inception of IDEA in 1975, evaluation teams have expended most of their efforts to determine whether a student was eligible for special education.

In an effort to redirect the teams toward more useful ends, Congress added language to IDEA in 1997 requiring that the evaluation focus as well on the content of the child's individualized education program, including information related to enabling the child's participation and progress in the general curriculum. So, to develop an appropriate IEP for a specific student, teams must employ finer-grained assessments that measure a student's mastery of specific skills, to pinpoint those that

require **special** education intervention. All of the students' needs for special education and related services must be identified, whether or not they are commonly linked to the suspected disability.[10]

IDEA IEPs focus on the unique educational needs of the individual eligible student and the specially designed instruction and services to meet those unique needs. S-B IEPs, on the other hand, focus entirely on goals designed for others—for nondisabled students who perform at or near age/grade level. The "I" in both IDEA and IEP stands for "individual," a central fact that should not be overlooked. S-B IEPs violate the basic spirit and intent of IDEA to the extent they focus on anything other than the needs of the individual student who has a disability.

Some IEP teams try to have the best of both worlds. They develop goals with the needs of the individual student as their main focus, and then are required to search through the standards, looking for one from which each goal might have been (but wasn't) derived. Precious time is wasted for no purpose.

One of the most serious problems in deriving IEP goals, and therefore services, from standards is that meaningful parent participation is limited at best, denied at worst. Full and equal parent participation in IEP development is a critical element in IDEA, and anything that limits that participation violates the law. Parents may be told that the student's goals must be derived from, or at least aligned to, general education standards, but this is **not** true. Additionally, parents may not have sufficient access to the standards to be familiar with what the S-B IEP advocates are proposing as the goals for their child.

False hopes may be generated for parents who view the grade level standards and come to believe/hope their child may achieve those, when in fact that is not realistically possible, given our present knowledge and practices. This is clearly not a desirable outcome of the IEP development process.

The most critical question of all is whether an S-B IEP can appropriately address the real-word unique educational needs of the students.

After all, that is what the IEP and the IDEA itself are intended to do. Is there time in an S-B IEP for teaching essential functional skills such as toileting, dressing, personal hygiene, grooming and holding a job? If so, is it **enough time** to treat functional issues as the priorities they are?

Does an S-B IEP allow for a special education curriculum, rather than the general education curriculum, when a students' unique needs require it? For example, a student who is both deaf and blind needs a unique communication system and other unique supports across all settings. A student who is blind needs orientation and mobility training, perhaps including using a dog guide, a cane or more "advanced" technology. What benefit accrues to anyone from finding a general education standard under which these essential goals/services can be subsumed?

FROM S-B IEP ADVOCATES

The key to S-B IEPs is the alignment of the student's goals to the student's grade level academic content standards. Some S-B IEP advocates allow for a number of purely functional, nonacademic goals which do not have to be aligned. Others do not. All agree that alignment to general education academic standards must happen to some degree. The question of whether instructional time is being allotted appropriately must be raised.

Many S-B advocates believe that IDEA's requirement that the IEP provide "access to the general curriculum" is central, and that "access" means to allow a student to participate in an activity somehow related to what the nondisabled students are doing. Courtade-Little and Browder (2005) illustrate how Lester, who has severe disabilities, can address a sixth through eighth grade science standard, the essence of which is that "Gravity is a force [i.e.], the effects of the earth's gravitational pull and the motion of objects in the solar system [sic]" (p. 16). Lester will **help select the objects** his classmates will use in relevant experimentation and will **drop each** when told to do so. Lester may or may not

make great use of this dropping skill (assuming he masters the goal) in his later life. Participation in this experimental learning may or may not be the best use of the limited instructional time in science which is available to Lester.

In another example of relating (aligning) an activity to what others are doing Courtade-Little and Browder present the case of Camilla. Camilla is a 12-year-old seventh grader who has significant cognitive disabilities. She is a nonreader who does not communicate verbally, but who uses an alternative communication (AAC) device to greet people. Her IEP focused on increasing her use of 20 math and science words and symbols which were to be programmed into her AAC system. One of her "access" goals for science and social studies was to learn to select a picture on the computer from an array scanned from science or social studies text.

One more example of alignment as a parallel activity offered by Courtade-Little and Browder is Ramona, who has significant cognitive disabilities and is included in a tenth-grade English class even though she has no reading skills. The state standards for tenth-grade English target "understanding symbolism in poetry and other literature," and therefore Ramona's S-B IEP team will develop a goal for her using picture symbols to teach her the "more abstract symbols of poetry" (p. 13-14). They do not deal with the why or how of depicting abstract symbols. The alternate assessments used in Ramona's state test only academic, not functional, skills.

POSSIBLE DISADVANTAGES OF S-B IEPS

S-B IEPs may pose certain risks to parents, teachers and students who have disabilities, as well as possibly running afoul of IDEA.

Parents: Terms such as "developmental delay" have led many parents to ask when their child will catch up from this delay. Special educators have long used and developed euphemisms designed to lessen the impact of negative terms such as mental retardation and many others. The S-B focus on academic, grade level standards may well encourage some parents to have high expectations.

While it is helpful to have high expectations, it is clearly harmful if they are unrealistically high.

The S-B IEP process may lead parents to believe or feel that striving toward grade level academic standards is mandated by federal law, and that therefore truly individualized, appropriate goals (even if far from grade or age level) are not to be pursued. If this happens, the parents have inadvertently compromised their own ability to advocate for services that actually address their child's unique needs. The focus on academic standards and goals detracts not only from the students' unique needs but also from the specialized, individualized interventions to which they are entitled.

Teachers: Teachers and other IEP team members are properly concerned about making the best possible use of their time. Finding a standard under which a goal might have been, but was not, written does not qualify as best use. However, to first examine a standard and then create a somehow related goal defies the primary principle of first and foremost addressing the child's unique needs.

Another concern of IEP teams is that S-B IEPs are portable only to the extent the standards are the same in the new district (or state) as in the old, even though the student's needs have not changed.

Students: Many, perhaps most, IDEA-eligible students' needs are primarily in the areas of functional skills, basic skills, modifications and accommodations. Prior to 1997, according to Thurlow and Quenemoen (2011) IEPs provided special education services and an individualized curriculum different from that for nondisabled students. Then, "the 1997 and 2004 IDEA reauthorizations reinforced the new focus for IDEA of the same goals and standards applying to all students" (p. 137).

What IDEA actually says is that the IEP must "meet the child's needs that result from the disability to enable the child to be involved in and progress in the general education curriculum and meet each of the other educational needs that result from the child's disability."[11] The annual goals include academic and functional goals.

Millions of IDEA students have needs related to their disabilities which are not part of the general curriculum. These are the needs most likely to be overlooked or downplayed in the development of an S-B IEP. These functional skills include caring for one's body and clothing, daily living skills such as simple meal preparation, washing dishes, recycling, laundry, housecleaning, using public transportation, pedestrian skills, shopping, eating out, money management, sex education, job skills and more.

Advocates of S-B IEPs recommend that these functional skills be practiced within the context of general education academic routines. The wisdom, practicality and benefit of this approach may be questioned. The importance of direct instruction in vital functional skills is well established.

These functional daily living skills, plus many not enumerated, should be given priority over any other goals/objectives except the most basic pre-academic and academic skills related to the daily living skills. For students who have moderate and more severe disabilities, our responsibility is to provide the skills and knowledge they need to live, work, and play as independently as possible. The functional skills that are essential for them must be taught most carefully, using sequential small steps, often derived from task analyses and precise pedagogical techniques. Then these skills must be generalized across settings, persons and situations. They must be practiced to mastery and incorporated into regular routines. This kind of instruction requires an intense, skilled teaching focus, and it cannot be fragmented or subordinated to academic goals designed for other children.

IDEA students who have S-B IEPs based on the general curriculum are at risk of receiving only nonsequential fragments and tidbits from a watered down version of a curriculum designed for children who do not have disabilities.

These functional, daily living skills and many others are seldom, if ever, included in a general curriculum, unless the standards are so vaguely and broadly stated that anything and everything could be subsumed under them, e.g., "Navigate the world in school," "Live productively in one's environment" or "Relate to the person, places and activities in the community," etc. General curriculum statements such as these are useless, as is the process of copying them onto an S-B IEP.

Previously we discussed Lester, who selected and dropped objects in a seventh-grade science project; Ramona, who used picture symbols to learn the abstract symbols of poetry in tenth-grade English; and Camilla, who was to increase her use of 20 math and science words programmed into her alternate communication system. These activities arguably are not part of a cohesive, integrated curriculum. Nor do they appear to be leading to goals focused on unique needs of the individual students.

Special educators and parents must beware of S-B IEPs or anything else that threatens the right of a child who has a disability to a free appropriate public education. A huge part of "appropriate" means that the services are focused on meeting the unique educational needs of that child, and this is not the case with S-B IEPs.

References

Courtade-Little, G. & Browder D. (2005). *Aligning IEPS to academic standards.* Verona, WI.: Attainment Co.

Deno, E. (1970). Special education as developmental capital. *Exceptional Children, 37,* 229–237.

Diamond, S. (1993). Special education and the great god, inclusion. *Beyond Behavior, 4,* 2, 3–6.

Dunn, L. M. (1968). Special education for the mildly retarded—Is much of it justifiable? *Exceptional Children, 35,* 5–22.

Kauffman, J. M. (2010). *Curtains for special education: An open letter to educators.* Unpublished.

Stainback, W. & Stainback, S. (1984). A rationale for the merger of special and regular education. *Exceptional Children, 51,* 102–111.

Thurlow, M. & Quenemoen, R. (2011). Standards-based reform and students with disabilities. In J. M. Kauffman & D. P. Hallahan (Eds.), *Handbook of Special Education.* N.Y.: Routledge.

Will, M. (1984). Let us pause and reflect—but not too long. *Exceptional Children, 51,* 11–16.

Zigmond, N. & A. Kloo (2011). General and special education are (and should be) different. In J. M. Kauffman, & D. P. Hallahan, Eds (2011). *Handbook of Special Education.* Routledge, N.Y.

Notes

1. See, e.g., National Commission on Excellence in Education. *A Nation at Risk: The Imperative for Educational Reform.* (Washington, DC: Government Printing Office, 1983) and National Science Board Commission on Pre-College Education in Mathematics, Science and Technology, *Educating Americans for the 21st Century.* (Washington, DC: National Science Board, 1983).

2. http://www.corestandards.org

3. http://www.corestandards.org/frequently-asked-questions

4. http://www.corestandards.org/assets/application-to-students-with-disabilities.pdf

5. *Brown v. Bd. of Education,* 74 S.Ct. 686, 347 US 483 (1954).

6. *City of Cleburne v. Cleburne Living Center,* 105 S.Ct. 3249, 473 US 432 (1985).

7. 20 USC §1400(c)(5).

8. 34 CFR 300.39(b)(3)(iii).

9. See, e.g., *Onamia ISD #480,* 48 IDELR 235, (SEA MN 2007).

10. 34 CFR 300.304.

11. 20 USC §1414(d)(1)(A)(i).

CHAPTER SEVEN

New twists and old conundrums

teachers, administrators, academics, parents and other interested persons engage in lively discourse about special education policy and practice. This is good, as it encourages research on effective practices and inspires people to examine important social and political issues relating to education of children with disabilities. In 2004, Congress added a few interesting new twists to IDEA that will generate discussion, debate and confusion for some time to come. In this chapter, we will examine several features of IDEA that are likely to impact students' IEPs, and we will revisit some areas of continuing disputes in interpretation of the law.

SCIENTIFICALLY BASED INSTRUCTION

Amendments to the Elementary and Secondary Education Act of 1965, commonly known as No Child Left Behind Act of 2001 (NCLB), holds states accountable for high achievement for **all** students, including categories of students who have not achieved at high levels in the past. IDEA amendments expressly tie the aims and methods

of special education to NCLB. Both laws include powerful accountability measures for students with disabilities, and both mandate the use of scientific research based educational practices. We used to speak of law and best practice, as if they were unrelated. NCLB and IDEA have forced us to reconsider; federal law now offers incentives to adopt research-validated practices and potential penalties for failure to do so. We would be remiss if we did not emphasize this change and its implications for special educators. To develop truly effective IEPs, to ensure compliance with the law, and to select the best teaching methods for students with disabilities, school personnel, parents and state education agency staff should be familiar with the theory and practice of research based education.

What Does Scientifically Based Mean?

The emphasis in IDEA and NCLB on scientifically based instruction presents schools with an important question: What is scientifically based instruction? Scientifically based instruction, which may also be called research-based, research-validated, or evidence-based instruction, includes educational practices shown through a substantial body of research to improve student learning outcomes. Studies that yield credible evidence about what works conform to the following characteristics:

▶ **Relevant research question:** The research should address a question directly related to the educational effectiveness of a clearly defined practice, i.e. does the practice produce or contribute to student learning gains?

▶ **Experimental or quasi-experimental design:** Only through these study designs is it possible to infer a causal relationship between an educational intervention or strategy and a learning outcome. Correlational research does not demonstrate causation.

▶ **Replicable study design:** The design, procedures, data collection and analysis should be described in sufficient detail to enable replication of the study. The research report should also indicate fidelity of implementation of the intervention.

▶ **Alternative explanations ruled out:** The study must be designed so that outcomes cannot be attributed to causes other than the educational strategy being studied. This means controlling for other variables that might affect learning outcomes for study participants.

▶ **Generalizable findings:** To the extent that study participants accurately reflect the characteristics of a larger student population, research findings can generalize to that population. The most generalizable research uses randomly selected participants.

▶ **Peer review and publication:** Researchers establish the credibility of their work through peer-review, the process of subjecting their work to the scrutiny of other experts in their field, and publication in scholarly journals.

▶ **Confirmation of findings through replication:** The more studies that demonstrate the same effect or outcome

of an educational strategy, the stronger is a claim that the strategy causes the outcome.

Identifying, Selecting and Using Scientific Curriculum and Instruction

Schools should use scientifically based instruction that improves student achievement. But how can teachers determine what methods meet that requirement, and where can they find curricula? The elephant on the table in the discourse about scientific research-based curriculum and instruction is that relatively few commercially available curriculum materials rest on a solid research foundation. This situation is changing, however, due in part to the mandates of NCLB.

The current upsurge in scientific research in education does not entirely solve the problem. Even if scholarly journals were bursting with high-quality research on the effectiveness of educational practices relevant to students with disabilities, the information would not have immediate utility for teachers, related service providers and parents. Spanning the research-to-practice gap is challenging because primary research articles do not necessarily offer practical information, and teachers and parents have limited time and opportunity to loiter in university libraries, searching through scholarly journals. The best available options are to:

1. Carefully and critically review publishers' descriptions of the research basis for their curriculum materials.

2. Pursue professional development opportunities.

3. Read practitioner's journals that publish practical articles.

4. Consult personnel at state departments of education, especially those responsible for administering Title I, special education, and such grant-funded school improvement initiatives as Reading First.

5. Mine the internet, where boundless information is available.

Consumers of these resources need to shop with a critical eye, as snake oil is more readily available than research-validated remedies! Readers should be particularly wary of materials that speak of educational practices in terms of philosophy or opinion rather than evidence of effectiveness.

A detailed discussion of education research is beyond the scope of this book. On page 163 we have listed useful resources, several of which are free to download.

PREVENTING THE NEED FOR SPECIAL EDUCATION

The proportion of all the nation's students identified as disabled and IDEA-eligible rose steadily from 1976–77 through 2004-05, increasing from just over 8% to 13.8%. Beginning in 2005–06 the special education population began a steady decline, reaching 13.1% in 2009-10. Since 2000-01 there have been major shifts in the percentages of special education students within certain categories. Autism Spectrum Disorder has quadrupled from 1.5% to 5.8%. Other Health Impaired doubled from 4.8% to 10.6%, largely due to the popularity of the diagnoses of ADD and ADHD. The big drop has been in Specific Learning Disability from 45.4% to 37.5%. The differences among states are notable. Rhode Island, for example, identifies over 18% of the student population as disabled but Texas only 9.1%.[1]

The IDEA differentiates between children who struggle in school because they have disabilities and need specially designed instruction and those who struggle from lack of adequate instruction. High-quality special education is absolutely essential—legally and ethically—for children with disabilities. Although they are not eligible for special education, children without disabilities who experience learning difficulties also need effective and strong curriculum and instruction. IDEA authorizes states to use two mechanisms— early intervening services and response to intervention (RTI)—to distinguish children with disabilities who need special education from children with learning problems who progress once they receive better instruction.

Supporting All Students

It is useful to view early intervening services and RTI in the context of current trends in school reform. First, the federal government and the education research community increasingly advocate the use of curriculum and instructional methods shown through rigorous research to be effective. Second, the US Department of Education has invested heavily in strengthening reading readiness and instruction in the primary grades through grants to the states. Third, education researchers have developed models of whole-school reform calculated to address the academic and behavior support needs of all children, with or without disabilities, who are at risk for failure.

Though they vary in specific detail, such whole-school improvement models all: (a) incorporate research-based interventions that address basic academic skills or student behavior and discipline; (b) employ curriculum-based and norm-referenced measures to monitor all students' achievement; and (c) provide supplemental, intensive instruction for students who need it. Figure 7.1 illustrates a typical three-tiered model.

Tier 1 is the general curriculum, which incorporates evidence-based methods in the regular classroom. Instruction at this level is intended to prevent problems by providing the most effective teaching to all children. Given appropriate curriculum faithfully implemented by well-prepared teachers, the majority of students can achieve at or near grade level standards. Ongoing progress monitoring informs teacher decision making and alerts staff to students who do not meet grade level standards in this strong learning environment.

Tier 2 offers supplemental instruction to children who for a variety of reasons are progressing at a slower than expected rate. Perhaps as many as 15–20 percent of students may need Tier 2 services in addition to—not instead of—the regular curriculum. These children work in small groups of 4–6. Teachers use systematic and continuous assessment to monitor student progress. Children should not flounder in Tier 2 indefinitely. If they do

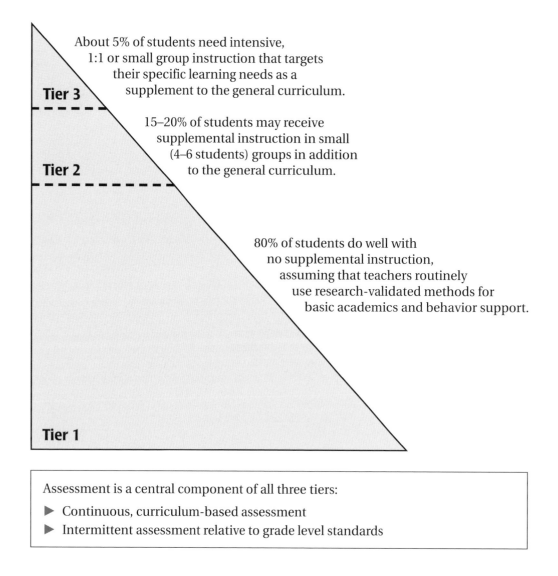

FIGURE 7.1 Tiered Intervention

Tier 3

About 5% of students need intensive, 1:1 or small group instruction that targets their specific learning needs as a supplement to the general curriculum.

Tier 2

15–20% of students may receive supplemental instruction in small (4–6 students) groups in addition to the general curriculum.

80% of students do well with no supplemental instruction, assuming that teachers routinely use research-validated methods for basic academics and behavior support.

Tier 1

Assessment is a central component of all three tiers:

▶ Continuous, curriculum-based assessment
▶ Intermittent assessment relative to grade level standards

not make good progress within a few weeks, they need to move on to Tier 3.

Tier 3 offers intensive, individually-designed instruction to individuals or very small groups of students with similar specialized needs. It serves the small percentage of students who were unable to progress adequately in the general curriculum even with supplemental instruction. Such slow or nonexistent progress raises suspicion of disability and should trigger a referral to special education.

The early intervening services and response to intervention processes encouraged by IDEA are

readily integrated with a whole school tiered system of student support.

Response to Intervention—LD Eligibility

In amending the IDEA, Congress sided with researchers who advocate an alternative to the discrepancy model of diagnosing learning disabilities that special educators have used almost exclusively for the past thirty years. IDEA now provides that schools may not be required to consider whether a child has a severe discrepancy between achievement and intellectual ability in oral expression, listening comprehension, written expression, basic reading skill, reading comprehension, mathematical calculation, or mathematical reasoning.[2]

Instead, schools may adopt a response to intervention (RTI) approach, which IDEA describes as "a process that determines if the child responds to scientific, research-based intervention as a part of the evaluation procedures."[3] If rigorous and continuous assessment shows that a student is progressing well, it is likely that the student does not actually have a learning disability but only needs more intensive and high-quality teaching. If a student continues to struggle even given stepped up instruction and more individual attention, it is likely that the student has a learning disability.

It is important to note that RTI cannot be the sole measure in a special education evaluation. IDEA continues to require that special education evaluations use a variety of assessment tools and strategies to gather relevant functional, developmental and academic information. Other information to review in determining whether a student has a disability and needs special education includes information from parents, classroom assessments, state assessments, teacher observations and standardized testing that the evaluation team deems necessary to determine whether a student has (or continues to have) a disability and, if so, to identify the student's unique special education needs.

The trap that awaits the unwary in implementing such innovative practices as tiered student support systems, early intervening services and RTI is the perception that such programs can meet the needs of all children. They cannot! IDEA continues to require individualization. These programs cannot legally substitute for or delay individual and comprehensive evaluations, as described in the statute and regulations, for students with suspected disabilities. Several recent rulings have made it clear that a students' participation in an RTI program cannot be allowed to delay an evaluation for IDEA eligibility. When a district suspects or has reason to suspect the student may have a disability, the entitlement to an evaluation arises and it must be conducted timely.

Nor can the district legally substitute for or delay the development and implementation of truly individualized educational programs, specifically described and conscientiously implemented in accordance with IDEA requirements.

Early Intervening Services

In order to prevent overidentification of disability, the IDEA permits states to spend up to 15% of their federal special education grants to develop and implement scientifically based approaches to reading instruction and behavior support for students at risk who have not been identified as eligible for special education.

These are called "early intervening services" and they should use supplemental instructional materials that have been developed to support and enhance the comprehensive core curriculum. NCLB requires that the core curriculum must meet rigorous scientific standards. The supplementary materials are aligned with and reinforce the research-based core.

These early intervening services are for children K–12 who have not been identified as needing special education, but who do need additional support.

What this means is that districts can use a substantial part of their federal special education dollars to fund general education services that may reduce the need for special education. Early intervening programs have both preventive and screening functions. They may forestall the development of learning or behavioral disabilities in some children by providing supplementary services to children at risk. It is important to note that early intervening services do not create an entitlement to special education, nor are they a substitute for special education.

Congress designed the early intervening services provision of IDEA to complement NCLB programs, although IDEA funds may not supplant NCLB funds. Early intervening services may include educational and behavioral evaluations, services and supports. The services may be provided at any grade level, but the law emphasizes scientifically based literacy instruction and behavioral interventions for student in kindergarten through third grade and professional development to prepare staff to use these methods.

Early intervening services may indeed prevent disability in some children, but they will certainly not eliminate the need and the legal right of other children with disabilities to special education. Teachers and other staff must be alert for children who flounder even while receiving early intervening services; this would constitute reason to suspect disability and thus require timely referral for special education evaluation.

Neither the IDEA nor the proposed regulations describe what early intervening services might look like, but current best practice should guide schools in their development and implementation. It is safe to anticipate they will resemble tier two services in the three-tier school improvement model described above. IDEA emphasizes literacy and behavior support but does not prohibit early intervening programs that address other academic skills.

FAPE AND QUALITY OF SERVICES

What is FAPE?

The purpose of IDEA is to make a free appropriate public education available to all children with disabilities. They are entitled to special education and related services designed to meet their unique needs, and to prepare them for further education, employment, and independent living.

The special education and related services must (a) be provided at public expense, under public supervision and direction, and without charge; (b) meet the standards of the State educational agency; (c) include an appropriate preschool, elementary school, or secondary school education in the State involved; and (d) be provided in conformity with the individualized education program.

Nothing is more fundamental to IDEA than the principle that every child with a qualifying disability is entitled to FAPE, but while the

meanings of free and public are clear, the meaning of appropriate is a little blurry. How do we know what is appropriate?

"Appropriate" is not necessarily "ideal." Though we might wish to afford every child an opportunity to maximize his or her potential, the IDEA does not require this. In the landmark *Rowley* case, the United States Supreme Court held:

> . . . Insofar as a State is required to provide a handicapped child with a 'free appropriate public education,' we hold that it satisfies this requirement by providing personalized instruction with sufficient support services to permit the child to benefit educationally from that instruction. Such instruction and services must be provided at public expense, must meet the State's educational standards, must approximate the grade levels used in the State's regular education, and must comport with the child's IEP. In addition, the IEP, and therefore the personalized instruction, should be formulated in accordance with the requirements of the Act and, if the child is being educated in the regular classrooms of the public education system, should be reasonably calculated to enable the child to achieve passing marks and advance from grade to grade.[4]

The Measure of Benefit

An IEP need not provide a superior education or maximize student potential, but it must offer meaningful educational benefit. How should we measure benefit? In the past, the courts have been split on this question and have quibbled about whether the measure should be prospective or retrospective, or whether trivial benefit (whatever that is) should be enough to satisfy IDEA requirements, or whether it was necessary to demonstrate some objectively measurable academic progress.

It is not a merely rhetorical question to ask whether setting the bar at an ill-defined minimal level is sufficient for students with disabilities today. It is a real question, and the answer is arguably no. It is hard to believe that Congress could have intended to establish high academic standards and an outcome-oriented educational policy, as it did with NCLB, but also endorse a policy requiring that

IEPs provide only a modicum of benefit for students with disabilities. Recent IDEA amendments appear to demonstrate an intent to strengthen special education services and to improve learning outcomes. IDEA 1997 appeared to hold districts to a higher standard by: (a) emphasizing the support of students in the general curriculum, (b) including students with disabilities in large-scale assessments, (c) requiring progress reports at regular intervals, and (d) providing that a lack of progress should trigger IEP revision. IDEA 2004 retained those provisions and added more that should encourage districts to take another look at appropriateness and benefit. Congress has not retreated from the position that special education should, to the extent appropriate for individual students, provide services that enable them to be involved in and make progress in the general curriculum.

Furthermore, the numerous explicit references to NCLB and to scientifically based instruction in IDEA 2004 suggests a determination to strengthen special education practices and to hold schools accountable for improving the academic achievement of all students, including those with disabilities.

Some courts have looked beyond mere procedural compliance and minimal benefit to examine both the substantive quality of the services students receive and demonstrated student benefit. The Sixth Circuit discussed this issue at length in *Deal v. Hamilton Co. Bd. of Ed.*[5] Its analysis, unlike many, reviews the big picture of IDEA, including all sections of the statute and its legislative history sections. It is worth reviewing in some detail:

> The facile answer to the question [of benefit] is that a school district is only required to provide educational programming that is reasonably calculated to enable the child to derive more than *de minimis* educational benefit. . . . At some point, however, this facile answer becomes insufficient. . . . A school district clearly is not required to "maximize each child's potential commensurate with the opportunity provided other children" . . . The Third Circuit, however, has held that an IEP must confer a "meaningful educational benefit." . . . [W]e agree that IDEA requires an IEP to confer a "meaningful

educational benefit" gauged in relation to the potential of the child at issue.

Rowley is the only Supreme Court decision to have addressed the level of educational benefit that must be provided pursuant to an IEP. Nothing in *Rowley* precludes the setting of a higher standard than the provision of "some" or "any" educational benefit; indeed, the legislative history cited in *Rowley* provides strong support for a higher standard in a case such as this, where the difference in level of education provided can mean the difference between self-sufficiency and a life of dependence.

An examination of the IDEA followed, and the court quoted the Findings section, where Congress noted that implementation of IDEA had suffered from low expectations for students with disabilities and "an insufficient focus on applying replicable research on proven methods of teaching and learning for children with disabilities." Furthermore, the statute authorized funding for teacher preparation, staff development and research all focused on the development and use of effective practices in special education. The court continued:

> At the very least, the intent of Congress appears to have been to require a program providing a meaningful educational benefit towards the goal of self-sufficiency, especially where self-sufficiency is a realistic goal for a particular child. Indeed, states providing no more than some educational benefit could not possibly hope to attain the lofty goals proclaimed by Congress.

The court faced head on school districts' natural preference for choosing the less costly of possible service options:

> Left to its own devices, a school system is likely to choose the educational option that will help it balance its budget, even if the end result of the system's indifference to a child's individual potential is a greater expense to society as a whole.

Because of this conflict of interests, "judicial intervention is necessary to fulfill congressional intent and serve the public interest" in disputes over expensive services, the court in *Deal* concluded.

Some legal scholars and a few lower courts agree with the *Deal* Court that the 1997 and 2004 Amendments to IDEA raised the standard for "appropriate" higher than the *Rowley* standard. However, the majority view of higher courts is that the *Rowley* standard is still the law, and that if Congress wishes to set a higher standard, it must do so explicitly.

Thorny Issues of FAPE: Some Things Old, Some Things New

Methodology

Methodology is inextricably entwined with appropriateness, and it will continue to be an issue with children who do not progress satisfactorily with the methods their schools have selected. As the court pointed out in *Deal*, "Indeed, there is a point at which the difference in outcomes between two methods can be so great that provision of the lesser program could amount to denial of a FAPE."

Issues of methodology have a uniquely polarizing effect, and many disputes between schools and parents about appropriate methodology have ended up in the courtroom. In *Rowley*, the US Supreme Court explained that: "Courts must be careful to avoid imposing their view of preferable educational methods upon the States. The primary responsibility . . . for choosing the educational method . . . was left to state and local educational agencies in cooperation with the parents . . . " The Court then noted that IDEA expressly requires states to disseminate and adopt promising educational practices. Clearly, the Court assumed that schools know about and employ effective, research-based methods.

It would appear that, in light of *Rowley* and based on the increasingly explicit statutory language about scientifically based instruction, when it can be shown that a school has chosen educational methods and strategies not based on credible, scientific research, courts owe no deference to the school's choices of curriculum and instruction. Should any doubt about this remain, IDEA 2004

includes new language in the section outlining required IEP components. Each IEP must now contain:

> (IV) a statement of the special education and related services and supplementary aids and services, *based on peer-reviewed research to the extent practicable,* to be provided to the child, or on behalf of the child, and a statement of the program modifications or supports for school personnel that will be provided for the child—
>
> > (aa) to advance appropriately toward attaining the annual goals;
> >
> > (bb) to be involved in *and make progress in* the general education curriculum . . . and to participate in extracurricular and other nonacademic activities; and
> >
> > (cc) to be educated and participate with other children with disabilities and nondisabled children [new language in italics].[6]

Congress has taken an unambiguous stand on methodology; schools must use effective methods.

State education agencies and schools are already scrambling in response to NCLB to improve teaching, learning and assessment, but it may take a while for the realization to set in that high expectations apply for all categories of students, including those with disabilities. At the same time, parents hope for the best possible education and outcomes for their students with disabilities. They will continue to press for the use of effective methods regardless of whether schools are prepared to provide them. Consequently, we can expect that disagreements between schools and families over methodology will continue into the indefinite future.

The student's disability category may be a significant determinant of whether a court will closely examine a district's choice of methodology. The areas that most frequently give rise to methodological disputes are specific learning disabilities, autism spectrum disorders, hearing impairments and deafness, and emotional-behavioral disabilities.

Parents of students with autism have been more successful than most in methodology-based challenges, perhaps because autistic children often make no measurable progress at all when the school chooses unsystematic or loosely-structured methods. It is difficult for a court to disregard the complaints of parents whose children do not benefit from the special education methods the school chose. A growing body of research demonstrates that 1:1 applied behavior analysis (ABA) is the most effective approach to use with most autistic children. The wiggle room for districts in the area of autism is the IDEA term "to the extent practicable." ABA is time and labor intensive and consequently expensive. Many districts have adopted programs that incorporate elements of ABA but with a higher student-staff ratio and fewer hours of service than the research recommends. To the extent that schools can achieve positive outcomes, courts may defer to their choices.

Students with learning disabilities, many of whom can make some progress regardless of what methods their teachers use, have had variable success in methodology disagreements. If a district can show that a student appears to get some benefit, as indicated by passing grades (often just barely), courts have in the past often looked no further. Many existing commercial curricula—some designed for whole school adoption and other for special education use—incorporate research-based principles and strategies. In the past, some school personnel have chosen other methods for a variety of reasons. They may use whatever methods they learned in their teacher preparation programs. They may use methods that they enjoy teaching, or that they think are fun for the children. In order to comply with IDEA they may have to put aside such considerations and use methods that have demonstrably promoted measurable learning gains.

A particularly interesting realm of methodology-related disputes involves students with hearing impairments. In these cases, choice of methodology implicates politics as well as program efficacy. One faction of the deaf community rejects what they see as stigma in the "medical model" of deafness. Instead, they identify themselves as a distinct cultural group with its own language,

American Sign Language (ASL). Since 1997, IDEA has required that IEP teams consider a set of special factors that includes:

> . . . in the case of a child who is deaf or hard of hearing, consider the child's language and communication needs, opportunities for direct communications with peers and professional personnel in the child's language and communication mode, academic level, and full range of needs, *including opportunities for direct instruction in the child's language and communication mode.*[7] [italics added].

Behavior

Misbehavior, as any teacher would readily attest, is a constant challenge in the classroom and other school settings, and students with disabilities probably contribute more than their fair share of school discipline problems. Of course, some children with disabilities violate rules or act out for reasons indistinguishable from the reasons those without disabilities misbehave. Others, however, exhibit problem behaviors that are directly or loosely tied to their disabilities. Some disabilities limit the ability to pick up behavioral norms and skills by observation. Some disabilities impair self-control or the ability to anticipate consequences. Children who have disabilities that cause or contribute to inappropriate behavior need explicit instruction and guided practice to meet expectations. And many children with disabilities misbehave out of frustration, or to distract attention from their academic skill deficits. They may take on the role of class clown, or they may be disruptive, sullen, or withdrawn. At issue in such cases is not behavior but academic learning and success.

IDEA requires districts to conduct evaluations that assess children in all areas of suspected disability. In addition, the regulations state that evaluations should be sufficiently comprehensive to identify all of a student's needs for special education and related services, even those not commonly associated with the suspected disability.[8] This provision seeks to ensure that districts gather enough relevant information to inform IEP development. IEP teams must consider the use of positive behavioral interventions and supports and other strategies to address behavior that impedes a student's learning or that of others.[9] Neither the statute nor the regulations indicate what "consider" means, but it surely does not imply talk without action. The goal is to alter the behavior so that the student and other students in the class can learn. In order to achieve that goal, the district should assess behavior (in all relevant school settings) and include behavioral intervention or other services in the student's IEP.

If a student commits an infraction, and the school proposes exclusionary discipline for more than 10 days, IDEA requires a Manifestation Determination. If the team concludes that the student's behavior was a manifestation of disability, i.e., that it was "caused by or had a direct relationship to" a disability, or that the district had failed to implement the student's IEP, the IEP team must develop a Behavior Intervention Plan (BIP). Neither the statute nor its regulations define BIP or explain how it differs, if at all, from the behavior support that should already be in the IEPs of students with a history of misbehavior. This policy vacuum has caused consternation in the few judicial cases in which BIPs were at issue.

Recently, several cases have focused on the appropriateness of BIPs. Courts have been generally liberal in their holdings. If the IEP addresses the need for change in behavior and contains strategies to use, the failure to provide a BIP does not violate IDEA.[10] A federal circuit court found that academic progress was adequate to show that a student who had autism had received FAPE, even though the behavioral problems remained severe.[11] Another court held that the district must address only in-school behavior and not behaviors that interfere at home or in the student's private placement.[12]

In *Alex R. v. Forrestville Valley Comm. Unit Sch. Dist. #221,* a disabled child's behavior deteriorated over several years until he became violent and posed a serious safety risk to staff and other students. The district responded with a series of meetings, program modifications and changes in placement. None of the strategies helped. The

Seventh Circuit Court acerbically pointed out the dearth of regulatory definitions and guidance, and concluded that it could not "create out of whole cloth" specific requirements for BIPs. The court treated the BIP requirement as procedural and concluded that the district's ineffectual plans satisfied IDEA requirements.[13] The Eighth Circuit Court has ruled that a BIP need not be in writing, provided it is actually implemented.[14]

When the law in insufficiently specific, as it is on the topic of behavior support and BIPs, we advise districts to draw upon the best, research-based practices available. Effectiveness in altering student behavior is not a matter of intuition or chance but is subject to observation, measurement and experimentation. A growing body of research on behavior support efforts points to the efficacy of whole school behavior support programs along the lines of the three-tier student support model discussed above. They incorporate positive behavior interventions and strategies, as IDEA requires, and are designed to address the behavioral instruction and service needs of all students through the use of research-validated strategies. Such a system nips in the bud many problems and offers expanded service opportunities for students who exhibit significant behavioral difficulties. Given the emphasis of IDEA on scientifically based practices, and the repeated allusions in the law to positive behavioral interventions and supports, we advise districts to implement well-researched programs and to include in students' IEPs behavioral goals and services designed to assist students to reach those goals.

Deletion of Mandatory Objectives

Prior to 2004, IDEA mandated the inclusion of measurable short-term objectives in IEP. It required IEP teams to define intermediate steps toward annual goals and establish an accurate assessment system to monitor a student's progress throughout the year. Unfortunately, special education personnel often filled IEPs with dozens of goals and objectives, sometimes imported wholesale from a computer program, from general curriculum standards, or from commercial curriculum materials, rather than focusing on the narrower set of specific skills and knowledge that individual students needed for meaningful participation in the general curriculum. Producing the goals and objectives took a great deal of teacher time—time that would have been better spent in instruction—and the IEPs often ended up being too cumbersome to be useful. Teachers and their professional organizations felt beleaguered by an imagined legal mandate to produce these bloated documents. The sensible solution would have been to clarify the law so that IEP teams could understand the utility of lean IEPs, narrowly tailored to address the special education needs of individual children.

Instead, Congress responded to the demands for paperwork reduction by eliminating short-term objectives from many IEPs. The good news is that many, perhaps most, districts recognize the value of short-term objectives, benchmarks or progress markers and are widely continuing to employ them. Those who choose to abandon them can be confident of IDEA compliance only by careful adherence to the letter of the law: (a) **Are all goals,** not just those addressing academic needs, **truly measurable?** (b) Do the goals address the individual student's learning needs, as identified in the present levels of performance (PLOPs)? (c) Are the goals demonstrably geared toward enabling the students to make progress in the general curriculum? (d) **How will the student's progress be measured** so that it is possible to determine whether the services are effective? (e) When will you give to parents reports describing the student's progress toward annual goals?

Without short-term objectives, it will much more difficult to gauge the student's progress and decide whether it is necessary to modify instruction or the IEP. With or without short-term objectives, the IEP will have to be defensible. If a parent files a complaint or requests a due process hearing, the district will need evidence that the IEP is being implemented, that the methods in use are scientifically based, and that the student is progressing appropriately.

DENIAL OF FAPE

A school substantively denies FAPE, as discussed above, when an IEP does not confer meaningful benefit on a student with a disability. Other district actions or inactions can also represent a denial of FAPE.

Procedural Violations

According to the Supreme Court in the *Rowley* decision, FAPE has both procedural and substantive components. Does or should this mean that any procedural deficiency in IEP development can be the basis for declaring a program inappropriate? School administrators reasonably fear an affirmative answer would leave districts vulnerable to endless litigation and expense. Congress addressed this concern in IDEA 2004, which now provides that a procedural violation denies FAPE only if the violation (a) impeded the child's right to a FAPE, (b) significantly impeded parents' opportunity to participate in decision making, or (c) caused a deprivation of educational benefits.[15]

While hearing officers clearly cannot find a denial of FAPE in minor procedural errors that have no impact on students' or parents' IDEA rights, school districts are not off the hook for gross violations of IDEA procedural requirements. Fortunately for school districts, courts and hearing officers are capable of distinguishing harmless errors from those procedural flaws that prejudice parents' and students' rights. The IDEA provision closely parallels judicial understandings of the procedural-substantive balance.

The Ninth Circuit Court of Appeals thoroughly reviewed the issue in *W.G. v. Target Range Sch. Dist.,* where it held that procedural errors invalidated the IEP and entitled the parents to reimbursement for the private schooling they had obtained. The court discussed the reasoning by which a court could find an IEP fatally flawed because of procedural errors:

When a district fails to meet the procedural requirements of the Act by failing to develop an IEP in the manner specified, the purposes of the Act are not served, and the district may have failed to provide a FAPE. The significance of the procedures provided by the IDEA goes beyond any measure of a child's academic progress during the period at issue.

Predetermination

One of the most common and serious IDEA violation occurs when a district selects, before the IEP meeting, the student's services or placement. Chapter Two discussed this problem and presented some real-world examples of meetings in which the district had predetermined services or placement. We revisit the issue here because of the ubiquity and gravity of this violation. IDEA **demands** that: (a) parents **must** have a voice in decisions about their children's special education; (b) school personnel **must** listen to and sincerely consider parents' concerns and preferences; (c) the student's needs **must** determine what services are offered; and (d) the placement decision **must** follow and be based on the IEP.

A typical predetermination scenario appeared in a Hawaii case in which the hearing officer wrote:

> [I]t is apparent that the DOE had predetermined the physical location of Kelii's placement. The parents were the only team members who knew Kelii. There was no team discussion about the physical location for Kelii's placement and no discussion about potential harmful effects. . . . Nor was there a consideration of alternatives. . . . Predetermination of a child's placement is a violation of IDEA because it deprives the parents of meaningful participation in the IEP process.[16]

In a clear example of predetermination, a district special education director coerced the IEP staff into selecting services and placements only from a preprinted list, based on budget and logistic concerns, regardless of what they believed the student actually needed. This procedure violated Section § 504 Regulations.[17]

In *Knable v. Bexley City Sch. Dist.,* the school failed for nine months to develop an IEP for a student who had been found eligible for special education as a child with a severe emotional-behavioral disability. The dispute revolved around placement, and the parents met with staff from the neighborhood school several times to discuss placement options. The district recommended a day treatment program, but the parents believed their son needed to be in a residential setting. Despite the parents' repeated requests, the district did not convene an IEP meeting. The district prepared a draft IEP only after the parents enrolled their son in a residential treatment facility. The Sixth Circuit Court rejected the district's argument that the parents caused the delay by refusing the district's chosen placement. The district's procedural violation of failing to hold an IEP meeting, and to develop an IEP, had deprived the student of educational opportunity and thus denied him FAPE, the court concluded.[18]

The Sixth Circuit Court dealt with a similar situation in *Deal v. Hamilton Co. Bd. of Ed.* as mentioned in Chapter Two. The parents of a young child with autism paid for 40 hours per week of home-based, one-on-one applied behavior analysis (ABA). The child also attended a district preschool. At the end of his first school year, the parents met with district staff to discuss extended school year services and requested that the district pay for the ABA program. The district refused and offered instead its own program for autistic children. The parents continued to provide intensive ABA services, insisting this was the appropriate program, and the district was steadfast in its refusal. The parents requested a due process hearing. The hearing officer found that the district had an unwritten policy of refusing to provide ABA for any child, regardless of individual needs, and of substituting its own less costly program. The dispute eventually made its way to the Court of Appeals, which ruled in favor of the parents. By categorically predetermining the child's services and placement, the district effectively excluded the parents from involvement in IEP development and denied FAPE to the child. According to the court:

Participation must be more than a mere form; it must be meaningful. . . . Despite the protestations of the Deals, the School System never even treated a one-on-one ABA program as a viable option. Where there was no way that anything the Deals said, or any data the Deals produced, could have changed the School System's determination of appropriate services, their participation was no more than after the fact involvement.[19]

One of the most risky procedural errors is to exclude parents from genuine participation in decision making. Schools have often treated parents as passive observers, while staff made decisions. Even worse, some school personnel display adversarial attitudes toward parents. This is contrary to the design of the law. The IDEA establishes a rich array of parent rights and has upheld the rights of parents as partners with the schools in making educational decisions about students with disabilities. In 1997 and again in 2004, Congress reaffirmed and strengthened the parents' role in decision making. Infringing parents' right to participate in decision making constitutes a denial of FAPE. The US Supreme Court explained:

> It seems to us no exaggeration to say that Congress placed every bit as much emphasis upon compliance with procedures giving parents and guardians a large measure of participation at every stage of the administrative process . . . as it did upon the measurement of the resulting IEP against a substantive standard.[20]

When courts fail to find predetermination, it is usually because they believe that parents participated in a meaningful way, the school personnel had open minds, or placement options were seriously discussed. District personnel can come to the meeting with suggestions and opinions, but must be open to more than one course of action.

The lesson from these cases is simple: Procedural requirements are not simply paper formalities that districts can neglect with impunity. Courts and hearing officers are growing especially impatient with district predetermination of services or placement which subverts the "evaluation → IEP → placement" sequence of IDEA and/or precludes genuine and meaningful parent involvement.

Failure of IEP Implementation

Parents sometimes express frustration because they believe the school is not fully or correctly implementing their child's IEP. School staff may feel similarly frustrated when the district cannot or does not make available services that the IEP team has decided the student needs.

The federal appellate courts that have addressed the question are in essential agreement that a school is to be granted some leeway in IEP implementation. But how much? If an IEP specifies 20 hours a week of special education and the student receives 19, is that sufficient? 15? 10? And so on. If the IEP calls for small group reading instruction, is a group of 20 small? 10? 6?

The Fifth Circuit Court requires a failure to implement substantial or significant provisions of the IEP in order to find a violation,[21] while in the Eighth Circuit Court, IDEA is violated when the school fails to implement an "essential provision of the IEP that was necessary for the child to receive an educational benefit." Applying this standard requires consideration of both the shortfall in services and the progress of the child.[22]

The Ninth Circuit Court has adopted a "materiality" standard, i.e., more than a minor discrepancy between what was provided and what the IEP required. This standard does not require a showing of educational harm, but the child's progress or lack of it may be considered in determining the materiality of the failure.[23] The dissent in this case argued vigorously that such a standard was unworkably vague, and inconsistent with the language of IDEA, which says services must be provided "in conformity with" or "in accordance with" the IEP.[24] The dissent proposed a per se rule where **any** deviation in implementation of the IEP would violate IDEA.

Some understanding of how these lines are drawn can be gleaned from a sampling of actual implementation failures. In an easy case, the district offered only 1½ hours a week of reading instruction to a student for whom 20 hours of intensive reading teaching per week had been recommended. Private reading services were awarded.[25]

A district denied FAPE when it failed from September to January to provide the 20 hours per week of special education required by the IEP, failed to give prior written notice of a proposed amendment to the IEP, and did not ensure that the reading teacher attended the entire IEP amendment process.[26]

FAPE was denied when daily "special education teacher support services" were provided on only 74 of 97 days,[27] and when a student whose IEP said no time was to be in general education was placed there 32% of the time.[28] FAPE was also denied by a failure to provide: (a) specified instructional materials;[29] (b) Braille, mobility training, and progress reports;[30] and (c) peer tutoring.[31]

The failure to implement behavior intervention plans (BIPs) is a common problem, and legal decisions are often based on the egregiousness of the failure and its behavioral consequences. When some teachers didn't know that a BIP existed and others were misinformed about its provisions, a violation was found.[32] Similarly, if misbehavior which has resulted from a failure to implement the BIP has serious consequences, such as severe injury, a violation will probably be found.

The district staff responsible for IEP implementation must be informed of their specific responsibilities, as well as the modification and supports required by the IEP. In a Minnesota hearing the district did not have an appropriate plan for offering the concrete, positive reinforcers the student's IEP required. In a finding of interest to many schools, the general classroom behavior rules did not meet this IEP's requirement for individualized, clearly defined behavioral limits.[33] Another issue in the implementation of BIPs is that frequently a BIP is implemented, if at all, by only

one teacher and not by all the other adults in the student's daily life at school.[34]

The frequent intertwining of IEP development and implementation issues was well illustrated in a case involving the provision of physical therapy and speech/language therapy. The district: (a) did not monitor how much therapy was given to students with severe disabilities; (b) provided only "consultation" in lieu of actual therapy because of staffing shortages; and (c) provided only medically necessary physical therapy and ignored educational needs, due to a contract with an outside agency.[35]

A language arts teacher's failure to implement the test-retake provision in a student's IEP constituted a denial of FAPE, when the teacher did not have a copy of the IEP and the wording in the IEP was unclear.[36] FAPE was also denied when an unqualified teacher who had no degree in education, no certification in any state and no experience in special education, was unable to implement an IEP.[37]

Often, the failure to deliver all the services specified on the IEP is due to related service personnel's absence or to scheduling problems. Other problems commonly occur when district personnel, some or all, simply fail to use the IEP to guide educational activities and services.

IEPs are the heart and soul of IDEA. However, legally compliant IEP development and content are wasted when a district fails to implement the IEP.[38]

CONSEQUENCES OF DENIAL OF FAPE

District personnel rightly fear a legal finding that a student's program is inappropriate. Such a finding can be very expensive if the child's parents have given up on the public school and unilaterally placed their child in a private school. The US Supreme Court in *Florence Co. Sch. Dist. Four v. Carter* spoke loudly and clearly to those districts that fear the financial consequences of failing to make a free, appropriate program available to a student who has a disability:

... [P]ublic education authorities who want to avoid reimbursing parents for the private education of a disabled child can do one of two things: give the child a free appropriate public education in a public setting, or place the child in an appropriate private setting of the State's choice. This is IDEA's mandate, and school officials who conform to it need not worry about reimbursement claims . . .[39]

The relief measures that courts most frequently order upon finding that districts have denied FAPE are reimbursement for private school placement and compensatory education.

Reimbursement for Costs of Private School

Reimbursement for a unilateral placement in a private school is one of the most common equitable remedies available to parents when a district fails to make FAPE available to their child. In *Burlington Sch. Comm. v. Mass. Dept. of Ed.*, the US Supreme Court established the rule that parents are entitled to reimbursement for private school placements when the district's offered program is not appropriate under *Rowley,* and the private placement is appropriate.[40] The Court added, in *Carter,* that private placement need not be state-approved and suggested (but did not hold) that reimbursement may be limited to that which is reasonable.

The Ninth Circuit Court dealt with this issue in *Capistrano Unified Sch. Dist. v. Wartenberg.* A 16-year-old boy with learning disabilities, attention deficit disorder and a conduct disorder had a long history of school failure and behavior problems. After the district offered an IEP that seemed to provide even fewer services than the several previous unsuccessful IEPs, the parents enrolled their son in a private school and sought reimbursement from the district. The district alleged that their offered IEPs were appropriate, and that the boy's continuing academic failures resulted from misbehavior rather than disability. After rejecting this theory, the court applied the *Burlington* test, and awarded full reimbursement of private school expenses to the parents. Particularly persuasive was the fact that, after years of dismal failure, the boy began making academic progress in the highly structured environment of the private school, which offered a high teacher-student ratio, teacher and classroom continuity throughout the day, and a comprehensive behavior plan.[41]

Initially silent on the question of reimbursement for unilateral placement, IDEA adopted the *Burlington* rule and now explicitly provides that parents may receive reimbursement for unilateral placement, if the district "had not made a free appropriate public education available to the child in a timely manner prior to that enrollment."[42]

However, parents who unilaterally place their children in private schools do so at their own risk, as there is no assurance of reimbursement. Reimbursement may be reduced or denied if:

▶ the parents did not notify the district of their dissatisfaction with the IEP and their intent to enroll the student in a private school at the most recent IEP meeting, or if they did not give the district notice in writing at least 10 business days before removing the student from public school.

▶ before the parents removed the student from the public school, the district notified the parents in writing of its intent to evaluate the student, but the parents did not make the student available for such evaluation; or

▶ upon a judicial finding that the parents' actions were unreasonable.[43]

Reimbursement for the private school placement will not be denied if

▶ the district prevented the parents from giving notice;

▶ the parents did not receive notice of the notice requirement;

▶ the parent is illiterate or unable to write in English; or

▶ compliance with the notice requirements would likely result in serious emotional harm to the student.[44]

The Fifth Circuit Court decision in *Cypress-Fairbanks Ind. Sch. Dist.* illustrates the risk parents incur when they seek reimbursement for unilateral placement in private school. In that case, the court applied a four-part test to the district's program, asking whether: (1) the program is individualized on the basis of the student's assessment and performance; (2) the program is administered in the least restrictive environment; (3) the services are provided in a coordinated and collaborative manner by the key stakeholders; and (4) positive academic and nonacademic benefits are demonstrated. The court quickly answered yes to the first three questions and then concluded that the answer to the fourth question was also yes because the child, who had attention deficit hyperactivity disorder (ADHD) and Tourette Syndrome, had earned passing grades and was able to engage in some routine tasks without supervision. The court not only denied reimbursement to the parents, but also ordered the parents to pay costs of litigation, a highly unusual result.[45]

Another issue that arises in the private placement reimbursement is whether the parent-selected private school must meet the LRE requirements of IDEA in order to be appropriate, and therefore reimbursable. Three Circuit Courts—the Third, Sixth, and Eighth—have held LRE does **not** apply to private placements. The other circuits have not yet ruled.[46]

Compensatory Education

If a student did not attend private school, tuition reimbursement is not an appropriate remedy for district failure to provide a FAPE. Increasingly, the courts have held that compensatory education is an equitable way to compensate a student for the loss.

In one Minnesota case, a federal district court awarded compensatory damages as a consolation prize for a family that had sought private school tuition reimbursement. The school had failed for two years to provide an appropriate program because the student's IEP did not include present levels of performance, and did not address all of the student's individual needs. The court, however, refused to order reimbursement for the private school into which the parents had unilaterally placed their son, because that school also failed to provide an appropriate program. Instead, the court awarded two years of compensatory education in the public school.[47]

Compensatory education can include supplementary instruction or therapy services during school hours, after school tutoring or other services, or extended school year. Courts can also order compensatory education after a student ages out of special education. In one such case, the district, in addition to other serious IDEA violations, had denied an aide to a student who could not attend school without one and thus deprived her of a FAPE for three years. When she turned 22, the school claimed it had no further obligation to her. The court held that she was entitled to three years of compensatory education beyond her 22nd birthday and said the IEP team should determine the exact nature of those services.[48]

No clear standard exists for determining a fair amount of compensatory education. In *Reid v. District of Columbia,* the court ordered compensatory education for a 16-year-old student with severe learning disabilities. The district conceded that it had failed the student by not referring him to special education though his reading achievement was in the bottom 5% in reading. Even after being found eligible for special education, he continued to decline, and the district responded first with ineffective incremental increases, and later reductions in special education services. A hearing officer found that the student had been denied FAPE for 4 ½ years and ordered 810 hours of compensatory education, an hour for every day of services denied. The court of appeals said the determination of the amount of damages should be a qualitative rather than a quantitative process; the basis of the decision should be the facts of the individual situation and the students needs rather than a standardized formula. Furthermore, the court explained, the compensatory education must actually compensate rather than aim for a low standard such as "some" benefit.[49]

Of course, compensatory education cannot truly compensate for inappropriate special education or failure to deliver IEP services any more than compensatory damages can compensate for the loss of a leg crushed in a car accident.

Damages

In some cases, parents have sought monetary damages in actions against school districts for failure to provide FAPE. Courts have generally held that damages are not available under the IDEA because the statute does not expressly authorize the award of damages, but a few interesting cases have left the door ajar.

In *Emma C. v. Eastin*[50] a federal district court in California, holding that damages might be available, declined to dismiss a class action suit in which a group of children sought compensatory damages. The court looked at the IDEA section authorizing courts to "grant such relief as the court determines is appropriate" (20 U.S.C. § 1415(e)(2)) and found no bar to damages. Furthermore, the court noted a US Supreme Court decision[51] holding that monetary damages were available under Title IX of the Education Amendments of 1972 (20 U.S.C. §§ 1681), a statute that also lacked specific authorization of damages. In that case, the Court said that "The general rule, therefore, is that absent clear direction to the contrary by Congress, the federal courts have the power to award any appropriate relief in a cognizable cause of action brought pursuant to a federal statute."

In some circumstances, parents may seek money damages under other laws, such as the federal tort claims statute, Section 1983, or Section 504 of the Rehabilitation Act of 1973, for IDEA violations. In one such case, a federal district court found an administrator personally liable for unreasonably changing a student's placement without first determining whether that placement would be appropriate. The court held that the parents did not need to demonstrate heightened culpability such as reckless disregard, but that negligence

was sufficient to sustain a Section 1983 claim.[52] (See earlier discussion of *Mark H. V. Hamamoto* awarding damages under § 504.)

Exhaustion of Administrative Remedies

Normally, a parent must exhaust IDEA administrative remedies (i.e., go to a hearing) before pursuing a civil action, but there are exceptions to this rule. When a mother sued a school district under Section 1983 for intentional infliction of emotional distress through its "deliberate indifference" and failure to implement the IEP of her autistic son, since no remedy is available under IDEA for a parent's alleged emotional injury, the court held that the mother was not obligated to exhaust administrative remedies.[53]

In another case, *McCormick v. Waukegan Sch. Dist. #60*, a student suffered permanent and life-threatening injury when a teacher ignored the IEP. The student had a genetic metabolic disorder that reduced his stamina and his ability to participate in vigorous activity. His IEP specified that he was to have adapted PE with limited exertion. A PE teacher disregarded the IEP and insisted that the student run laps and do pushups, threatening him with a failing grade if he did not comply. As a result, he incurred permanent kidney damage that created a need for dialysis. His parents brought suit under IDEA, and both state and federal tort laws seeking damages for his physical and emotional injuries. The court held that exhaustion of remedies was not required, explaining:

> The nature of his claim is not educational; no change to his IEP could remedy, even in part, the damage done to Eron's body. By adding an intentional infliction of emotional distress claim to his complaint, Eron only seeks to recover for the arguably outrageous actions of Neterer, the physical education instructor. He does not allege any ongoing emotional difficulties that might be addressed through IDEA. After closely examining the "theory behind the grievance" in Eron's complaint, we are convinced that it would be futile for Eron to exhaust the administrative process under the circumstances of this case because IDEA does not provide a remedy for

his alleged injuries, which are non-educational in nature.[54]

Enlightened self-interest dictates the necessity of IDEA compliance, both procedural and substantive, as failure to comply can be far more costly than the development and scrupulous adherence to an appropriate IEP.

LEVEL PLAYING FIELD

Before IDEA, students with disabilities and their parents were all but powerless to challenge the decisions that schools made. Congress set out to change that in 1975, when it wove an elaborate web of substantive and procedural rights for eligible students and their parents into IDEA (then called the Education for All Handicapped Children Act). The intent was to level the playing field so school districts could not roll over parents in a lopsided game. Parents were to be, as the US Department of Education explained, equal participants with the schools. In most districts, the reality of school-parent partnership departs from the ideal, and courts have often emphasized the judge-made rule of deferring to the professional choices of educators at the expense of the statutory scheme of parent involvement. So how level is the playing field now?

In a move many believe to have tilted the playing field, the Supreme Court ruled in *Schaffer v. Weast*[55] that the party challenging an IEP has the burden of proof, unless the state provided otherwise prior to 2005. This means the parent, who has far less access to records and other relevant information than does the district, must produce more persuasive evidence than does the district in order to prevail. This plus the Supreme Court's denial of expert witness fees[56] to a prevailing party now places the parent in a difficult-to-impossible position in the view of many.

Parent Consent

One important parent right under IDEA has always been the obligation of the district to secure parent consent before initial evaluation and before initial placement in special education. Consent means that:

(a) The parent has been fully informed of all information relevant to the activity for which consent is sought, in his or her native language, or other mode of communication;

(b) The parent understands and agrees in writing to the carrying out of the activity for which his or her consent is sought, and the consent describes that activity and lists the records (if any) that will be released and to whom; and (c)(1) The parent understands that the granting of consent is voluntary on the part of the parent and may be revoked at any time.[57]

IDEA also includes a clause that relieves districts of the obligation to hold an IEP meeting or develop an IEP if parents have not given consent.[58] If taken literally, this suggests that parents would have to consent to special education and related services before knowing what special education and related services the district proposes to offer. Of course, this conflicts with the requirement for informed consent and could lead to backward, circular and time-wasting situations in which the parent consents, the IEP team meets and develops an IEP, the parent disagrees with the IEP and revokes consent, the team meets again and revises the IEP, etc. Presumably the intent of Congress was to accommodate parents who do not want their children to receive special education at all, and to protect districts from liability if such parents changed their minds and sought retroactive services. This is reasonable; school districts should not be liable for failure to provide services that parents have unambiguously rejected. It is not reasonable to expect parents to give blind consent.

In a situation where parents have joint custody and educational decision making authority, the federal office of Special Education Programs (OSEP) has at least twice asserted that if one parent consents to special education services and the other does not, the district may **not** serve the child. This rule raises an interesting question: If special education is beneficial to eligible children who need it, and if IDEA is about what is appropriate for children, why should the negative parent have veto power? It will be interesting to see how courts of the future deal with this situation. We should all note that OSEP's views do not have the force of law, but may be given some deference.

Parent Participation

Integral to the design of IDEA is the substantive involvement of parents in assessing student needs and planning how to address those needs. In its Findings section, IDEA 2004 states that:

> (5) Almost 30 years of research and experience has demonstrated that the education of children with disabilities can be made more effective by . . .
>
> > (B) strengthening the role and responsibility of parents and ensuring that families of such children have meaningful opportunities to participate in the education of their children at school and at home. . . .[59]

State education agencies and local school districts must have in place policies and procedures that ensure the opportunity for parents to participate in meetings related to the identification, evaluation, program and placement of their children. "Participate" is the operative term. The school must enable meaningful participation in discussion and decision making. Mere attendance at meetings satisfies neither the spirit nor the letter of the law. The requirement applies to all meetings in which decisions will be made except for routine meetings among staff to discuss day-to-day instructional planning necessary to implement an existing IEP.

Courts enforce the parent participation mandate inconsistently. The Ninth Circuit case, *W.G. v. Target Range Sch. Dist.,* established the rule that, unlike most procedural errors, diminishing the parents' role or excluding parents from decision making is per se a denial of FAPE.[60] Recent decisions affirm the essential role of parents in designing their children's special education. Precluding parent participation through staff predetermination of services or placement egregiously violates IDEA. School districts should be aware that courts have become more alert to this problem and less likely to excuse it.

Professionals Versus Parents

Ever since the Supreme Court decision in *Rowley,* courts have noted their own lack of expertise in education and repeated the assertion that courts should not substitute their own ideas for the professional judgment of educators. Some courts have overgeneralized that principle and have deferred to the decisions of educators at the expense of the parents' role. In a recent case, an administrative law judge (ALJ) had disregarded the testimony of the parents' expert witnesses and ruled in favor of the school district. A federal district court disagreed, and entered summary judgment for the parents. In reversing the trial court's decision, the Fourth Circuit Court of Appeals made the astounding statement that:

> The ALJ correctly recognized that while [school] and [parent] experts disagreed, IDEA requires great deference to the views of the school system rather than those of even the most well-meaning parent.[61]

A conscientious reading of the IDEA, its legislative history, and its implementing regulations produce no support for this sweeping diminution of the parents' role; in fact, it is utterly contrary to the structure of the law and its plain language.

Perhaps regretting its rash decision in *A.B.,* the Fourth Circuit Court reached the opposite conclusion only a year later. In *Henrico Co. v. Z.P.,* a hearing officer determined that a district had denied FAPE to a child with autism by using the TEACCH curriculum, from which he did not benefit, rather than the parents' preferred ABA methodology. The district defended its choice with testimony about the successful use of TEACCH with children who have autism. The federal district court criticized the hearing officer's fact-finding as "irregularly made" because it favored the parents' witnesses over the generic testimony of the district's witnesses. The court of appeals reversed, again emphasizing the obligation of federal courts to give deference to the factual findings of hearing officers, and citing with approval the hearing officer's assertion that determinations of appropriateness must consider the needs of the individual child:

To conclude that the hearing officer erred simply because he did not accept the testimony of the School Board's witnesses, an argument that the School Board comes very close to making, would render meaningless the due process rights guaranteed to parents by the IDEA. . . . [I]f the hearing officer had relied on the parents' witnesses to conclude that the [district's] program was a bad one, then we might agree with the School Board's position that the hearing officer's findings do not warrant any deference. The hearing officer, however, accepted and acknowledged that students had benefitted from the Twin Hickory program. . . . The hearing officer relied on the testimony of the parents' witnesses to conclude that Z.P.'s unique problems made the Twin Hickory program inappropriate for Z.P.; the hearing officer did not conclude that the Twin Hickory program was inappropriate for all autistic students. Given the basis for the hearing officer's conclusion that the IEP did not provide Z.P. with a free appropriate education, it was entirely proper for the hearing officer to rely primarily on the testimony of the parents' witnesses.[62]

Placement

A significant number of IDEA cases present a fact pattern where the parents believe the public school is not providing FAPE to their child, and they eventually remove the child to a private school, often a special education school serving children with similar disabilities. The parents then seek reimbursement, and the district argues they are not so entitled because the specialized school is not the LRE. The question presented sounds deceptively simple: Does the LRE preference of IDEA apply to a private, parentally chosen specialized school when the public school has not provided FAPE?

Twenty years ago, the US Supreme Court held in *Burlington v. Dept of Ed.,* that parents' violation of the IDEA's "stay-put" provision (regarding placement) did not bar reimbursement for the private school they had selected when the district failed to provide FAPE.[63] In 1993, the US Supreme Court ruled in *Florence Co. Sch. Dist. Four v. Carter* [64] that the IDEA requirement that districts' programs must meet state standards does not apply to parent placements. In that case, the

parents had unilaterally removed their ninth-grade daughter from the public school and placed her in a private academy that served only children with disabilities. The court awarded reimbursement to the family and did not discuss LRE.

Between the *Burlington* decision of 1985 and *Carter* in 1993, a New Jersey state court heard a case *(Lascari v. Ramapo Indian Hills Reg. H.S.),* where the parents had removed their child to Landmark, a residential school well known for its outstanding program for students who have LD. The district argued that Landmark was not the LRE, and therefore the parents could not receive reimbursements. The court rejected that argument and awarded tuition reimbursement.[65]

Prominent among the few cases that have actually analyzed this issue of whether a parent's placement must meet the LRE preference of IDEA is *Cleveland Heights-Univ. Heights City Sch. Dist. v. Boss.* Based on *Burlington* and *Carter,* the Sixth Circuit Court held that the failure of the specialized school—Landmark—to meet the LRE preference of IDEA did not bar the parents from receiving full reimbursement.[66]

The Third, Seventh and Eighth Circuits Courts also recognize that LRE was not intended to promote integration with nondisabled peers at the expense of an appropriate education, and that therefore LRE does not apply when the district has failed to make FAPE available.[67,68,69] Surprisingly few cases have squarely addressed this issue. In those cases in which the issue has arisen, the courts have sometimes held, without a stated rationale, that the schools in which the parents placed their children were not the LRE compared to the public school, e.g., the Fourth Circuit Court held without analysis in *A.B. v. Lawson*[70] that the LRE **does** apply to parents' placements. It is hard to understand how—or even if—these courts reconciled their decisions with the Supreme Court's decisions in *Burlington* and *Carter,* or with the plain language of IDEA.

If LRE did apply to parents' placements made after the district failed to provide FAPE, the parents would be on a severely tilted playing field. In their search for an appropriate program for their child, they would not be able to select a highly specialized school that exclusively served children whose disabilities were similar to those of their child. In other words, they would be barred from seeking the exact sort of program designed to meet their child's unique needs. Surely that cannot be the intent of IDEA.

Attorney's Fees

An area in which IDEA 2004 undermines parents is in attorney's fees. In 1986, IDEA was amended to allow prevailing parents to recover reasonable attorney's fees in successful hearings and court actions. The IDEA amendments of 1997 and 2004 excluded IEP meetings and state complaint resolution from the proceedings for which parents might recover attorney's fees, and also provided for a reduction in awards under certain circumstances. Additionally, IDEA now authorizes courts to award reasonable attorney's fees to state education agencies or local school districts if (a) the parents' case is frivolous, unreasonable or without foundation; (b) if litigation is prolonged inappropriately; or (c) if the purpose of the actions is improper, such as to harass or delay.[71]

Schools and parents are not equally positioned in special education disputes. School districts have easy and constant access to legal advice and services at taxpayer expense. Many parents, on the other hand, have great difficulty finding an attorney knowledgeable about special education law, and even more difficulty marshalling the financial resources to pay the costs of a hearing and possible appeals. The changes in IDEA in 1997 and 2004 regarding attorney's fees tip the balance even further in the districts' favor. The threat of awarding attorney's fees to school districts can have a chilling event on parents' exercise of their rights; the reality is that some parents have now effectively lost access to due process hearings and civil suits.

Fortunately, IDEA also requires states to offer mediation services[72] and state complaint investigations.[73] Mediation allows parents and schools to formulate mutually acceptable solutions to disagreements through a negotiation process facilitated by an impartial trained mediator. Mediation works well when both parties are interested in identifying common interests and reaching a win-win solution. State complaint investigation, a robust dispute resolution mechanism, takes the problem out of the hands of the parties and turns it over to the state education agency, which investigates the facts that sparked the disagreement and determines whether the district was in compliance with IDEA. Both mediation and state complaint investigation processes are available to parents at no cost.

Very few parents can prevail in a hearing or in court without using expert witnesses, which typically cost thousands of dollars. Nevertheless, in 2006 the US Supreme Court ruled in *Arlington v. Murphy*[74] that parents, when they prevail, may not recover the costs of their experts. In a strong dissent Justice Breyer argued that the legislative history of IDEA establishes that Congress intended that prevailing parents would recover expert fees as well as attorney fees. Apparently he was correct. The IDEA Fairness Restoration Act (S. 613 and H.R. 1208) was introduced in Congress in 2011 and, as of this writing, is widely predicted to become law. If it passes, Congress will have overridden the Supreme Court and assured parents who prevail under IDEA that they can recover experts' fees as well as attorneys' fees.

CONCLUSION

The IDEA has evolved throughout its 35-year history. Congress has occasionally subtracted from it but more often has added to it, with the express purpose of strengthening special education and reaffirming the substantive and procedural rights it confers upon children with disabilities and their parents. Debate and confusion ensue with every change. Advocacy groups and professional organizations busily promote interpretations that favor the perceived interests of their constituencies. Special educators squeeze IDEA update workshops into their busy schedules and hope that the forms don't change too much this

---

FIGURE 7.2   IEP Gospel Truths

▶ A legally appropriate IEP is individualized and reasonably calculated to allow the student to receive educational benefit.

▶ IEP development must proceed in accordance both with the IDEA and with its regulations.

▶ An IEP that is flawed in substance or procedure exposes a district to the risks of litigation and such expensive remedies as private school costs or compensatory education.

---

time. Eventually, the system regains its equilibrium and focuses again on the old familiar conundrum: How can we simultaneously comply with the complexities of the law, involve parents in decision making, and focus on delivering a Free Appropriate Public Education to students with disabilities?

One solution is to develop and implement streamlined, serviceable IEPs in accordance with the IDEA principles we have outlined in this book. Better IEP development and service delivery protects the interests of all concerned. First, it minimizes the risk of conflict with families and the loss of time and money spent in dispute resolution. Second, it promotes successful learning outcomes. Third, it increases the likelihood of compliance with such other laws as Section 504 and NCLB.

The recipe for correct and successful IEPs (see Figure 7.2) includes incorporation of evidence-based methodology, identification of each student's unique needs, specification of services necessary to address those needs, and goals and objectives that serve both as targets to aim for and measures of well-tailored programs. It may not be as easy as 1-2-3, but it gets closer to that with each legally correct and educationally useful IEP.

Notes

1. http://www.edexcellence.net/publications-issues/publications/shifting-trends-in-special-education.html (May 2011)

2. 34 CFR 300.307(a)(1).

3. 34 CFR 300.307(a)(2).

4. *Hendrick Hudson Bd. of Ed. v. Rowley*, 102 S.Ct. 3034, 458 US 176 (1982).

5. *Deal v. Hamilton Co. Bd. of Ed.*, 392 F.3d 840 (6th Cir. 2004).

6. 20 USC §1414(d)(1)(A)(i).

7. 34 CFR 300.324(a)(2)(iv).

8. 34 CFR 300.304(c)(6).

9. 34 CFR 300.324(a)(2)(i).

10. *E.H. v. Bd. of Ed. of Shenendehowa Central Sch. Dist.*, 361 F.App'x 156 (2nd Cir. 2009).

11. *Lathrop RII Sch. Dist. v Gray*, 611 F.3d 419 (8th Cir. 2010).

12. *Doe v. Hampden-Wilbraham Reg. Sch. Dist.*, 715 F.Supp. 2d 185 (D Mass. 2010).

13. *Alex R. v. Forrestville Valley Community Unit Sch. Dist. #221*, 375 F3d 603 (7th Cir. 2004).

14. *Sch. Bd. of Independent Sch. Dist. No. 11 v Renollett*, 440 F.3d 1007 (8th Cir. 2006).

15. 20 USC §1415(f)(3)(E).

16. *Kelii H. v. Dept. of Ed., Hawaii*, 50 IDELR 94 (D HI 2008).

17. *Ellenville (NY) Central Sch. Dist.*, 43 IDELR 145 (OCR 2004).

18. *Knable v. Bexley City School District*, 238 F.3d 755 (6th Cir. 2001).

19. *Deal v. Hamilton Co. Bd. of Ed.*, 392 F.3d 840 (6th Cir. 2004).

20. See n.4.

21. *Houston Indep. Sch. Dist. v. Bobby R.*, 200 F.3d 341 (5th Cir. 2000).

22. *Neosho R-V Sch. Dist. v. Clark*, 315 F.3d 1022 (8th Cir. 2003).

23. *Van Duyn v. Baker Sch. Dist. 5J*, 481 F.3d 770 (9th Cir. 2007).

24. 34 CFR 300.323(c)(2).

25. *Grossmont Union High Sch. Ass'n*, 47 IDELR 144 (SEA CA 2006).

26. *Anchorage Sch. Dist. v. Parents of M.P.*, 45 IDELR 253 (Alaska Superior Ct. 2006).

27. *New York City Dept of Education*, 48 IDELR 112 (OCR 2006).

28. *Termine v. William S. Hart Union High Sch. Dist.*, 249 F. App'x 583 (9th Cir. 2007).

29. *Poudre Sch. Dist.*, 43 IDELR 16 (SEA CO 2004).

30. *Sch. Union No. 92*, 43 IDELR 93 (OCR 2004).

31. *Clark County (Nev.) Sch. Dist.*, 42 IDELR 247 (OCR 2004).

32. *Jefferson Co. (KY) Pub. Sch.*, 43 IDELR 144 (OCR 2004).

33. *Onamia Indep. Sch. Dist. No. 480*, 48 IDELR 235 (SEA MN 2007).

34. See, e.g., *Guntersville City Bd. of Ed.*, 47 IDELR 84 (SEA AL 2006).

35. *Konocti (CA) United School Dist.*, 40 IDELR 49 (OCR 2003).

26. *Hemlock (MI) Pub. Sch. Dist.*, 51 IDELR 170 (OCR 2008).

37. *Damian J. v. Sch. Dist. of Philadelphia*, 49 IDELR 161 (ED PA 2008).

38. This section of Chapter Seven on non-implementation of IEPs was drawn in large part from Bateman, B. (2011). Individual education programs for children with disabilities. In J.M. Kauffman & D.P. Hallahan (Eds.), *Handbook of Special Education*. New York, NY: Routledge.

39. *Florence Co. Sch. Dist. Four v. Carter*, 114 S.Ct. 361, 510 US 7 (1993).

40. *Burlington Sch. Comm. V. Mass. Dept. of Ed.*, 105 S.Ct. 1996, 471 US 359 (1985).

41. *Capistrano Unified Sch. Dist. v. Wartenberg*, 59 F.3d 884 (9th Cir. 1995).

42. 20 USC §1412(a)(10)(C)(ii).

43. 20 USC §1412(a)(10)(C)(iii).

44. 20 USC §1412(a)(10)(C)(iv).

45. *Cypress-Fairbanks Independent School District*, 118 F.3d 245 (5th Cir. 1997).

46. See *C.B. v. Special Sch. Dist. No. 1*, 636 F.3d 981 (8th Cir. 2011).

47. *Brantley v. Ind. Sch. Dist. No. 625*, 936 F. Supp. 649 (D MN 1997).

48. *Melvin v. Town of Bolton Sch. Dist.*, 100 F.3d 944 (2nd Cir. 1996).

49. *Reid v. Dist of Columbia*, 401 F. 3d 516 (DC Cir. 2005).

50. *Emma C. v. Eastin*, 985 F.Supp. 940 (ND CA 1997).

51. *Franklin v. Gwinnett County Pub. Sch.*, 112 S.Ct. 1028, 503 US 60 (1992).

52. *Goleta Union Elementary Sch. Dist. v. Ordway*, 166 F. Supp. 2d 1287 (CD Cal 2002).

53. *Blanchard v. Morton Sch. Dist.*, 420 F.3d 918 (9th Cir. 2005).

54. *McCormick v. Waukegon Sch. Dist. #60*, 395 F.3d 564 (7th Cir. 2004).

55. 546 US 49 (2005).

56. *Arlington v. Murphy*, 126 S.Ct. 2455, 548 US 291 (2006).

57. 34 CFR 300.9.

58. 34 CFR 300.300(b)(4)(ii).

59. 20 USC §1401(c)(5)(B).

60. *W.G. v. Target Range Sch. Dist. #23*, 960 F.2d 1479 (9th Cir. 1992).

61. *A.B. v. Bd. of Educ. of Anne Arundel Co.*, 354 F3d 315 (4th Cir. 2004).

62. *Henrico v. Z.P.*, 399 F.3d 298, (4th Cir. 2005).

63. *Burlington Sch. Comm. V. Mass. Dept. of Ed.*, 105 S.Ct. 1996, 471 US 359 (1985).

64. *Florence Co. Sch. Dist. Four v. Carter*, 114 S.Ct. 361, 510 US 7 (1993).

65. *Lascari v. Ramapo Indian Hills Reg. High Sch.*, 560 A.2d 1180 (Sup. Ct. NJ 1989).

66. *Cleveland Heights-University Heights City School District v. Boss*, 144 F. 3d 391 (6th Cir. 1998).

67. *C.B. v. Special Sch. Dist. #1*, 636 F.3d 981 (8th Cir. 2011).

68. *Bd. of Murphysboro v. Ill. Bd. of Ed.*, 41 F.3d 1162 (7th Cir. 1994).

69. *Ridgewood Bd. of Ed. v. N.E.*, 172 F.3d 238 (3rd Cir. 1999).

70. *A.B. v. Lawson*, 354 F.3d 315 (4th Cir. 2004).

71. 34 CFR 300.517.

72. 34 CFR 300.506.

73. 34 CFR 300.507-8.

74. 548 US 291 (2006).

Index

scenarios, 109–20

Section 504 students and, 56, 119–22, 153, 158

sins of, 58, 87, *87*

teams, 25–45

"the Right Way," *12, 74*

"the Wrong Way," *12,* 71–87, *74*

timelines, *13, 45,* 108

transition components, 60, *92,* 103–4

updates to, 14, 20, 28, 33, 39, 64, 73, 87–90

"individually-designed instruction," 140

Individuals with Disabilities Education Act (IDEA)

1997 amendments, 11–12, 73, 104, 123, 131–35, 143–45, 149, 157

2004 amendments, 11–12, *13,* 15–17, *18,* 21, *22,* 25–26, 37, 48, 52–55, 64, 73, 124, 131, 143–49, 155–58

Appendix A excerpts, 51–52

components of, 11–21

discipline decisions and, 17–18, 34, 64, 145–46

parental rights under, 13–22, 153, 157

process sequence and, 11–22

informed consent. *See* parental consent

instructional plans, 25–36, 49, 52, 59–64, 72–81, 91–106, 137–52

insurance (private), 20, 65

interim alternative educational settings, 17–18, 34, 106

Internet (information's availability on), 104, 138

interventions (tiered), 139–42, 146

interviews (in evaluations), 14, 66, 104

invitations (to IEP meetings), 25–45

Irving Ind. Sch. Dist. v. Tatro, 57

Jim, sample transition plan, 104, *105*

Joe, IEP example, 108, *109–10*

J. R., IEP problems, 82

Kevin, IEP problems, 83

Knable v. Bexley City Sch. Dist., 148

labeling, 11, 13, 72, 78

See also evaluations

language issues, 13–14, 49, 64, 145–46

language therapy, 19, 27–32, *40, 42–43,* 53, 56, 63, 67–68, 79–83, 98, 150

learning disabilities

diagnoses and assessments of, 14–16, 28, 50, 57, 78, 111, 119, 139–40

schools designed for, 130, 151–52, 156–57, *158*

least restrictive environments (LREs), 16–17, 72, 129–31, 152, 162

See also placement

local education agencies (LEA)

due processes hearings and, 61, 147–57

IEP team membership and, 12–17, 27–40, 54

meeting reviews by, 20–40

provision of services, 27, 38, 41, 53–54

representatives of, *39,* 47, 66, 72, 92

teachers designated by, 26–28, 54, 99

See also district responsibilities; placement

Lovitt, Thomas, 80

Macomb Co. v. Joshua S., 57

mainstreaming, 16, *22,* 131, 162

See also general curriculum

Manifestation of Determination, *18,* 34, 146

Maria, case study, 109–19

McCormick v. Waukegan Sch. Dist. #60, 153

mediation services, 14, 20, 41, 157

See also dispute resolution processes

medical treatment, 57–58, 65

See also related services

meetings

alternative modes, 33

annual, 17, 33–37

attendance at, 12–17, 25–40, *43*

decision-making, 34, 38–41

documentation of, 20, 30, 39

duration of, 33

efficiency, 33, 35, 43–44

formats of, 33

invitations to, 25–28

LEA review, 20–40

location of, 33

parental rights and, 26, 34–35, 38–41, 154–57

preparation for, 35, 41–44

setting for, 33

students at, 29

timing of, 154

written input at, 32–33, 54

Megan, IEP example, 108, *115*

mental health issues, 15, 58, 111, 130

mental retardation (MR), 134

methodology

disagreements over, 64, 123, 155

IDEA 2004 amendments and, 59

inclusion in IEPs, 144–45, 158

instructional, 71, 77, 123, 144–45

parentally-preferred, 64, 155

for related services, 98–99

school authority over, 64, 99

mobility training, 50, 56, 106, 108, 134, 150

National Reading Panel, 54

needs

description of, 12–27

types of, 28, 32–33, 37, 49–51, 53, 64–66

needs determination

clustering of needs, 94, 102, 106

evaluation, 13–22

parental consent, 13–22, 26, 33–45, 59, 67, 90, 154

problematic statements of, 73–74

No Child Left Behind Act of 2001 (NCLB), 52–55, 59, 61–62, 123, 125, 129, 131–32, 137

non-academic activities, 53, 109

nondisabled persons (participation with), 17, 40, 48–50, 61–62, *92,* 134–35, 144, 156

non-verbal children, 62, 64, 134

notice (prior written), 21, 34, 41, 43, 150

objective measures, 76–78, 99, 123–34

objectives, description of, 48, 51–53, 60

problematic statements of, 76, 85, 101–2
   reports to parents, 62–63
progress reporting, 62–63
psychiatric services, 56, 58
psychiatrists, eligibility and, 15

race discrimination and, 130
Reading First (program), 138
reading instruction, *13,* 54, 59, 71, *117, 126,* 126–27, 138,
   141, 149–50
reading media, 49
"reasonable accommodations," 56, 76, 120–22, 151,
   156–57
records (educational), 14, 20–21, 29, 37–40, 67, 100, 154
reevaluations
   descriptions, 64
   parental consent for, 14, 20
   timing of, 14, 33, 89–90
Rehabilitation Act of 1973, 119, 122, 153
   See also Section 504
Reid v. District of Columbia, 152
reimbursement
   attorneys' fees, 20–21, 157
   denial of, 151–52, 156, 161
   private school tuition and, 19–20, 33, 61, 82, 146–47,
      151–52, 156
related services
   amount of, 47–48
   compensatory, 142, 144, 150
   description of, 11
   district responses, 56–61, 87, 98
   funding, 19–20, 162
   goals and objectives, 35, 52, 63, 77
   in IEPs, 12, 15, 34, 48, 50, 52–53, 91, 93, 132–33
   IEP team representatives and, 27–29, 52
   meetings and, 34, 52–53
   problematic statements of need, 71–72, 75–76, 132
   program planning, 15–17
   reimbursement, 19, 142, 144, 162
   rulings on, 55
   types of, 56–58, 64
report cards, 48, 62–63
reports
   periodic, 48, 62
   progress, 51–52, 62–63, 76, 95–97, 102, 113, 124
research
   peer-reviewed, 48, 53–54, 59, 123, 138, 144
   relevant questions, 138
   study designs, 138
research-to-practice gaps, 54–55, 99, 123, 137–45
residential placements, 16, 19, 38, 47, 55, 58, 146,
   151–52, 156
resolution sessions, 11–12, 20–21, 38–45, 157
resource rooms, 17, *31, 39, 43,* 55, 71–73, 94
response to interventions (RTIs), 13–14, 139–41
Reusch v. Fountain, 58
review officers/panel, 57, 63, 67, 90
Rowley, Amy, 16
Rowley standard, 16, 54, 79, 99, 123, 142–44, 147, 151,
   155, 161
Ryan, IEP problems, *86,* 86–87

school boards. *See* local education agencies (LEA)
schools
   authority of, 27, 99
   student transfers, 16–*18,* 145–46, 154
scientifically-based instruction
   definition of, 137–38
   uses of, 11, 54, 99, 137–38, 141–47
screening (IDEA provision), 13, 141
Section 504, 56, 119–22, 153, 158
self-advocacy skills, 104, *105, 122*
sex discrimination, 15, 130
Shaywitz, S., 54, 77
short-term objectives
   deletion of, 146–47
   elimination of, 11, 124
   examples of, *80–81, 84–86,* 108, *113, 118*
   goals and, 51–52
   IDEA 2004 changes and, 146–47
   IDEA excerpts, 48, 51–52
   in IEPs, 48, *50*
   paperwork reduction and, 66, 123
   progress reporting, 51–52, 62–63, 102, 124
sign language, 145
SLD eligibility, *13*
Smith, C., 94
social behaviors, 80, 84, 97, 106–8
socialization goals, 53, *84, 121*
special education services
   certification of, 54, 150
   cost of, 11
   definitions, 11–12
   district responses, 56–61
   funding, 19–20
   IEPs and, 25–44, 48–68
   IEP sequence, 93–106
   parental refusal of, 14
   problematic statements of need, 75–76
   program planning, 15–17, 77–79, 89–97
   related services and, 12, 15, 34, 48, 50, 52–53, 71–72,
      75–76, 91, 93, 132–33
speech therapy, 19, 27–32, *40, 42–43,* 53, 56, 63, 67–68,
   79–83, 98, 150
Spielberg v. Henrico County Public Schools, 38
staff
   adversarial attitudes, 11, 149
   certification of, 54, 150
   in-service training and, 99, *109*
   meeting participation and, 26, 28, 33
   safety risks, 146
   See also teachers
standards-based IEPs, 125–35
standards (grade-level), 48, 52–54, 61–62, 93, 97, 105,
   139–41
state compliance investigators, 41, 90, 143–54
"stay-put" provision, 17, 20, 156, 162
Strick, L., 94
student response forms, 21
students
   gathering information about, 12, 14, *42–43,* 90, 141
   on the IEP team, 29
   meeting attendance, 33

Foundational cases in special education

Courts have decided thousands of cases involving IDEA, and nobody except special education attorneys could be expected to be familiar with them all. However, a few cases are so important in establishing, clarifying, or reinforcing principles of constitutional law or IDEA, that everybody involved in special education should be familiar with them.

Pre-IDEA cases that impact students with disabilities

PARC v. Pennsylvania, 343 F.Supp. 179 (ED Pa. 1972)
Held that denial of education to students who have intellectual disabilities violates the Equal Protection clause of the US Constitution.

Mills. V. Bd. Of Ed., 348 F.Supp. 866 (D DC 1972)
Like *PARC*, held that public schools must admit students who have disabilities, and includes many provisions (e.g. appropriate education and due process) which laid the foundation for landmark federal special education law, the Education for All Handicapped Children Act (the former name for the Individuals with Disabilities Education Act (IDEA). This case also established the principle that insufficient funds does not constitute a legal defense for failure to provide services.

Goss v. Lopez, 419 US 565 (1975)
Held that students have a property right in public education, and that he US Constitution required due process (proportional notice and hearing) before a student can be deprived of this right through suspension or expulsion.

In the IDEA era: Rowley and later

Bd. of Education v. Rowley, 458 US 176 (1982)
Children with disabilities eligible for special education are entitled to a free appropriate public education (FAPE), which includes:
(1) adherence to IDEA procedural requirements, and
(2) an IEP reasonably calculated to allow the student to receive educational benefit. This is the "benefit" standard.

Polk v. Central Susquehanna Intermediate Unit 16, 853 F. 2d 171 (3rd Cir. 1988)
The "educational benefit" entitlement of Rowley means more than a trivial benefit. It must be a meaningful benefit.

When a district fails to provide FAPE, it may be required to reimburse parents for a unilateral placement in a private school, if that private placement is appropriate.

NOTE: The majority of circuit courts that have ruled on the question have held that the LRE requirement need not be met for a private placement to be deemed appropriate and therefore reimbursable.

Florence Co. Sch. Dist. Four v. Carter, 510 US 7 (1993)
A private placement need not be state-approved to be reimbursable, as long as it provides an appropriate program. In this case, the court approved a private placement in a special school for students who had learning disabilities. The court did not address the LRE issue, i.e., whether the more restrictive private school was the LRE.

Forest Grove Sch. Dist. v. T.A., 129 S.Ct. 2484 (2009)
Held that a private placement may be reimbursable when a district does not provide FAPE, and the private placement does, even if the student had not previously received special education services through the public school, despite language in the IDEA that appeared to limit reimbursement to students who had previously received special education through the public school district. A district has an obligation to identify and offer FAPE to all students with disabilities, and failure to do so cannot "immunize" a district against IDEA remedies.

Timothy W. v. Rochester Sch. Dist., 875 F.2d 954 (1st Cir. 1989)
The school believed it need not serve a student whose disability they presumed made him unable to benefit. The court said all children with a disability are entitled to FAPE, regardless of the nature or severity of the disability. This is the "zero reject" principle.

Daniel R.R. v. State Bd. of Ed., 874 F.2d 1036 (5th Cir. 1989)
The least restrictive environment (LRE) principle is a two-fold inquiry:

(1) Can education be achieved satisfactorily in the regular class?
(2) If not, is the student mainstreamed to the maximum extent appropriate?

This formulation establishes the appropriateness of the IEP as the primary consideration, and the restrictiveness of the placement secondary. Consider four factors in determining the appropriateness of regular class placement:
(1) identify what accommodations have been made;
(2) ask if the student can benefit from regular education;
(3) weigh that benefit against benefit from special education; and
(4) examine the possible disruptive effect of the student on others.

Other circuits have their own tests for LRE, but *Daniel R.R.* is both representative and thorough.

Cedar Rapids Comm. Sch. Dist. v. Garrett F., 526 US 66 (1999)
The US Supreme Court upheld its earlier ruling in *Tatro*, 468 US 883 (1984) that related services, which a school district must provide to the student, are services the student needs in order to benefit from special education. The sole exception is services that **must** be performed by a physician. In this case, even the intensive and extensive nursing services required for Garrett were related services, which the district had to provide at no cost to the parents.

Honig v. Doe, 484 US 305 (1988)
Schools may suspend students with disabilities for up to 10 days with ordinary due process. Suspension for more than 10 days is, in effect, a change in placement, which requires the school to use IDEA process for change in placement. If the parents request a due process hearing, the student must remain in the present placement until the proceedings are completed. This is the "stay put" provision.

NOTE: Congress later incorporated the principles of Honig v. Doe into IDEA.

Winkelman v. Parma City Sch. Dist., 550 US 516 (2007)
The right to a FAPE does not belong solely to students with disabilities. Parents have rights, both procedural and substantive, including the entitlement to a FAPE for their children. Parents may enforce these rights in court on their own behalf.